DAVE ROBERTSON
DEPARTMENT OF POLITICAL SCIENCE
INDIANA UNIVERSITY - BLOOMINGTON
1/77

CONDORCET *Selected Writings*

THE LIBRARY OF LIBERAL ARTS

CONDORCET

Edited, with an introduction, by

THE LIBRARY OF LIBERAL ARTS

Selected Writings

KEITH MICHAEL BAKER

PUBLISHED BY
The Bobbs-Merrill Company, Inc. INDIANAPOLIS

The Bobbs-Merrill Company, Inc.
4300 West 62nd Street
Indianapolis, Indiana 46268

First Edition
First Printing 1976
Designed by Irving Perkins

Library of Congress Cataloging in Publication Data

Condorcet, Marie Jean Antoine Nicolas Caritat, marquis de,
    1743–1794.
    Condorcet.

    (The Library of liberal arts ; LLA 159)
    Bibliography: p.
    1. Philosophy—Collected works.
B1992.E5 1976   194   75–38680
ISBN 0-672-60381-0

Contents

CONDORCET: Selected Writings

I THE ACADEMICIAN UNDER THE OLD REGIME

II THE PHILOSOPHE DURING THE FRENCH REVOLUTION

III   CONDORCET IN HIDING

Introduction

The aim of this book is quite simply to make available to students a selection of some of the more important writings of Condorcet on philosophy, politics, social science, and history. His *Sketch for a Historical Picture of the Progress of the Human Mind*, often regarded as the very epitome of Enlightenment thought, is well known in the English-speaking world. But the great body of his writings remains untranslated; and, apart from a modern translation of the *Sketch*, those few works that have been rendered into English exist only in old, rare, or fragmentary translations. The new selection presented here attempts to convey the fundamental ideas and the range of interests of a man who was in one short career mathematician and political theorist, man of letters and social reformer, scientific statesman and revolutionary deputy: a man who, if he is still recognized by historians as the last of the great philosophes of the Enlightenment, is now also being discovered by contemporary social scientists as one of the founding fathers of modern social science.

THE FORMATIVE YEARS

Marie-Jean-Antoine-Nicolas Caritat, marquis de Condorcet, was born on 17 September 1743 in Ribemont, Picardy.[1] His father, a military noble who bore the name of an ancient family, was killed shortly after the child's birth. His mother, widowed for a second time, compensated for this loss by smothering the child in a mantle of piety. Dedicated to the virgin for his protection, he was apparently kept in white dresses until the age of eight. To this display of piety Condorcet reacted by becoming in later life a convinced atheist.

Sent to the Jesuit school at Reims at age eleven, Condorcet entered the University of Paris in 1758, where he studied mathematics and philosophy at the College of Navarre. His education over in 1760, the young nobleman was expected to follow family tradition by embarking on a military career. This he refused to do. Despite family objections, he returned to Paris and took up lodgings with Girault de Kéroudou, his former teacher at the College of Navarre, under whose guidance he prepared for a scientific career.

In doing so, Condorcet naturally found his scientific aspirations fixed on membership in the powerful Paris Academy of Sciences, the center of scientific life in France and, indeed, in Europe.[2] Although the first mathematical paper he submitted to the academy (in October 1761) made no great impression on the academicians, a second mathematical paper, presented early in 1764, was far more favorably received. This was followed in 1765 by a work on the integral calculus, published with the approbation of the academy and praised in the annual report of its activities (even though Condorcet was not yet a member) for the elegance and profundity of the mathematics contained therein. In 1769, on the strength of his mathematical achievements, Condorcet was admitted to membership of the Academy of Sciences as a junior academician.

In the Academy of Sciences, Condorcet found a powerful friend, patron, and mentor in the mathematician and philosopher, Jean d'Alembert. It was with d'Alembert's support that the young mathematician made his way in the world of the great scientific academies of Europe. It was under d'Alembert's eye that he published his early scientific works. Furthermore, it was principally as a result of d'Alembert's intrigues that he was named assistant secretary of the Academy of Sciences in 1773 and became its permanent secretary in 1776. With that appointment, Condorcet became the principal spokesman for institutionalized science in France until the suppression of the Academy of Sciences by the Revolution twenty years later.

From d'Alembert, too, Condorcet learned that the implications of the role of the scientific intellectual extended beyond the secure position of the Academy of Sciences in the hierarchical social order of the old regime. Under d'Alembert's influence, the young mathematician became a member of that reforming group of men of letters in eighteenth-century France who so powerfully redefined the social role of the philosopher that they have ever since been referred to simply as the "philosophes." Condorcet himself gave a vivid description of this "party of humanity" in a celebrated passage of his *Sketch for a Historical Picture of the Progress of the Human Mind*, written almost a quarter of a century later.

> Soon there was formed in Europe a class of men who were concerned less with the discovery or development of the truth than with its propagation, men who whilst devoting themselves to the tracking down of prejudices in the hiding places where the priests, the schools, the governments, and all long-established institutions had gathered and protected them, made it their life-work to destroy popular errors . . . using in turn all the weapons with which learning, philosophy, wit, and literary talent can furnish reason; using every mood from humor to pathos, every literary form from the vast erudite encyclopedia to the novel or the broadsheet of the day; . . . never ceasing to demand the independence of reason and the freedom of the press as the right and the salvation of mankind; . . . and finally, taking for their battle cry—*reason, tolerance, humanity* (pp. 228–29).[3]

Condorcet's initiation into the philosophe group was largely accomplished in the salon of Julie de Lespinasse, with whom d'Alembert lived on the rue de Belle-Chasse from 1765 until her death in 1776. From the salon on the rue de Belle-Chasse, d'Alembert organized a determined effort to infiltrate the influential French Academy with men of letters favorable to the philosophe cause, a campaign which eventually resulted (after a bitter struggle) in Condorcet's election to the academy in 1782. In this salon, Condorcet met the leading men of letters among the philosophes, and the members of the liberal Parisian elite who favored their ideas. Here he met Turgot, the statesman and social reformer who was to become the second major influence on the young mathematician's career by introducing him to the economic theories of the physiocrats and the reforming principles of enlightened administrators. It was from the rue de Belle-Chasse, too, that d'Alembert and

Condorcet set out in 1770 on a crucial visit to Ferney, where the aged Voltaire gave his enthusiastic approbation to the latest recruit to the philosophe cause. Voltaire's enthusiasm was tempered by a certain nervousness, however, when Condorcet's anonymous *Letters of a Theologian*, published in 1774, were widely attributed to himself. "The author takes my defense; I would rather be slandered than defended like this," Voltaire complained. "This is a declaration of a hideous war. . . . I want neither the glory of having penned it nor the punishment that will follow." [4] The *Letters of a Theologian* deployed a radically subversive wit, a vitriolic pen, and a disdainful scientific expertise in the service of a savage anti-clericalism. They insisted on the philosophes' responsibility to serve notice of man's natural rights at the very foot of the throne. They were, indeed, a declaration of war. And with this declaration, the young mathematician opened a second career as political pamphleteer and social reformer.

By 1774, then, Condorcet had established himself as a mathematician, academician, philosophe, and pamphleteer. D'Alembert had offered him the model of a scientific career and the vision of an independent role for the man of letters to enlighten the public and address the throne. Turgot now presented him with a tougher, more technocratic vision of the relationship between power and enlightenment, together with a program for the regeneration of French government and society through the determined use of royal power. "To do good, one must have at least as much power as goodwill," Condorcet had written to Turgot in one of his earliest letters, while the latter was still royal intendant of Limoges. [5] In 1774, when Turgot became head of the financial administration of the monarchy as Controller-General, the power to do good seemed at hand. With Turgot translated to Versailles, Condorcet burst into a fury of action in support of the minister's reforms.

Turgot aimed at both immediate and long-term changes. [6] His most immediate goal was to create a national economy on laissez-faire principles, free of government intervention and local restrictions, with ready movement of goods and services in response to market conditions. In eighteenth-century circumstances, such a goal implied radical changes. It implied the creation of a free trade in grain, in defiance of a widespread popular conviction that it was the moral responsibility of government to control the grain market in such a way as to ensure the availability of the principal means of subsistence at traditional prices. It implied the elimination of the traditional guilds and corporations controlling the trades, even though these privileged institutions were generally regarded as integral parts of a traditional society constituted not by individual citizens but by corporate bodies, orders, and Estates. It implied the abolition of the *corvée* (the hated forced-labor tax that took peasants away from their fields to work reluctantly, and inefficiently, on the roads) in favor of a general tax levied on all: this despite the fact that such a tax threatened the existence of fiscal privileges in a society based on the principle of privilege and hierarchy. And, finally, it implied the creation of a unified national system of weights and measures based on scientific principles; the building of a network of canals in accordance with the most advanced engineering techniques; the applications of science to particular problems ranging from cattle-plague to the desalinization of sea-water: in short, the mobilization of science and scientists in the service of the state.

As friend and disciple of Turgot, as his unofficial scientific attaché, passionate adviser, and reckless propagandist, Condorcet played his part in support of these reforms. When, in 1775, Turgot's introduction of free trade in grain coincided with the effects of a bad harvest to produce a chain reaction of bread riots throughout northern France (suppressed by the Controller-General with a determined show of force), Condorcet defended Turgot's policy against its critics in a scathing series of polemics enunciating the "scientific" principles of laissez-faire economics. He made the arrangements for experiments to determine a scientific basis for a reformed system of weights and measures, pressing emphatically for such reform. He participated in hydrodynamic experiments to determine the engineering principles of canal construction. He carried out a series of feasibility studies (as they would today be called) evaluating the practicability and potential effects of proposed canals in particular areas. And when, in 1776, Turgot introduced the celebrated Six Edicts, which included abolition of guilds and corporations and suppression of the *corvée*, Condorcet fanned the flames of debate with a pamphlet so irresponsible that Turgot himself did everything he could to suppress it!

While the Controller-General was pressing for these immediate reforms, he was also planning to transform the entire system of government in France by introducing a hierarchy of representative assemblies ranging from local assemblies at the village level to a national assembly representing the whole realm.[7] Citizens would be admitted to these assemblies according to a property qualification; and they would meet together, not in the traditional form of an assembly of Estates, but as a single body without distinction of rank or order. The assemblies would carry out certain administrative functions on a local level, while advising the government on matters of national policy. With the nation enlightened by a system of public instruction, Turgot insisted, such bodies would come to represent a society of citizens equal before the law and contributing to the rational conduct of public affairs in accordance with their status as property owners and their capabilities as rational beings.

This comprehensive project of political reform was discussed by Turgot in the circle of his close associates and a draft memorandum explaining it to Louis XVI was composed. But before it could be presented to the King, Turgot had fallen from power (in May 1776). Finally published in 1787, the so-called *Memorandum on the Municipalities* was to have a significant influence on the political reforms carried out by the government on the eve of the French Revolution. It also provided the broad matrix within which Condorcet's political ideas developed.

Turgot's fall from power left Condorcet in despair. "This event has changed the whole of nature for me," he wrote to Voltaire from Ribemont. "I no longer take the same pleasure in this beautiful countryside where he would have brought forth happiness. . . . How far we are fallen, my dear and illustrious master, and from such a height." [8] After two years of passionate political activity in the cause of reform, the mathematician found himself abruptly returned to his mathematics. Not surprisingly, his work lagged. Although a committee was appointed in 1778 to examine his long-planned treatise on the integral calculus, that work remained unfinished. It was not until 1784 that Condorcet published another paper in the *Memoirs* of the Academy of Sciences. When he finally did so, however, it was in an urgent spurt of activity on a new subject, the calculus of probabilities. In the application of this calculus to social affairs, Condorcet found a means of reconciling his two great passions: mathematics and the public good.

The development and implementation of this conception of social science henceforth became the central focus of his thought and action.

THE MORAL AND POLITICAL SCIENCES

Condorcet was ready for an initial statement of his developing conception of social science in 1782, when he delivered his reception speech at the French Academy. Invoking his authority as permanent secretary of the Academy of Sciences, he presented his view of the indefinite advance of the human mind and the relationship between scientific and social progress. In doing so, he drew the attention of his audience to the sciences he regarded as the peculiar achievement and responsibility of his age: "those sciences, almost created in our own day, the object of which is man himself, the direct goal of which is the happiness of man." These sciences, Condorcet insisted, were the essential link between scientific and social advance. They would follow the same methods and enjoy a progress no less sure than that exhibited by the physical sciences:

> In meditating on the nature of the moral sciences, one cannot indeed help seeing that, based like the physical sciences upon the observation of facts, they must follow the same methods, acquire an equally exact and precise language, attain the same degree of certainty (p. 6).

This revolutionary claim, Condorcet maintained in his notes for a revised edition of his reception speech, would naturally be greeted with hostility by those with a vested interest in an irrational social order. Inevitably, the truths of the moral sciences would be accepted more slowly than those of the physical sciences. For that reason, it was all the more necessary to demonstrate the validity of their claim to scientific status. To do so, Condorcet elaborated a rather eclectic philosophy of probability drawing upon a number of strands in Enlightenment thought. Developed in a series of manuscript notes still remaining among his papers, sketched out in a fragmentary way in the notes to his reception speech in 1782, this philosophy was first systematically made public in 1785 in the *Essay on the Application of Mathematics to the Theory of Decision-Making*, the work which he intended to prove his conviction that the moral and political sciences were susceptible of all the precision and certainty of the physical sciences.

Condorcet began by invoking the common eighteenth-century distinction, suggested by Locke and most radically developed by Hume, between truths of reason and truths of fact. In the case of all scientific statements, it is necessary to distinguish between the rational certainty *(évidence)* of propositions and their "reality" (empirical basis). If such statements can be given axiomatic form as a series of propositions each deriving from the preceding one (the goal of all rational scientific endeavor), they can be regarded as truths of demonstration enjoying the same kind of certainty as mathematics. Insofar as they purport to describe empirical reality, however, they depend for their validity upon two conditions: first, an observed correlation with a constant order of facts in experience; second, the assumption that a particular phenomenon, or series of phenomena, which was observed yesterday will recur today and tomorrow in similar circumstances. As truths of experience, in this sense, all scientific statements are merely probable. They possess "only that kind of degree of certainty which is a true probability mathematically expressed. This certainty is essentially different from the strictly defined certainty of the mathematicians" (p. 18).

On the basis of this distinction, Condorcet developed his case for the scientific status of the moral and political sciences. He did so in a number of different ways. His most general claim was that the *principles* of morals and politics were no less certain than those of the physical sciences. Perhaps the clearest statement of this view can be found in the notes he later wrote for an edition of Voltaire's works (not included in this selection). While he never explicitly elaborated the logic involved here, Condorcet was convinced (with many of his contemporaries) that the first principles of morals and legislation could be formally derived from the very *definition* of man as a sensate being endowed with reason.

They are in effect the necessary result of the properties of sensitive beings capable of reasoning; they derive from their nature; from which it follows that it is sufficient to suppose the existence of these beings for the propositions founded on these notions to be true; just as it is sufficient to suppose the existence of a circle to establish the truth of the propositions which develop its different characteristics. Thus the reality of moral propositions, their truth relative to the state of real beings, of men, depends entirely upon this truth of fact: that men are sensitive and intelligent beings.[9]

Read in the light of the distinction suggested in the notes to Condorcet's reception speech, this passage can be interpreted in the following way. It is enough to posit the existence of a sensitive being capable of reasoning to demonstrate the validity of certain moral principles as logical propositions. It is therefore enough to verify empirically the factual existence of such beings to establish the validity of these principles "relative to the state of real beings". The basic fact of man's physical nature (that is, the existence of the body) is proven by constant experience. Probable truth though it may be, it is nevertheless as certain and as constant as the most certain and constant truth of the physical sciences: the fact that the sun will rise tomorrow. It follows, then, that "if we examine the small number of facts necessary to establish the first foundations of ethics, of political, civil, or criminal legislation, or of administration . . . we shall see that these facts are as general and as constant as the facts of the physical order" (p. 19).

With this reasoning, Condorcet made an adroit leap from the *is* to the *ought*. The first principles of morals and politics once established, the art of legislation and administration would become the rational task of deriving particular consequences, in particular circumstances, from general truths. Yet these abstract truths are often vague in practice; in matters that require precise observation or are susceptible to numerous possible outcomes, they do not necessarily extend beyond a statement of first principles. It was therefore essential to develop a science of rational conduct (a *social art*) that would make it possible to order the contingencies of the social world in accordance with the first principles of the moral and political sciences (or, as Condorcet was later to call them, the first principles of *social science*). To do so, Condorcet turned to the calculus of probabilities first suggested by Pascal, later developed in a fundamental work by Jakob Bernoulli (*Ars conjectandi* [The Art of Conjecturing] published posthumously in 1713), and finally brought to mathematical fruition by Laplace in a series of papers published in the 1770s and 1780s.[10]

All our truths, Condorcet ultimately concluded, are but probabilities. In the last analysis, he maintained with Hume, this is even true of mathematical and other forms of demonstrable reasoning, which, while they provide truths more reliable than any others, are nevertheless "based on the constancy of the laws observed in the operation of our understanding" (p. 42). It follows that the degree of certainty we attain in any statement depends upon the greater or lesser probability that the relevant facts have a common cause, the greater or lesser probability that the fact regarded as a cause is indeed the cause. This is no less true of the moral sciences, Condorcet maintained, than of the physical sciences. "Thus it is from the more or less constant order of facts observed in moral as in physical phenomena that the kind of certainty derives that pertains to reality" (p. 18).

Suppose a phenomenon has occurred a hundred thousand times, for example, and failed to occur once. My expectation that it will recur is less than it would have been if the phenomenon had occurred two hundred thousand times and failed to occur once. But while the probability of the expected event is different in these two cases, Condorcet argued, the mathematical "certainty" (or precision) with which these probabilities can be expressed is the same. "The science in general is as certain because I know exactly in the same manner the degree of certainty that I obtain; but the degree of certainty of the result is not the same" (p. 19).

Condorcet's argument that the moral sciences can equal the physical in reliability hinges, in effect, on this distinction between the "certainty of a science" and the "certainty of its results." At any given time, the results of the moral sciences may be less probable than those of the physical sciences. If the observation of facts is more difficult in human affairs, and their order consequently less easy to elicit, the moral sciences may in given cases acquire fewer precise truths. If the order of observed facts is itself less constant than that revealed by the physical sciences, then their actual results will be less probable. Yet the probability of these results can in theory be expressed and evaluated in terms of the calculus of probabilities. Thus subjected to mathematical evaluation, the propositions of the moral sciences can be as certainly and precisely expressed as can the truths of the physical sciences. It was therefore theoretically possible to bring the moral and physical sciences together on a sliding scale of probabilities that could at all stages be expressed and evaluated with mathematical precision.

For Condorcet the mathematician, then, the calculus of probabilities provided an answer to the challenge of the pyrrhonian skeptics, the threat of whose arguments had constantly endangered the philosophes' attempt to develop a philosophy of social action. All the reasoning by which we direct our judgment and our conduct is indeed based merely on probability, he acknowledged in the *Essay on the Application of Mathematics to the Theory of Decision-Making*.

> But this conclusion, far from leading us to discouragement and indolence, as did the old pyrrhonism, must produce the contrary effect. For it follows that all our knowledge, of whatever kind, is founded on probabilities the value of which it is possible to determine with a kind of precision. In seeking to determine these probabilities, we no longer act or make judgments in accordance with a vague and mechanical impression, but we follow an impression subjected to calculation, the relationship of which to other impressions of the same kind is known to us.[11]

Seizing upon the calculus of probabilities as the essential link between the moral and physical sciences, Condorcet bound them together in a unified mathematical conception of science theoretically applicable to the whole realm of human experience. The measured precision of probable belief replaced the Cartesian certainty of demonstration in this mathematical model of science. Yet Condorcet nevertheless remained, in a sense, a Cartesian. His aim was to recover for science—and to integrate into a unified mathematical conception of science—even those areas of knowledge thrown to the skeptical dogs by Descartes. There is no one, he argued in the *Essay*, who has not at some time or another found his opinions changing, not according to new motives or a revised argument, but simply as a result of the impression of time, circumstances, and events. If we were able to substitute for this habitual and instinctive process of adjustment the precise evaluation of the grounds for our beliefs, "our reason would cease to be the slave of our impressions" (p. 64). The result, the philosophe was convinced, would be a science in which the contingencies of human life and action could be finally subjected to mathematical rule. In such a promise, Condorcet found hope for the social science of which the eighteenth century dreamed, the science that was to be the essential condition of a rational and enlightened social order.

THE THEORY OF RATIONAL CHOICE

In his pamphlet, *On the Influence of the American Revolution on Europe* (1786), Condorcet welcomed events in America as a sublime affirmation of the rights of man and as a demonstration of the importance of a written declaration of such rights as the constitutional basis for enlightened government. Yet of the four cardinal rights of man that Condorcet laid out in the introduction to this work, it is interesting that he regarded as least important (and most problematic) the right to contribute, directly or indirectly, to the formulation of social policy and the enactment of the laws. Zealous republicans had regarded this right as the most important of all, Condorcet admitted. Indeed, he maintained, its equal enjoyment *by each man using his reason* should be regarded as the ultimate goal in a just social order. "But it loses its most precious advantages if prejudices divert those who must exercise it from the narrow paths traced for them by the immutable laws of justice; and, in terms of public happiness, a republic with tyrannical laws can fall far short of a monarchy" (p. 74).

This statement defines the fundamental problem of the *Essay on the Application of Mathematics to the Theory of Decision-Making*. For Condorcet, the rights of man included the right to choose the laws, but only the right to do so rationally. As permanent secretary of the Academy of Sciences, he found his ideal of political decision-making in the idealized republic of science in which votes were weighed, not counted. He regarded politics as a matter not of *will* but of *reason*. A majority vote was only justified, he was convinced, if a proposition declared to be true by the greater number was likely to be more correct than one declared to be true by the lesser number. The purpose of the *Essay* was to develop a theory that would ensure the rationality of the decisions made by a representative assembly. As such, it was the central work in Condorcet's liberal political theory: the work to which he constantly returned in drawing up his later constitutional schemes. Long neglected by historians—as it was ignored by contemporaries—this massive and often bizarre book has finally been recognized by contemporary social scientists as a classic in the development of mathematical social science.[12]

The central question of the *Essay on the Application of Mathematics to the Theory of Decision-Making* can be stated as follows: on what grounds can it be justifiable to subject individual citizens to a law that has not been directly and unanimously voted by all, or to a decision that they believe is contrary to their own interests? Condorcet found the answer to this question in a mathematical guarantee: "a very great probability of the truth of this decision is the only reasonable and just grounds according to which one can demand such submission" (p. 44). The purpose of the *Essay* was to demonstrate mathematically that it was possible to provide this guarantee to the represented.

> Thus our principal task here is to discover the probability that gives assurance of the validity of a law passed by the smallest possible majority, such that one can believe that it is not unjust to subject others to this law and that it is useful to submit oneself to it. . . . Then, too, the citizen obeying this same law would feel that while he is obliged as a necessary condition of the social order not to conduct himself in a certain category of actions simply according to his own reason, he at least has the advantage of following only those opinions which, setting his own judgment aside, he must regard as possessing the degree of probability sufficient to direct his conduct (p. 59).

The represented citizen possessed of this guarantee would in this respect be in a very similar position to the dissenting citizen of Rousseau, who would also set his own judgment aside in deference to the general will (or, as Condorcet would say, the "public reason"). Clearly, another of the aims of the *Essay* was to answer Rousseau's strictures against representation in terms very close to his own.

To achieve this purpose, Condorcet elaborated what has been called a "theoretical operational model" of collective decision-making. Suppose an assembly of voters having equal enlightenment and intelligence, each expressing his opinion in good faith, each (like Rousseau's citizen) thinking his own thoughts without influencing another's. Given the number of voters, the probability that the opinion of each voter will be true, and the majority required for a decision, it is possible mathematically to calculate:

1. the probability that the assembly will not produce a false decision;
2. the probability that it will produce a true decision;
3. the probability that it will produce any decision, true or false;
4. the probable truth of a decision reached (a) by an unknown majority; (b) by a known majority.

It is important to understand what is involved in these different probabilities. In making a new law, for example, it is necessary to ensure a high probability that there will not be a false decision (1). But this, in itself, is not enough. The function of an assembly is to make decisions. It is therefore important that the danger of false decision (1) not be averted at the cost of having no decision at all (3). Similarly, it is as important to ensure that a good law will receive an appropriate majority (2) as it is to prevent a bad law from doing so. Thus there must be adequate assurance that a law is rejected because it is bad, and not because no decision can be reached (3). Finally, when a law is adopted, either by any majority or by a prescribed majority (4), there must be adequate assurance that it is indeed a good law.

Given this model, Condorcet proposed that the probability of a voter's opinion being correct can be expressed as greater than one-half if he is regarded as more likely to make a correct judgment than an erroneous one. Similarly, it can be expressed as less than one-half if the voter appears more likely to make an erroneous judgment than a correct one. Now if in an assembly the probability that each voter's opinion is correct exceeds a half, Condorcet argued, it can be shown mathematically that the probable truth of a decision passed by a simple majority increases with the number of voters. Conversely, if it is less than one-half, the larger the assembly the smaller the probability that a majority decision will be true.

But what is a "true" decision in this context? And how can the likelihood of a voter to make a "true" decision be measured? Modern theorists of decision-making would tend to answer the first question by defining a "true" or "correct" decision as the voting result that most accurately expresses the voter's preferences, or the "strategy" that maximizes the desirable outcomes. But Condorcet does not take such an approach. He does not discuss "true" decisions in terms of their outcomes; nor does he wish to identify them merely with the correct expression of voters' preferences. He is interested not in the precise statement of preferences as a matter of will, but in the correct evaluation of choices as a matter of rational judgment. No matter how closely a decision corresponded to the preference of the voters, it would not in his view be a true (or enlightened) decision unless the voters themselves were enlightened. In other words, Condorcet defines a "true" decision implicitly as the decision that would be made by truly enlightened men in accordance with reason and justice. Stripped of its mathematical trappings, his argument is simply that more enlightened assemblies make truer (or more probably true) decisions.

This point becomes clear when Condorcet turns to the critical problem for the mathematics of the *Essay*: that of evaluating the actual probability of the opinions of the individual voters composing an assembly. Here, Condorcet suggested that such an evaluation could be accomplished by "empirical means." In practice, this meant setting up an examining tribunal, composed of very enlightened persons, to review the decisions of any given assembly and estimate the truth of its decisions. From this estimate, it would be possible to work back mathematically to the probable truth of the opinions of the voters composing it. The problem with this suggestion is obvious. Since the reliability of the findings of this examining tribunal could itself only be assessed by another examining tribunal, there would be an infinite regress of hypothetical assumptions as to the probability of voters' opinions.

Nevertheless, Condorcet derived important political conclusions from the mathematics of the *Essay*. Under existing conditions, he argued, a numerous popular assembly could not be composed only of enlightened men. The risk of false decisions in a popular assembly could be minimized by requiring proportional majorities, but only at the cost of increasing the danger of reaching no decision at all. From this reasoning, Condorcet concluded that a pure democracy would be appropriate only "to a people much more enlightened, much freer from prejudices than any of those known to history. For every other nation, this form of assemblies becomes harmful, unless these assemblies are limited in the exercise of their power to decisions directly relating to the maintenance of security, liberty, and property: matters upon which a direct personal interest can adequately enlighten all minds" (p. 49).

Condorcet found this conclusion reinforced by another aspect of his analysis of voting which has in recent years attracted much attention among social scientists interested in the theory of decision-making. This involved complex decisions that can be broken down into a series of more simple propositions to be voted on, or in which there are more than two alternative ways to cast a vote. The classic case of such decisions is an election between three candidates. Here a candidate who attains a simple majority of the votes is not necessarily the true choice of the voters when they are asked to express their preference more precisely by comparing every candidate singly with every other. This voting paradox had been noticed by the chevalier de Borda, one of Condorcet's contemporaries in the Academy of Sciences, a few years before the publication of the *Essay*.[13] But Condorcet developed its analysis in what is now regarded as his principal contribution to the theory of collective decision-making.

From this analysis, Condorcet drew two principal conclusions. He first insisted that in order to achieve a rational decision, it was of fundamental importance that the question be correctly put to the vote in such a way that complicated decisions were reduced to a series of votes on simple propositions. It followed from this that the power to frame the questions to be submitted to an assembly was crucial: yet it "has been almost everywhere left to chance, or given as a power or right attached to a particular office, rather than imposed as a duty that demands wisdom and precision" (p. 56). Condorcet was to pay considerable attention in his constitutional schemes to the manner in which this responsibility was to be exercised.

Secondly, Condorcet insisted, it is necessary that the voters be more enlightened, the more complicated the decisions submitted to them. Otherwise, the procedures required to prevent a false decision would serve to perpetuate abuses and bad laws by making any decision impossible. How then was it possible to arrive at an adequate assurance of the truth of a decision passed by majority vote? To answer this question, it was first necessary for Condorcet to decide what constituted adequate assurance in a given situation. In the case of legislation, he argued that it would be justifiable to discount a risk of a bad law that was no greater than a risk of death regarded by most men as negligible. Arguing that a man of thirty-seven is usually no more afraid of sudden death than a man of forty-seven, and estimating that the risk of such death increased between these two ages by $1/144768$, Condorcet concluded that a probability of $144767/144768$ that a law passed by the minimum majority in an assembly would be true, would be adequate assurance of the validity of such a law. This probability, he contended, would be relatively easy to secure in a small assembly of enlightened voters but almost impossible in a larger assembly of less enlightened voters.

It followed ultimately from this conclusion that only where the great majority of voters in a society was at least enlightened enough to choose the elite of more enlightened men competent to make truly rational decisions, and only where this elite in its turn was truly free from prejudice and error, could a truly rational politics be achieved in a representative constitution.

> Thus, provided a society possesses a large number of enlightened men, free from prejudice; and provided that the right of the great number lacking sufficient enlightenment is limited to choosing those whom it considers wisest and best informed, to whom the citizens consequently entrust their right to decide on questions beyond their competence, an adequate assurance of decisions conformable to truth and reason can be attained (p. 62).

For Condorcet, the mathematics of the *Essay* made it possible to justify national reliance on the superior judgment of an enlightened elite in terms of the general principle of political consent. It also made it possible to transform political decision-making from an exercise of will into the collective discovery and implementation of truth. This vision of a rational politics was to inform his career throughout the difficult days of the French Revolution.

RATIONAL POLITICS

The problem of representation, the crucial problem of the *Essay on the Application of Mathematics to the Theory of Decision-Making*, became a matter of immediate practical importance in France in 1787. In that year, the Controller-General, Calonne, recognizing the impending bankruptcy of the government, announced the program of reform that set off the course of events leading two years later to the French Revolution. Central to Calonne's proposed reforms (and to those of his successor, Brienne) was the creation of provincial assemblies composed of representatives elected by and among landowners without distinction of rank and Estate. This reform, echoing as it did Turgot's *Memorandum on the Municipalities*, Condorcet welcomed with enthusiasm. Since these provincial assemblies could ultimately send representatives to a national assembly (again without distinction of rank and Estate) he regarded their creation as infinitely preferable to the demand for the calling of the antiquated Estates-General that would preserve the privileges of the clergy and the aristocracy by meeting as three separate Estates. Thus, while many liberals were joining the campaign of the parlements for the Estates-General, Condorcet was waging a consistent campaign against it. As part of this campaign, he developed a comprehensive program for detailed constitutional change, published in his *Essay on the Constitution and Functions of the Provincial Assemblies* at the very end of 1788. This lengthy work was Condorcet's most comprehensive treatise on political theory. It developed in detail his concern to make representative political institutions responsible for the rational conduct of politics. But by the time it was published, it had already been left behind by events. To Condorcet's great apprehension, the government had been compelled to call the Estates-General for 1789.

In the remaining months before the Estates-General met, Condorcet had two principal aims. Bombarding the electorate with pamphlets, he attempted to avert impending disaster by enlightening the population on the rights of man and the principles of rational politics. At the same time, he presented himself for election, first in the assembly of the nobility of Mantes (where he held property) and then in the assembly of the nobility of Paris. In both these assemblies, Condorcet participated in drawing up the traditional *cahiers de doléances*; in neither was he chosen to represent his fellows at Versailles. Not until after the fall of the Bastille and the collapse of the traditional city government in the capital did Condorcet win elective office, as a member of the new municipal assembly of Paris. There he played a conspicuous part in the efforts of that assembly to maintain order and calm as the Revolution threatened, with the October Days, to drift into anarchy.

Anarchy, its causes and dangers, dominated the academician's thinking in the waning months of 1789. If its dangers were evident everywhere, its causes were not far to seek. Condorcet found them in irresponsible leadership and an ignorant populace. Rational politics and peaceful constitutional change required the leadership of an enlightened elite and the educated participation of a population instructed in the nature and limits of its rights. The elaboration of such a rational political order was the aim of the Society of 1789, a club founded early in 1790 by Condorcet and his associates (a group closely linked to Lafayette) in an attempt to counterbalance the influence of more radical leaders in the Jacobin Club. Its purpose, as Condorcet argued in the prospectus for the *Journal of the Society of 1789*, was to develop the principles of the "social art"—"that science for which all other sciences work." Equating rational politics with peaceful solutions, social science with political order, the members of the Society of 1789 hoped at once to guarantee the political achievements of 1789 (hence the name of their society) and substitute rational discussion for the threat of further unrest.

Not surprisingly, given the abstract character of its aims, the Society of 1789 was short lived and had little influence. But it represented a conception of rational politics that Condorcet was to pursue throughout his career. The establishment of complete equality between men and women, and the creation of an educated populace through the provision of public instruction for all, were central to that conception. Of the many articles Condorcet published in the *Journal of the Society of 1789*, one of the most interesting is his essay, *On the Admission of Women to the Rights of Citizenship*, which represents the clearest statement of his feminism.

It has often been assumed that Condorcet became a convinced feminist under the influence of Sophie de Grouchy, whom he met and married in 1786. This remarkable woman, who shared his passion for liberty and taste for philosophy (she later translated Adam Smith's *Theory of Moral Sentiments*), doubtless encouraged Condorcet in the formulation of his views on equal rights for women. But the notes he wrote for a revised edition of his reception speech at the French

Academy would seem to indicate that he was already a convinced feminist before his marriage. In this respect, Condorcet shared in a larger upsurge of feminism on the eve of the Revolution, to which he gave perhaps the clearest expression and the most radical political formulation.

In the notes to his reception speech, and in a series of political writings culminating in *On the Admission of Women*, Condorcet suggested a number of basic arguments for the rights of women. These rights, he insisted, are required by reason and justice. The rights of men result simply from the fact that they are sentient beings endowed with the capacity to form moral ideas through the exercise of reason. "Women, having these same qualities, must necessarily possess equal rights. Either no individual of the human species has any true rights, or all have the same. And he who votes against the rights of another, of whatever religion, color, or sex, has thereby abjured his own" (p. 98). But what of the traditional arguments for the inequality of women? Physically, Condorcet argued, women are doubtless weaker than men. But should this be grounds for inequality? Emotionally, there are many differences between the sexes. But are these anything but the result of education and socialization? Excluded by the laws from the conduct of public affairs, women have naturally been socialized to act and react differently from men. But should the effects of such exclusion be accepted as an argument for its continuation?

Intellectually, Condorcet admitted, it can indeed be said that no woman has ever demonstrated genius in the arts and sciences. Perhaps this phenomenon is the result of inferior education and lack of opportunity; perhaps it has an ultimate physiological basis. In one of his last writings, *Fragment on the New Atlantis*, Condorcet was to suggest this as an important area of research for scientists. But in any case, he argued, this phenomenon suggests only that women may be inferior to a small class of exceptionally gifted men, not that they are in any way inferior to the great mass of male humanity. "Since it would be completely absurd to restrict to this superior class the rights of citizenship and the eligibility for public functions, why should women be excluded from them any more than those men who are inferior to a great number of women?" (p. 98).

These considerations apart, there remained one principal objection to equal rights for women: the argument that the exercise of public functions would take them away from the home and the fulfillment of their natural duties. But this argument, Condorcet maintained, had no more force than the contention that the exercise of political rights would take the peasant from his plow or the artisan from his workshop. A woman enlightened by the exercise of her political rights would be better fitted to educate children and raise free men. Indeed, the freedom of men to exercise their natural rights, in accordance with an independent reason, could not be sustained in the long run unless their wives and mothers enjoyed the same rights. It was for this reason that when Condorcet came to discuss the question of public instruction, he placed enormous emphasis on the equal education of men and women.

Condorcet developed his ideas on this subject in a series of articles published in the course of 1791 in a journal entitled *Bibliothèque de l'homme public* (The Public Man's Library). The educational views developed in these *Memoirs on Public Instruction* stand at the heart of his vision of a just society, rational democratic politics, and indefinite social progress. Given legislative form in the influential plan for public instruction which Condorcet presented to the Legislative Assembly in April 1792, they represent the culmination of the educational discussions of the Enlightenment. Although never adopted in the precise form proposed by Condorcet, this educational plan influenced the shape of French education throughout the nineteenth century and into the twentieth.

The title of the *Memoirs on Public Instruction*, the first of which is printed in this volume, was in itself a programmatic statement. In speaking of *instruction*, rather than *education*, Condorcet was invoking a distinction fundamental to educational debate in the eighteenth century. *Education* implied the formation of the whole personality: the inculcation of ideas, beliefs, and attitudes through control of the entire environment of youth, in accordance with the model of communal education among the ancients. Many revolutionaries were prepared to argue that such education was the only effective method to form citizens worthy of the new state. *Instruction* implied what we would normally think of today as schooling: the communication of ideas, techniques, and skills necessary for the conduct of everyday life, and the encouragement and training of talent appropriate for the various occupations and professions. This alone, Condorcet insisted, must constitute the responsibility of the government in a modern society.

Communal education among the ancients rested upon the existence of a slave class that freed the small body of citizens for civic functions; it was founded upon the assumption that citizens existed only to be molded for service to the state. Neither of these conditions, Condorcet maintained, could exist in modern society. Here, where everyday economic functions must be carried out by citizens no less equal in their rights than those relieved of the economic necessity for such labor, where social differentiation implies a need for a differentiated system of public instruction to meet the needs of all social classes, the attempt to form all citizens in a rigorously identical mold would be utterly inappropriate. It would also be entirely contrary to the true principles of liberty—the liberty of the individual thinking being to form his own ideas—which the ancients never understood. Thus Condorcet placed it beyond the power of government to inculcate beliefs by teaching current opinions as dogmatic truths. Even the constitution was to be presented as a statement of present political fact rather than as the object of a new civic religion. The aim of public instruction was to be limited to teaching men and women how to think, not telling them what to think. "The duty of the public authority is to arm the full force of truth against error, which is always a public evil. But it does not have the right to decide where truth resides or where error is to be found" (p. 127). For that reason, Condorcet argued, the actual content of public instruction—heavily weighted toward scientific education as the best means of training the critical intelligence and the independent mind—should be determined by scientists and scholars organized independently of government authority.

To public instruction, thus defined, Condorcet assigned two principal tasks: the maximization of the sum of knowledge and ability available to society as a whole, and the maintenance of equal rights. Men are by nature unequal; as society becomes more complex, social dependence increases, and so do the effects of natural inequalities. This is particularly true, Condorcet recognized, of inequalities of intellect. Education cannot diminish the intellectual superiority of particular individuals; indeed it can only foster that superiority for the advancement of society as a whole. "It would indeed be a fatal love of equality that feared to

extend the class of enlightened men and to increase their enlightenment" (p. 108). In Condorcet's vision of the good society a hierarchical
system of public instruction, open to all in proportion to their means and
abilities, would enable every individual to acquire the knowledge and
skills of which he is capable. The arts and crafts would thereby be
promoted by public training in skills formerly regarded as guild secrets;
the professions would be advanced by opening them to the talents; and
an army of researchers would be trained to further social progress
through the advancement of science. Knowledge would increase,
enlightenment would become widespread, and human progress would
continue indefinitely.

But while the benefits of natural inequalities would be maximized for
the good of all, the pattern of dependence and subjection such
inequalities had always implied would be eliminated. The citizen who
knew arithmetic enough for the conduct of his own life would not be
dependent upon someone more learned for health and happiness; the
individual instructed in the elements of civil law would not be enslaved
by the most enlightened of lawyers; the person who had learned to
exercise his native powers of reasoning would not be deprived of his
natural rights by the power of a demagogue. Elementary instruction,
open to all, would therefore extend a true equality of rights by
destroying the dependence that goes with ignorance. It would establish
a real liberty of individual choice and action by preparing every citizen
to fulfill the common functions of everyday social life. And it would
create the conditions for the rational conduct of politics by preparing
every citizen to exercise the civic responsibilities entrusted to all and to
recognize the necessity of delegating more complicated responsibilities
to those more enlightened. The conditions would be created, in short,
for the rational politics toward which Condorcet constantly endeavored
to turn the conduct of the French Revolution.

POLITICAL FAILURE

In October, 1791, Condorcet entered the Legislative Assembly. He
did so as an avowed republican. Convinced by the abortive flight of

Louis XVI to Varennes that royal defiance would continue to breed anarchy and prevent the peaceful fulfillment of the Revolution, the academician had broken from his former friends with a sensational declaration of republicanism in July 1791. He found new allies among Brissot and his associates, who became the principal leaders of the new assembly. With the Brissotins, Condorcet pressed vigorously for the French declaration of war against Austria that came in April 1792. With the Brissotins, too, he waged an active campaign in the assembly against an irresponsible king, untrustworthy royal ministers, and a court suspected of counterrevolutionary plotting. The result of this campaign was to create a deadlock between the assembly and the crown that could only be broken by popular intervention. The first sign of that intervention came on 20 June 1792, when a crowd of armed demonstrators filed through the assembly to demand action against the king, before proceeding to the royal palace to harass their monarch. In this situation, the Brissotins found themselves caught between the anvil of parliamentary moderatism and the hammer of popular radicalism. They were also victims of their own failure of nerve. As popular demands for the suspension or deposition of Louis XVI mounted, the Brissotins found themselves lacking the will and unsure of the means to remove the king and save the principle of representative government. Personally convinced of the necessity and inevitability of the deposition of the monarch, Condorcet nevertheless found himself a reluctant witness to the revolution of 10 August 1792, which overthrew the monarchy by direct popular insurrection.

Elected once again to the Convention, which proclaimed the French Republic on 21 September 1792, Condorcet was to declare himself in favor of Louis XVI's guilt but against his execution: instead, he proposed the most extreme penalty short of death. In the meantime, he devoted himself to two principal concerns, the defense (ultimately unsuccessful) of his plan for public instruction and the drafting of his second great legislative scheme—the constitutional plan often known as the Girondin constitution. Elected to the constitutional committee of the Convention on 11 October 1792, Condorcet soon became the most influential and hard-working of its members. Largely responsible for the draft constitution that the committee eventually approved, he presented the plan to the Convention on 15 February 1793.

Condorcet's constitutional plan is complicated in its detailed provisions, but its main outlines are relatively simple. Certain of its conditions can be regarded as given, both in Condorcet's own thinking and in the particular political circumstances in which he wrote. The unity of the republic, a fundamental principle of the French Revolution, was now required by political necessity and the demands of national defense. It was a principle that Condorcet had constantly embraced. Representative government, as opposed to direct democracy, was necessitated by the very size of the country and its population. For Condorcet, it was also a matter of urgency to sustain the principle of representation against the claims of the Parisian crowd to exercise the direct right of popular sovereignty by force of insurrection. Universal male suffrage and the elimination of fiscal conditions of eligibility for public office had been virtually dictated by such insurrection on 10 August 1792. They were willingly accepted by Condorcet (who in the course of the French Revolution abandoned the idea of a restricted suffrage he had originally accepted from his mentor, Turgot), though he would doubtless have preferred Frenchmen to be ready to accord the same rights to women.

Given these conditions, the problem Condorcet attempted to solve in his constitutional plan can be stated, as he approached it, almost mathematically. How could the representatives of the people be made responsible in a way that would allow for the direct expression of popular opinion, without at the same time permitting a portion of the population to arrogate the right to speak in the name of all? How could the actions of the representatives and the deliberations of the people be organized in such a way as to formulate the collective reason of the greatest number, rather than to express merely the arbitrary will of the majority? How could this be done peacefully and rationally, avoiding tumult and disorder on the one hand, and the paralysis of government on the other?

Essentially, Condorcet's solution to these problems involved two main elements. The first was the creation of primary assemblies in every locality. These assemblies would be given the power to elect the members of the national assembly and the council of ministers; to accept or reject a constitution or constitutional amendments, or decide other issues submitted to popular referendum; and to initiate a demand for legislative action or a constitutional convention. Their deliberations would be organized in such a way as to maximize their reliability as a true expression of the common will (or, as Condorcet would prefer, the common reason) and minimize their potential for disorder. To achieve this first goal, Condorcet applied the reasoning of his *Essay on the Application of Mathematics to the Theory of Decision-Making*. Questions presented to the primary assemblies would be submitted to each assembly in exactly the same form, logically reduced to a series of propositions requiring a simple yes or no vote, and decided without prior discussion. These votes would then be mathematically combined to express the rational will of the whole people.

One advantage of such deliberations, Condorcet emphasized, was that they would also allow for short meetings attended by peaceful and industrious citizens, with no opportunity for trouble-makers to disturb the public good. At the same time, the creation of the primary assemblies would make it possible to institutionalize the right to revolution by a complex mechanism that would give citizens the means to effect revolutionary change under a legal, peaceful form. This mechanism would deprive any portion of the people of the pretext that it was taking direct action in the name of the whole. The process could be initiated by any fifty citizens demanding the convocation of a primary assembly to consider whether the legislative assembly should be required to take up a particular issue, or whether a constitutional convention should be called. And the problem of insurrection would thereby be solved constitutionally by provisions for permanent, legal revolution.

The second main element in Condorcet's constitutional plan was the creation of a unicameral assembly. Long an opponent of any system of the balance of powers, Condorcet maintained that such systems either destroyed themselves or depended for their operation upon an invisible constitution based on corruption and intrigue, or the existence of a two-party system. Neither of these was acceptable to the French nation, as Condorcet interpreted its need for a stable, rational regime. It followed, then, that legislative power was to be delegated to a unicameral assembly free of the complicated checks and balances dictated by the "fear of innovation, one of the most fatal scourges of the human race" (pp. 156–57). To ensure the rationality and responsibility of the decisions of this assembly, however, it was limited to a duration of two years between elections (though representatives were eligible for reelection), constrained by a form of procedure intended to minimize the possibility of rash and ill-considered action, and subject at any time to censure by the primary assemblies. Ministers elected by the people were to be answerable to the assembly without being its creatures; they were removable by that assembly, but only subject to ratification of that decision by an elected national jury. For the aristocratic principle of the balance of powers, Condorcet therefore substituted the eternal vigilance of an enlightened and informed population and a constitutional mechanism that would ensure the rationality of all political decisions.

Condorcet's speech explaining the provisions of his constitutional plan was the expression of a life-long concern with the relationship of reason and will in politics, the culmination of twenty years' reflection upon the principles of liberty and equality. But it had little effect. Seized upon by Brissot and his associates as a means of gaining the initiative from the radicals of the Jacobin Club, Condorcet's legislative proposals quickly fell victim to the struggle between the Girondins and the Jacobins for control of the Convention. Constantly interrupted by popular petition and political conflict, suffering lengthy postponements as the deputies moved to deal with the more pressing issues of domestic revolt and civil war, the debate dragged on rather incoherently until 2 June 1793 when a new popular insurrection purged the assembly of twenty-nine of the leading Girondins. Their control of the Convention thereby assured, the Jacobins lost no time in introducing their own constitutional plan, created like the world (it was remarked) in six days! Submitted to the Convention on 10 June, the Jacobin constitution was adopted after little discussion two weeks later.

To these events Condorcet reacted with an explosive pamphlet protesting the adoption of the Jacobin constitution and defending his own. Condemned for this action in the Convention, the *philosophe* fled into hiding before he could be arrested. He left behind him a last, unfinished appeal to the people to save themselves from the tyranny he now saw prepared for them, a fundamental restatement of his understanding of the relationship between social science and rational politics.

The *Essay on the Application of Mathematics to the Theory of Decision-Making* had been intended for the educated elite of the old regime: the elite of academicians and statesmen, liberal nobles and enlightened bourgeois, who had failed in the Society of 1789 to guide the conduct of the French Revolution according to rational principles. *A General View of the Science of Social Mathematics* was meant for a different audience: the mass of the French people whose ignorance of the true principles of the moral and political sciences had destroyed Condorcet's hopes for representative politics and now threatened to deliver France to the dictatorship of extremism. Published in a *Journal of Social Instruction* created to provide "that instruction which the false politics or indifference of our legislators has constantly refused us for three years," [14] the article was regarded by Condorcet as part of a desperate last attempt to free the people from the ignorance and error upon which political despotism must always depend.

To achieve this goal, Condorcet extended and generalized his conception of social mathematics into a "common, everyday science," applicable to every realm of social conduct. This science could only be developed, he admitted, by "mathematicians who have thoroughly studied the social sciences" (p. 189). But its utility and applications would be no more limited to the mathematicians who had created it than was the use of lunar tables for navigation restricted to the scientists who had developed the theory upon which such tables depended. Every man, in all his actions, is a gambler. Each individual automatically and intuitively balances the probabilities involved in his actions. The development and propagation of a mathematical social science grounded on the theory of probabilities would therefore enable men to substitute rational calculation for habitual and instinctive modes of thought and action. It would free men from passion and prejudice, deliver them from the mob-leader's art, and restore the empire of reason to social affairs. It would, in short, become the basis of a "social art" that would render democratic politics rational and rational politics democratic. Such, at least, was Condorcet's dream.

THE FUTURE OF HUMANITY

Driven into hiding near the Jardin du Luxembourg, the defeated philosophe embarked upon a justification of his political conduct in the course of the French Revolution, only to be persuaded by his wife to abandon a personal defense for a vindication of humanity at large. While the Terror reached its height in the streets around him, Condorcet found consolation in a project he had long planned and discussed, a comprehensive historical study of the nature and course of human progress. The hastily written introduction to that study, published posthumously in 1795 as the *Sketch for a Historical Picture of the Progress of the Human Mind*, immediately became the philosophe's most influential work. The defense and elaboration of the belief that had guided Condorcet's actions throughout his life, the *Sketch* became the starting point for much of the social theory of the nineteenth century.

The manuscript of the *Sketch* left among Condorcet's papers is dated 4 October 1793. He spent his remaining months of life drafting many chapters for the larger work to which the *Sketch* was only an introduction. While some of these fragments developed and substantiated Condorcet's view of progress in past epochs, others elaborated upon the means to further progress in the future. One outlined a project for a universal symbolic language of the sciences; another developed a decimal system of classification to be used for the organization and investigation of scientific data; still another explored the moral and social effects of techniques of birth control. One of the most important of these fragments, the *Fragment on the New Atlantis*, set forth Condorcet's hopes for the organization of scientific life in the new society. Despite this frenzy of activity, the vast *Historical Picture of the Progress of the Human Mind* was never finished. Fearing for the security of his asylum and the safety of those conspiring to hide him, Condorcet abandoned his writing and left his hiding place toward the end of March 1794. He sought refuge on the outskirts of Paris, where he was arrested in a country inn, his humble disguise betrayed (the story goes) by his demeanor and the aristocratic number of eggs he expected in an omelette. Imprisoned on 27 March 1794, he was found dead two days later.

The aim of the *Sketch for a Historical Picture of the Progress of the Human Mind* was to reclaim man's past in order to demonstrate his power to control the future. This meant that it was necessary to see history as a truly human past, which is to say a secular past, the product of human action and interaction rather than of divine intervention and inspiration. This meant, too, that it was necessary to find a principle of order that would reveal an intelligible past, the orderly creation of men rather than the haphazard product of chance and circumstance. Condorcet found this principle of order in sensationalist psychology: in the ability of man to receive and compare sensations, ordering them by the use of signs and the elaboration of ever more abstract linguistic systems, perpetually combining and recombining them to his own satisfaction or advantage. Prompted by man's first instinctive experience of external phenomena independent of his existence, fostered by the progressive development of social communication among men, accelerated by the development of modern science, this fundamental psychological capacity was the motor force of progress and the key to the true understanding of history. In this sense, Condorcet regarded the indefinite progress of humanity as implied in the very nature of man. The aim of the *Sketch* was less to explain the growth of reason itself—that growth was posited as natural—than to point to the destruction of the obstacles which had inhibited or distorted that growth. It was to demonstrate man's progressive emancipation, first from the arbitrary domination of his physical environment and then from the historical bondage of his own making.

Having thus reclaimed the past as a human past and revealed the logic of the development of human faculties behind the crimes and contingencies of history, it remained only to demonstrate man's potential for indefinite progress in the future. Essentially, Condorcet's hopes for the future rested upon two broad conclusions. First, he was convinced that the obstacles which had in the past threatened the advance and dissemination of reason were finally being destroyed under the impact of scientific, technological, and political revolution. Second, he believed that the discovery of the true principles of the moral and political sciences had made it possible to elaborate a rational "social art" that would foster social progress and scientific advance. Rational laws would destroy artificial conflicts of interests among individuals and nations, mitigate those that are ineradicable, and foster the natural sentiments of compassion and benevolence. An enlightened system of public instruction would inform men as to their true rights and interests, and arm every individual with the means of providing rationally for his needs. Social mathematics, propagated and practiced as a common, everyday guide to rational conduct, would teach everyone to estimate the consequences of his actions, thus avoiding the erroneous calculation of interest that lies at the heart of most antisocial behavior. And the rational organization of scientific research, independent of government intervention and purged of false social interests, would advance the frontiers of human knowledge beyond the power of the imagination to conceive.

All this, Condorcet insisted in the *Sketch*, was within man's grasp. "Everything tells us that we are now close upon one of the great revolutions of the human race. . . . The present state of enlightenment assures us that this revolution will have a favorable result, but is not this only on condition that we know how to employ our knowledge and resources to their fullest extent?" (p. 217). This was a revealing phrase. For although Condorcet's belief in indefinite future progress was based on the general assertion that observation of past events warrants extrapolation into the probable future, he was not strictly a historical determinist. Since in his view nature has endowed man collectively with the capacity to learn from experience, to understand its laws, and to modify their effects, the progressive emancipation of man from nature is itself natural. The growth of freedom is the only historical law. The *Sketch* not only demonstrated the power of the social art to direct and secure that freedom; it also made clear that it could succeed only as a democratic and collective art. Only if all are enlightened can any be free. Ultimately it is this emphasis upon the collective action of mankind, this concern with "the most obscure and neglected chapter of the history of the human race"—the progress of the mass of the people in society—that links Condorcet's conception of social science with his broad view of human history.

NOTES TO "INTRODUCTION"

1. The principal biographical studies of Condorcet are listed in the Bibliography. The present introduction draws largely on my own recent work, *Condorcet. From Natural Philosophy to Social Mathematics* (Chicago, 1975). Readers seeking more substantial documentation of points suggested here are invited to consult that work.

2. For a comprehensive study of the academy and its place in eighteenth-century French life, see Roger Hahn, *The Anatomy of a Scientific Institution. The Paris Academy of Sciences* (Berkeley, 1971).

3. In quotations cited in this way, page numbers refer to the present volume.

4. Voltaire to Claude Henri de Fuzée de Voisenon (August 20, 1774), letter 17984; Voltaire to Jean le Rond d'Alembert (August 17, 1774), letter 17975, in Theodore Besterman, ed. *Voltaire's Correspondence*, 107 vols. (Geneva, 1953–1965).

5. Condorcet to Turgot (June 29, 1770), Charles Henry, ed., *Correspondance inédite de Condorcet et de Turgot (1770–1779)* (Paris, 1883), p. 16.

6. On Turgot, see Douglas Dakin, *Turgot and the Ancien Regime in France* (London, 1939); Edgar Faure, *La disgrâce de Turgot* (Paris, 1961).

7. For a brief discussion of these schemes, and an indication of the range of interpretation to which they have been subject, see Gerald J. Cavanaugh, "Turgot: the Rejection of Enlightened Despotism," *French Historical Studies* 6 (1969–1970): 31–58.

8. Condorcet to Voltaire (June 5, 1776), letter 19014, in Besterman, *Voltaire's Correspondence.*

9. A. Condorcet-O'Connor and F. Arago, eds., *Oeuvres de Condorcet*, 12 vols. (Paris, 1847–1849): 4: 540.

10. For the general history of the theory of probability, Isaac Todhunter, *A History of the Mathematical Theory of Probability from the Time of Pascal to that of Laplace* (Cambridge and London, 1865), is still the standard work. Some of the philosophical problems that form the background to Condorcet's thinking about probability are well discussed by Ian Hacking, "Jacques Bernouilli's *Art of Conjecturing*," *British Journal for the Philosophy of Science* 22(1971): 209–229; "Equipossibility Theories of Probability," ibid., 339–355; and *The Emergence of Probability* (Cambridge, 1975). The relationship between the thinking of Condorcet and Laplace on probability is discussed by C.C. Gillispie, "Probability and Politics: Laplace, Condorcet and Turgot," *Proceedings of the American Philosophical Society* 116 (1972): 1–20.

11. *Essai sur l'application de l'analyse à la probabilité des décisions rendues à la pluralité des voix* (Paris, 1785), p. xciii.

12. See especially Duncan Black, *The Theory of Committees and Elections* (Cambridge, 1958); G.-G. Granger, *La mathématique sociale du marquis de Condorcet* (Paris, 1956); and G.-Th. Guilbaud, "Theories of the General Interest and the Logical Problem of Aggregation," in Paul R. Lazarsfeld and Neil W. Henry, eds., *Readings in Mathematical Social Science* (Chicago, 1966), pp. 262–307.

13. Alfred de Grazia, "Mathematical Derivation of an Election System," *Isis* 44 (1953): 42–51, gives a translation of Borda's paper.

14. *Journal d'instruction sociale. Prospectus* (Paris, 1793), p. 12.

CHRONOLOGY: *Condorcet's Life and Works*

1788   Publishes a number of pamphlets in support of the reforming measures of Brienne and against the calling of the Estates-General. Publishes the *Essai sur la constitution et les fonctions des assemblées provinciales.*

1789   Works to secure the election of enlightened representatives to the Estates-General. Participates in the drafting of the *cahier de doléances* of the nobility of Mantes and of Paris. Fails to win election to the Estates-General.

  Elected to the municipal assembly of Paris established after the fall of the Bastille.

1790   One of the founders of the Society of 1789. Edits the society's journal, to which he contributes a number of articles, including *Sur l'admission des femmes au droit de cité.*

1791   Publishes five *Mémoires sur l'instruction publique.*

  Declares in favor of a republic after the king's flight to Varennes.

  Elected to the Legislative Assembly, which opens its sessions on 1 October. Closely associated with the Brissotins. Becomes one of the leading figures in the assembly.

1792   Presents a comprehensive plan for public instruction to the Legislative Assembly (April). Becomes convinced of the necessity to depose Louis XVI constitutionally, but is unable to avert the overthrow of the monarchy by the revolution of 10 August 1792.

  Elected to the Convention, which opens its sessions on 20 September. Appointed to the Committee on the Constitution, which is charged with drafting a republican constitution.

1793   Presents a constitutional plan to the Convention (the "Girondin Constitution") in February. Protests against the purging of the Convention on 2 June and denounces the Jacobin Constitution.

  Publishes the *Journal d'instruction sociale*, containing the unfinished *Tableau général de la science qui a pour object l'application du calcul aux sciences politiques et morales.*

  Denounced in the Convention on 8 July, he goes into hiding. Spends his remaining months at work on the *Tableau historique des progrès de l'esprit humain.*

1794   Leaves his hiding place; arrested at Bourg-la-Reine, on the outskirts of Paris, on 27 March. Found dead in prison 29 March.

1795   Publication of the *Esquisse d'un tableau historique des progrès de l'esprit humain.*

Select Bibliography

WORKS BY CONDORCET

French editions:

Eléments du calcul des probabilités et son application aux jeux de hasard, à la loterie et aux jugements des hommes. Paris, 1805.

Esquisse d'un tableau historique des progrès de l'esprit humain, edited by O. H. Prior. Paris, 1933. Reprint with a new preliminary essay by Yvon Belaval. Paris, 1970.

Essai sur l'application de l'analyse à la probabilité des décisions rendues à la pluralité des voix. Paris, 1785. Reprint. New York, 1972.

Oeuvres de Condorcet. 12 vols., edited by A. Condorcet-O'Connor and François Arago. Paris, 1847–1849. Reprint. Stuttgart, 1968.

English translations:

An Authentic Copy of the New Plan of the French Constitution, as presented to the National Convention. . . . London, 1793. Obscure and unreliable, but the only complete translation of Condorcet's constitutional project.

Life of M. Turgot. London, 1787.

Life of Voltaire. London, 1790.

Notes on Book XXIX of "The Spirit of the Laws." In *A Commentary and Review of Montesquieu's Spirit of Laws. . . .* by Destutt de Tracy. Philadelphia, 1811.

Report on the General Organization of Public Instruction. In *French Liberalism and Education in the 18th Century,* edited by F. de la Fontainerie. New York, 1932.

Sketch for a Historical Picture of the Progress of the Human Mind, translated by June Barraclough with an introduction by Stuart Hampshire. London, 1955.

WORKS ON CONDORCET

Alengry, Franck. *Condorcet, guide de la Révolution française, théoricien du droit constitutionnel et précurseur de la science sociale.* Paris, 1903.

Baker, Keith Michael. *Condorcet. From Natural Philosophy to Social Mathematics.* Chicago, 1975.

Black, Duncan. *The Theory of Committees and Elections.* Cambridge, 1958. Contains an important discussion of Condorcet's theory of decision-making.

Bouissounouse, Janine. *Condorcet. Le philosophe dans la Révolution.* Paris, 1962. A short, popular biography.

Cahen, Léon. *Condorcet et la Révolution française.* Paris, 1904. Still the standard account of Condorcet's political career.

Gillispie, Charles Coulston. "Probability and Politics: Laplace, Condorcet and Turgot." *Proceedings of the American Philosophical Society* 116 (1972): 1–20.

Granger, Gilles-Gaston. *La mathématique sociale du marquis de Condorcet.* Paris, 1956. An important book.

Guilbaud, G.-Th. "Theories of the General Interest and the Logical Problem of Aggregation." Pp. 302–307 in *Readings in Mathematical Social Science,* edited by Paul R. Lazarsfeld and Neil W. Henry. Chicago, 1966. Like Black and Granger above, discusses Condorcet's contribution to the development of the theory of decision-making.

Koyré, Alexandre. "Condorcet." *Journal of the History of Ideas* 9 (1948): 131–152. A sympathetic view.

Manuel, Frank. *The Prophets of Paris.* Cambridge, Mass., 1968. Contains an excellent essay on Condorcet.

Reichardt, Rolf. *Reform und Revolution bei Condorcet. Ein Beitrag zur späten Aufklärung in Frankreich.* Bonn, 1973. An important study.

Schapiro, J. Salwyn. *Condorcet and the Rise of Liberalism.* New York, 1934.

Sée, Henri. "Condorcet, ses idées et son role politique." *Revue de synthèse historique* 10 (1905): 22–33. A succinct analysis.

GENERAL WORKS

Bury, J. B. *The Idea of Progress.* London, 1920.

Cassirer, Ernst. *The Philosophy of the Enlightenment.* Translated by Fritz C. A. Koellin and James P. Pettegrove. Princeton, 1951.

Cobban, Alfred. *A History of Modern France.* 3 vols. 3d. ed. Baltimore, 1963. Penguin Books, 1965.

———. *In Search of Humanity. The Role of the Enlightenment in Modern History.* New York, 1960.

Frankel, Charles. *The Faith of Reason: The Idea of Progress in the French Enlightenment.* New York, 1948.

Furet, François, and Richet, Denis. *The French Revolution*. Translated by Stephen Hardman. New York, 1970.

Gay, Peter. *The Enlightenment: An Interpretation*. 2 vols. New York, 1966–1969.

———. *Voltaire's Politics. The Poet as Realist*. Princeton, 1959.

Gillispie, Charles Coulston. *The Edge of Objectivity. An Essay in the History of Scientific Ideas*. Princeton, 1960.

Hahn, Roger. *The Anatomy of a Scientific Institution. The Paris Academy of Sciences*. Berkeley, 1971.

Lefebvre, Georges. *The French Revolution from its Origins to 1793*. Translated by Elizabeth Moss Evanson. New York, 1962.

Sydenham, M. J. *The French Revolution*. New York, 1965.

———. *The Girondins*. London, 1961.

Williams, David. "The Politics of Feminism in the French Enlightenment." Pp. 333–51 in *The Varied Pattern: Studies in the 18th Century*, edited by Peter Hughes and David Williams. Toronto, 1971.

NOTE ON THE TRANSLATIONS

With the exception of *Essay on the Application of Mathematics to the Theory of Decision-Making*, translated from *Essai sur l'application de l'analyse à la probabilité des décisions rendues à la pluralité des voix* (Paris, 1785), and the introduction and notes to the *Reception Speech at the French Academy* which remain among Condorcet's manuscripts in the Bibliothèque de l'Institut de France (MS. 855, ff.2–21), the French versions of the works translated here appear in *Oeuvres de Condorcet*, 12 vols., edited by F. Arago and A. Condorcet-O'Connor (Paris, 1847–1849).

The translation of Condorcet's *Sketch for a Historical Picture of the Progress of the Human Mind* by June Barraclough was first published in 1955 by Weidenfeld and Nicolson, London. It appears here by permission of both Mr. Arthur A. Cohen and Weidenfeld and Nicolson. *On the Admission of Women to the Rights of Citizenship* is a revised version of a translation published by Dr. Alice Drysdale Vickery as *The First Essay on the Political Rights of Women* (Letchworth, 1912). The remaining translations were made by the editor of this volume. Editor's notes (and occasional notes by Condorcet) follow each selection.

I wish to express my appreciation to Dr. Dora Bell who graciously made available to me her own draft translation of Condorcet's *Memoirs on Public Instruction*. And I should like to thank Robert Smith and Florence Thomas, who patiently typed my translations.

CONDORCET *Selected Writings*

I The Academician under the Old Regime

Reception Speech at the French Academy (21 February 1782)

Condorcet was admitted to the French Academy on 21 February 1782, after a bitter contest in which he defeated his rival by one vote. D'Alembert, who had used all his influence as permanent secretary of the academy on Condorcet's behalf, was so delighted at the outcome that he is said to have exclaimed: "I am happier at this victory than I would be if I had squared the circle!" In these circumstances, Condorcet clearly intended the speech he gave at the customary reception ceremony, a selection from which is printed below, to be a fundamental statement of his philosophical creed. Some measure of the significance he attached to this speech can be found in the fact that he prepared an anonymous introduction and notes for a second edition, elaborating and defending his views on human perfectibility, scientific advance, the relationship between scientific and social progress, the nature of the moral and political sciences, the equality of women, the achievements of the philosophes, and legal reform. The introduction and selected notes [A–L], never before published, are printed here for the first time.

[INTRODUCTION]

The discourse of the marquis de Condorcet before the French Academy is among those that have caused the most stir, much more perhaps because of the subject than the manner with which it is treated. One searches in vain for those grandiose flights of eloquence, those agreeable or striking images, those intellectual embellishments and flashes of ingenuity and wit, which qualify so many of these speeches as models for all kinds of eloquence. Its clear style—simple and grave, without neologisms or false shows of brilliance—is almost all the literary merit it possesses. But its subject is important. The author has set himself to prove that knowledge must always increase and spread among men, that the progress of humanity toward happiness and morality will follow the advance of enlightenment. He has also set himself to show that literature will lose little from this advance; and that if it does there is little cause for mourning, since this will be to the profit of reason. At least, this is how we have interpreted this part of his discourse, for the fear of displeasing those of his new fellow members who have not cultivated the sciences has apparently cast a veil (though, in truth, a rather transparent one) over this part of his discourse.

The opinion presented in this discourse is not new. It has been held by several celebrated men.[1] M. de Condorcet has merely set it forth in more detail and indicated the grounds for accepting it. Since the fate of humanity depends in great part on the truth or falsehood of this opinion, and even on the greater or lesser promptness with which the common run of men adopt it or reject it, it has been deemed useful to reprint this discourse with notes developing (or even sometimes challenging) the author's opinion. We do so, however, with the respect due to every man who usefully cultivates his time and his intellect, and who writes only what he believes. . . .

[RECEPTION SPEECH]

Gentlemen,

The honor of being admitted to your number must doubtless awaken illusions of self-glory in the man of letters who regards it as a recognition of his talents. But so glorious an honor can excite in me only the sentiment of gratitude. I know how much your just regard for the illustrious company which has favored me with the title of its interpreter has influenced your votes. In admitting me to your own assemblies, you have wished me to lack no means of responding in a worthy manner to the confidence that body has deigned to accord me.

I should like to ascribe your beneficence to the same sentiment of love for the sciences that prompted you to institute a public eulogy in memory of Fontenelle, the most celebrated of my predecessors in a career in which I march so far behind him.[2] You have believed that a philosopher who, without having enriched the sciences with any discovery, has contributed perhaps as much to their progress as the most fertile geniuses, must share with them in the same honors. And you have treated Fontenelle with as much respect as Descartes, because Fontenelle rendered common and popular the truths that Descartes revealed only to the wise.

This union between the sciences and letters, the bonds of which you seek to tighten, must be one of the distinguishing characteristics of this century. For the first time, the general system of the principles of our knowledge has been developed. The method of discovering truths has been reduced to an art, one could almost say to a set of formulae. Reason has finally recognized the route that it must follow and seized the thread that will prevent it from going astray.[A] These first truths, these methods spread through all nations and carried into two worlds, can no longer perish. No more will the human race see those alternations of obscurity and enlightenment to which it was long believed that nature had eternally condemned it. It is no longer in the power of men to extinguish the torch lit by genius. Only a global catastrophe could bring back the shades of darkness.

Living in this happy epoch, witnessing the final efforts of ignorance and error, we have seen reason emerge victorious from a battle that has been so long and arduous. And now at last we can exclaim: *truth has conquered; the human race is saved!* Each century will add new enlightenment to that of the century that has preceded it, and this progress, which nothing can henceforth halt or delay, will have no other limits than that of the duration of the universe.

Yet is there no boundary beyond which the natural limits of our mind will render all progress impossible? No, gentlemen, there is not. As enlightenment increases, methods of instruction will be correspondingly perfected; the human mind will seem to grow and its limits to recede. A young man now leaving school possesses more real knowledge than the greatest geniuses—not of antiquity, but even of the seventeenth century—could have acquired by long study. Ever more comprehensive methods succeed one another, bringing together within a narrow compass all the truths it occupied the men of genius of a whole century to discover. In all ages, the human mind will see before it an ever-infinite space; but the gulf which at each moment it leaves behind it—that which separates it from the period of its infancy—will constantly increase.[B]

Every scientific discovery is a benefit for humanity. No system of truths is sterile. We have gathered the fruit of our fathers' labors: let us beware of the belief that those of our contemporaries can remain useless. Let us enjoy in advance the happiness that they will one day confer upon our nephews, as a father sees with pleasure the growth of a tree that will extend its shade over his posterity.[C]

It would be easy for me to confirm this truth. Necessarily the witness of the progress of the sciences, I see each year, each month—one might almost say each day—marked equally by a new discovery and by a useful invention. This spectacle, at once sublime and consoling, has become the habit of my life and a part of my happiness. Those sciences, almost created in our own day, the object of which is man himself, the direct goal of which is the happiness of man, will enjoy a progress no less sure than that of the physical sciences. The idea, so sweet, that our nephews will surpass us in wisdom, as in enlightenment, is no longer an illusion.

In meditating on the nature of the moral sciences, one cannot indeed help seeing that, based like the physical sciences upon the observation of facts, they must follow the same methods, acquire an equally exact and precise language, attain the same degree of certainty.[D] All would be equal between them for a being foreign to our species, who would study human society as we study that of the beavers or the bees. But here the observer himself forms part of the society that he observes, and the truth can have only biased or prejudiced judges.

Thus the advance of the moral sciences will be slower than that of the physical sciences; and we should not be astonished if the principles upon which they are established have to force men's minds to receive them (to put it this way) while in physics men rush to accept new truths and even new errors.[E] But while opinion in the moral sciences, still uncertain, seems sometimes to regress and embrace the very errors it has abjured, the wise are occupied at a distance in enriching the system of human knowledge with happy discoveries. The voice of reason makes itself heard to enlightened men; it instructs children whose fathers have misunderstood it and it ensures the happiness of the generation that does not yet exist.

Thanks to printing, that preserving art which safeguards human reason, once a principle useful to public happiness has been discovered it becomes instantly the patrimony of all nations. In vain do obstinate men seek to reject a new truth set down in books: it survives the men who have disdained it; and, even as they believe it annihilated, it silently prepares its empire over opinions.

Perhaps the necessary progress of the physical sciences would have been sufficient to ensure that of the moral sciences and preserve us from the return of barbarism.[F] The union between these two orders of knowledge enlarges the sphere of the moral sciences, and can alone give to their facts the exactness, and to their results the precision, which distinguish the truths appropriate to the system of the sciences from the simple insights of reason.[G] It renders the scientists more worthy of respect by making their speculations more directly useful; it makes the philosophers more wise by accustoming them to that slow but sure advance to which the study of nature is subject, by teaching them to expect everything from time, the infallible effect of which is to bring happy revolutions and great discoveries.[H]

But since it is impossible to contest the general progress of all the sciences, why does a powerful voice arise to attack their utility? [3] Since the most remote times, each century has accused itself of being more corrupt than those that have preceded it. The view that human nature is subject to a constant process of degeneration seems to have been the common opinion in all ages of the world. It even dares to perpetuate itself among us, and in this very century eloquence has more than once employed its arts and its prestige in defense of this view.

Among these detractors of our century, whose motives I do not need here to analyze or reveal, I shall address myself solely to those virtuous men who despise the century in which they live because their soul is more afflicted by the spectacle of present evils than by the record of those past, those men who are angered against their contemporaries by the very excess of the interest they take in their happiness. If such men seem to foresee still greater evils for posterity, this is simply from fear that, unresponsive to the lessons of the wise, it will not know how to prevent the misfortune that threatens it.

I respond to them in this way. Do not accuse me of being insensitive to the evils of humanity. I know that its wounds still bleed; that the yoke of ignorance still weighs everywhere upon it; that wherever the virtuous man casts his eyes, misfortune and crime are there to sadden his view and break his heart. It is true that ignorance and error still live. But these monsters, the most formidable enemies of man's happiness, drag with them the mortal dart that has struck them, and their very cries, which terrify you, prove only how sure and terrible have been the blows they have received.

You believe us degenerate, because the austerity of our fathers has yielded place to that mildness which mingles with our virtues as with our vices, a mildness which seems to you too closely to resemble feebleness! But virtue needs to rise above nature only when it fights ignorance and the passions at one and the same time. Remember that enlightenment renders virtue easy. One might even say that love of the general good, and the courage to devote oneself to it, is the habitual state of the enlightened man.[1] In the ignorant man, justice is only a passion perhaps incompatible with gentleness. In the educated man, it is but humanity itself, subjected to the laws of reason. The project of rendering all men virtuous is chimerical: but why should one not one day see enlightenment combine with genius to create for happier generations a method of education and a system of laws that would render the courage of virtue almost useless? Governed by these salutary institutions, man would need only to listen to the voice of his heart and to that of his reason, to fulfill by natural inclination the same duties that today cost him effort and sacrifice—just as a worker without intelligence and without skill now executes with the help of machines the marvels of genius in the arts, the masterpieces that human industry abandoned to its own forces would never have equalled.[J]

This same mildness that you reproach in us has rendered wars rarer and less disastrous, has castigated as a crime that furious passion for conquest so long glorified with the name of heroism. It is to this mildness, finally, that we owe the consoling certainty that we will never again see those leagues of factious men still more fatal to the happiness of citizens than to the tranquillity of princes, nor those massacres, *those proscriptions of peoples,* that have sullied the annals of the human race.

Deign to compare your century to those preceding it. Attempt to see it with the eyes of posterity, and to judge it historically. You will see, in those ages whose virtues you mourn, a more primitive corruption uniting with ferocity in human customs, a baser greed showing itself with more audacity, vices almost unknown today shaping the character and the customs of whole nations, and even crime often counted among the number of common and everyday actions.

The judgments of historians are perhaps the least suspect proofs of the principles and manners of the times in which they have written. Consult those of past centuries. See upon what acts of barbarism, upon what injustices they have lavished their praise, even when fear or interest could no longer have dictated it. Observe in the details of their life the men whose virtues our fathers celebrated, whose panegyrics still resound among us. You will find few whom we could not reproach with actions that the public disgust would have branded in our own day with an ineffaceable opprobrium.

Yet you yourselves count these men among the virtuous. What? Is this not acknowledgment that their vices were those of their century; that to render them just it would have been sufficient to enlighten them? Pity them then, with us, for having lived in those times of ignorance in which the virtuous man—unable to find immutable and certain principles in a still primitive reason—was forced to take as his guide the opinion of his century, his virtue limited to forbidding (even in secret) the actions that this opinion had placed among the number of crimes.

See now, from one end of Europe to the other, how enlightened men combine all their efforts for the good of humanity, directing all their resources to this sole object with a courage and a concerted action unknown in any other country.[K] The barbarous practice of torture is almost abolished. The public voice, this voice so imperious when inspired by humanity and reason, demands other reforms in this part of the laws, and it will obtain them from the justice of sovereigns.[L]

The American, breaking his own chains, has imposed upon himself the duty to break those of his slaves. Of all free peoples, he has been the first to call all who cultivate the same land to the same rights and to the same liberty. The sovereign of Portugal, lamenting that he cannot imitate this great example completely, has at least ordained that in his vast estates man shall no longer be born a slave. Everything seems to announce that negro slavery, this odious remnant of the barbarous politics of the sixteenth century, will soon cease to dishonor our own.

That other slavery, which in former times deprived almost all men in Europe of the right to property, is being extinguished little by little in the countries where primitive customs and the feebleness of governments have preserved it. This fruit of anarchy will disappear with anarchy itself; and the public power, stronger and more unified, has driven before it the crowd of the oppressors.

The deaf, those unfortunate beings whom the privation of the sense which relates man to his like would condemn to imbecility and unhappy solitude, have found an unhoped-for resource in the happy application of philosophical analysis to the art of language. Returned to the ranks of men and of useful citizens, they become a touching and immortal monument to the philosophical genius that characterizes our century.

Succor directed by a beneficent and sure art has returned to life thousands of men abandoned to an apparent death, whom ignorance would have plunged still-living into the tomb. Societies of learned men, distinguished for their zeal and their enlightenment, watch over the health of the people and the preservation of the animals necessary to their subsistence. In these paternal institutions, the beneficence of monarchs has equalled, perhaps even surpassed, that which public spirit has inspired in popular constitutions.

The voice of humanity has dared to make itself heard even in the midst of the tumult of war: Cook's vessel, respected on the seas, has proved that France regards enlightenment as the common good of nations.[4] Already we see the barriers hindering commerce between different peoples lowered or removed. Harmful, especially to those who erect them, they serve only to foment national hatreds and to corrupt morality by the necessary contradiction they produce between duty and the hope of an easy gain, between the provisions of the law and the opinions of the people. Several sovereigns have finally recognized that the true interest of a nation is never separated from the general interest of the human race. They have recognized that nature could not have wished to found the happiness of one people on the unhappiness of its neighbors, nor to set in opposition two virtues that it equally inspires: love of the fatherland and love of humanity. They have felt that the true glory of a prince is measured by the felicity of his people. Legislators rather than monarchs, they have made absolute power the pure and sacred organ of an enlightened and beneficent reason.

How sweet it is for France to see its young king present the world with the spectacle of a sovereign who, in his first laws, has shown the desire to restore to his subjects that personal liberty, that freedom of property, those primitive rights, that man holds from nature and every constitution must preserve to him. How sweet it is to see a sovereign whose first political alliance accords a generous protection to a people still young and already so celebrated: a people forced by oppression to seek safety in liberty, whose first war has had as its goal only the equality of nations, the independence of the seas, and the maintenance (or rather the establishment) of a code still lacking for the security of commerce and the peace of Europe! [5]

In the midst of this war, undertaken for a cause so novel in the annals of the world, the destiny of France grants us a grandson of Henry IV and of Leopold of Lorraine, the two princes in modern history whose names have been dearest to their peoples.[6] Surrounded by domestic examples, living in the most enlightened of centuries, in the midst of a nation in which the most intense enlightenment is also the most equally distributed, he will grow with the happiness of this very nation; he will become the benefactor of a century still less infected than ours with the remnants of barbarism. Fear for him neither the seductions nor the pride of absolute power. Brought up under the eyes of a mother in whom the simple and natural graces temper the majesty of the throne, he will learn from her to value the respect one owes to his power less than the voluntary homage the heart loves to render to goodness. Like her, he will remember his grandeur only to pardon injuries, to ease misfortune, and to protect wronged innocence when lies are in everybody's mouth and fear has left the truth defenseless. It is for kings deprived of enlightenment that the intoxication of power is dangerous. In the eyes of an enlightened prince, what is sovereign power but an immense duty, even a harsh one, if the sentiment of the good that he has achieved does not come to console him? Perhaps the courage of virtue is less necessary to kings than enlightenment and a just spirit. In all men, ignorance is the most fertile source of vices: but it is especially for men endowed with supreme power that this truth is incontestable. It is for them above all that personal interest and justice, their happiness and that of their fellow citizens, are truly linked by an indissoluble chain. They alone can set against the feeble interests of their passions the opinion of the universe, whose anxious and severe eye observes and judges them, and the destiny of a whole people—threatened as it is by a moment of bad judgment or feebleness.

Among the philosophers who have regarded the progress of enlightenment as the sole foundation upon which the human race can base its hope for a universal and durable happiness, several have believed that this same progress could be harmful to that of the letters and the arts; that eloquence and poetry would languish in a nation occupied with science, philosophy, and politics.

Yet the principles of the arts are the fruits of observation and experience. They must perfect themselves to the extent that one learns to observe more methodically, precisely, and skillfully. In enlightening themselves, men acquire more—and more accurate—ideas: the distinctions they make between objects become at once finer and more precise. Thus languages must also perfect and enrich themselves, for their veritable wealth consists not in the number of words they employ but in the abundance of those expressing clear and precise ideas. They will, it is true, be less bold and less elaborate. The orator who demands only applause, or who seeks to seduce, will be able to complain of the austerity or coldness of languages. But they will offer a more flexible and more perfect instrument for those wishing only to enlighten men.

Enlightenment must have an equal influence on talent itself: it extends it and enlarges it. Picture Voltaire meditating upon a great work: he gathers around him all that his immense reading has revealed of the secrets of nature, the treasures he has derived from history, and the profound study he has made of opinions and customs. He seems not to dare to fight alone against the difficulties of his subject. And if he has been so great, if he is unique up until now in the history of letters, it is because he has combined an immense desire for glory with an inexhaustible thirst for knowledge, and has been able constantly to unite study and work, enlightenment and genius.

Sound judgment is increased by the cultivation of the sciences. And it is so necessary in the arts that the only men who have been placed among the first rank by the unanimous voice of all peoples are those rare individuals in whom sound judgment is no less striking than superiority of talent. It is perhaps the only quality that distinguishes the great man whom we admire from the extraordinary man who merely astonishes us.

Once taught to measure our esteem only on the basis of real utility, we will come to regard the fine arts as a means which reason can and must utilize to penetrate men's minds and extend its conquests. These arts, subject to the severest laws, will proscribe those beauties of convention founded on antique errors and on popular beliefs. But they will replace them with beauties more real, beauties that austere truth will not disavow. If frivolous minds wish to regard this change as signifying the decadence of the arts, the philosopher will recognize it as the sure effect of the advance of the human mind toward perfection. We shall perhaps lose some vain pleasures; but must man regret the playthings of his infancy?

The progress of reason is far from being antithetical to the perfection of the fine arts. Indeed, if this progress could come to a halt, if we were condemned to know only what our fathers have known, these arts would soon be annihilated. For since they are founded on imitation, how could they not themselves be brought to a halt, or fall into decay, if the objects they must depict did not constantly multiply; if, ever more closely observed and better known, these objects did not present the genius with new distinctions and novel combinations? Why was the reign of eloquence and poetry so short in Greece and Rome? It was because that of the sciences was not prolonged there. Their poets, to whom philosophy no longer furnished new ideas, were soon only feeble or exaggerated imitators of ancient poets; their men of letters knew only how to comment in artistically cadenced phrases on the maxims of the Academy or the Porch. The empire of letters will be more permanent among us because each age, marked by new truths, will open new sources of beauty to the talent of the poet or orator. Those great phenomena which struck the sight of the first men, awakening the genius of the first inventors of the arts, would have offered their successors only worn-out pictures beyond the power of talent to animate or renew, if philosophers—by tearing down the veil with which fables and systems so long covered the truth—had not opened the eyes of poets to a new world made greater by their discoveries. In the centuries given over to error, Ovid and Lucretius embellished with the poetic art the systems of Pythagoras and the dreams of Epicurus. Is the eternal law of nature finally revealed to us? Voltaire seizes his brush: he paints, with the palette of Virgil, the picture of the universe traced by Newton's compass.

You also, gentlemen, have constantly combatted by your works and by your example the opinion that regards the progress of the sciences as heralding the fall of the fine arts, an opinion which would be the cruellest mockery and a confession of their uselessness.

You have always called to sit among you men whom the sciences have made illustrious, men whose literary culture purifies taste and embellishes genius. The profound philosopher to whom we owe the most eloquent picture of the progress of the human race; the mathematician who first determined the laws according to which bodies obey the forces nature imprints upon them, resolving the most difficult problems that Newton left to his successors; the inventor of a new calculus, a glory which our century would otherwise have envied that preceding it: such a man became by your choice the spokesman of a company devoted to the cultivation of letters.[7] You have often heard him instruct and interest your assemblies by reading those eulogies in which one sees that accuracy and aptness of expression which the study of the exact sciences renders natural, united with a grace, a lightness, a skill which a writer who had made literature his sole endeavor could not help but envy. . . .

NOTE A.   The author seems to have seized clearly upon the distinctive character of our century. But he should have clarified and developed his ideas more fully. We shall attempt to supplement what he has said on this point. By principles of a science, we understand certain general rules by the aid of which men who cultivate that science learn to distinguish what is proved from what is not proved; to be careful not to extend the consequences of a fact or a general truth beyond its true limits; to know the kinds of proofs appropriate to each kind of truth and the degree of certainty resulting from them; to understand the kinds of truths to which particular methods can lead, and the degree of reliability or precision of these methods, which issue ultimately in the formation of an exact, precise language. There are general principles common to all the sciences, which we call logic. But there are also principles particular to each science.

It is doubtless the knowledge of the whole range of these particular principles that the author regards as an advantage reserved to our century. It is enough to be convinced of this truth to compare the works of physics, physiology, mineralogy, chemistry, botany, etc., with those of the last century. . . .

As to the methods which the author insists have been reduced to an art and even *to a set of formulae*, he says nothing but the truth. Indeed, this seems in some ways to characterize our century even more clearly. The mathematical sciences, mechanics, and astronomy were studied according to true principles before the end of the last century; we have only extended to other sciences the methods of reasoning already established in them. But it is in terms of methods of discovery that we have made the greatest progress. These methods are no substitute for genius, but they direct it and make it less dependent upon chance. Genius, if it is not guided by a method, owes to chance not the force to follow the road to truth but the fact that it has recognized that road. The expression *reduced to a set of formulae* is very appropriate to describe exactly the degree of perfection to which these methods have been developed. . . .

Now it is obvious that since printing necessarily prevents these principles and methods from being lost, and carries them to all corners of the globe, it is equally impossible to imagine either a political event that would annihilate at one blow all the lands to which knowledge has now been spread, or a situation in which sciences based on true principles and guided by true methods would give way to systems and vain subtleties.

NOTE B. These same reasons make the progress of the sciences necessary and inevitable. Ease of instruction, the necessary result of the discovery of the true principles of each science, must multiply the number of those cultivating them; and it is almost impossible that in any generation there should be no one with a genius for discovery. But even if that were to occur, there would still be men who would add to the stock of knowledge all the detailed truths that require only time and labor.

An objection could be made here. It could be argued that as the sciences become swollen with new truths, a situation would arise in which all the force of the human mind would be exhausted simply in acquiring the knowledge already known. A second objection could also be raised on the grounds that once we have discovered what is closest to us, the potential discoveries remaining would require so much more power of intelligence or so much more labor that they would become impossible. The author responds with two observations. He first observes that a young man now leaving school has amassed more real knowledge than the greatest geniuses of the preceding century. This is true, at least with the reasonable proviso that by "leaving school" the author means "having finished not only the courses of study in an ordinary college, but the courses comprising the whole of public education." In effect, it is easy to see that a schoolboy who has learned botany well from Linnaeus could know more plants, and know them better, than Tournefort at the end of his life; that a chemist who had followed Bergmann for two or three years would know all that is true in the works of Becher and Stahl, together with many things that they had never known; that the courses in mathematics taught in several schools comprise everything that Descartes, Pascal, and Newton knew in mathematics and much that is new. I have more than once seen very young men provide solutions of problems proposed by these great men, and these youths were persons of ordinary ability.

The author replies to the second objection by observing that methods are improved and generalized as the sciences advance. That is particularly evident in mathematics. It was argued, more than thirty years ago, that mathematics would make no more progress; yet since that time M. de Lagrange has made all his discoveries.

But the author should have observed that this scientific advance will of necessity not be uniform, even if we regard as negligible the influence of fashion upon the interests of different nations and different centuries in one science rather than another, or set aside the political influences which also affect the sciences. There must be periods in which a science remains for some time without making any progress. If it is founded on facts, a long period of time will sometimes be necessary to gather the new facts required to advance to some great discovery. Sometimes these facts themselves will be of the kind demanding a long period of years to be well observed. It is very possible, for example, that astronomy will appear on occasion to make little progress, if some great phenomenon remaining to be discovered can only be known by a long series of observations. Meteorology in general might be in the same situation.

It might even occur that mineralogy, once it has arrived at an exact knowledge of the nature of mineral substances, and the places they are found, will remain for a long time without giving us knowledge concerning their formation. In the sciences of calculation or experience, it is possible that the new method necessary for great advances might be beyond the power of a single man, that it can only be found after the redoubled efforts of several generations, or even that it is necessary for a decisive experiment to be prepared by a great number of smaller experiments. A half-century of experiments on electricity were required to make Franklin's discovery possible. During that period scientific progress, although almost insensible to all eyes, was no less real; and the sciences awoke from their sleep with a flash of brilliance.

Finally, it can happen that the physical sciences become dominated by a man with a grandiose imagination, skillful in forming hypotheses and dressing them up in a brilliant style, able to cast ridicule on the modest student of nature who stops at the details. Scientific progress will not be suspended, but it will be hidden. Vain delusions will occupy attention and the truth will not be advanced; but this eclipse will not last long.

NOTE C.   One cannot say of any science that it is immediately useful, but it becomes so when applied in practice. It is therefore almost necessary for the great speculations of scientists to remain long useless. But there are few that eventually cannot become useful. . . .

NOTE D.   This opinion is generally contrary to received ideas, and necessarily so. Two very powerful classes have an interest in combatting it: the priests and those who exercise authority. Indeed, if reason is sufficient to teach man to know himself and his true duties, and to avoid misunderstanding of the means he has of assuring his own happiness and that of his fellows, then priests are useless. If, on the other hand, the theory of the constitution of states and the sciences of legislation and administration have fixed principles—if, human nature being given and the ideas of right and justice well established, all these sciences consist in deducing the consequences of these principles in such a way that all particular questions relating to these subjects are decided by them—then there will remain almost no questions to be decided according to those vague principles of political utility or wealth. Almost nothing will remain arbitrary; government will scarcely be worth the effort; and the qualities of a great statesman will be education and exactness of mind rather than shrewdness and cunning.

Will it not therefore be useful to develop here the proofs of this opinion? It is necessary to distinguish in all the sciences, except pure mathematics and general metaphysics, between the rational certainty *(évidence)* and the reality of their truths. Whatever the nature of a proposition deduced from other propositions, if one has made an exact analysis of all the ideas entering into the argument, the conclusion will be equally certain *(évident)* and equally precise. As for its reality, it is easy to see that this is only the result of our experience of a constant order, strengthened by the observation that facts observed yesterday will be observed today if none of the circumstances has changed. The very existence of the body has only that kind of degree of certainty which is a true probability mathematically expressed. This certainty is essentially different from the strictly defined certainty of the mathematicians. But it is necessary to observe that certainty, strictly defined, extends only to the propositions I understand intuitively at a given instant. Those I have understood intuitively the preceding instant only have for me a second kind of certainty, a certainty founded on a constant order that I have observed, that every time I examine anew a proposition I remember having seen rigorously demonstrated I find it still self-evidently true. In just the same way, I judge that the body I have seen and touched exists, because I have observed that every time I have remembered having seen and touched a body, I have been able to see and touch it again in the same circumstances. This judgment has the same kind of certainty as the statement that the sun will rise tomorrow. Thus it is from the more or less constant order of facts observed in moral as in physical phenomena that the kind of certainty derives that pertains to reality. Consequently it is necessary to distinguish two aspects of this kind of certainty: i) the more or less constant order; ii) the certainty with which one knows this order. These two conditions have an effect, the one on the real and absolute certainty of a science, the other on its actual certainty.

Let us suppose, first of all, that a phenomenon has occurred a hundred thousand times and failed to occur once [in the same circumstances]: I therefore have a given probability that it will occur rather than not occur. From this point of view, my certainty is less than it would be if the phenomenon had occurred two hundred thousand times and failed to occur once. The science in general is as certain because I know exactly in the same manner the degree of certainty that I obtain; but the degree of certainty of the result is not the same. It follows that since the moral sciences are founded on facts and reasoning, their certainty will be the same as that of the physical sciences. If the observation of facts is more difficult in these sciences, if one can be less sure at any given instant of having discovered the order involved, they will at any given moment comprise fewer precise and certain truths. If the order of certain facts is less constant, then the results relative to these facts will be less certain.

But if we examine the small number of facts necessary to establish the first foundations of ethics, of political, civil, or criminal legislation, or of administration, and even of the facts which are necessary to establish the most important general truths—the limits of legislative authority (of whatever kind), which cannot go as far as to violate in a state of peace the rights that are anterior to society; the injustice of all slavery, as of all laws of intolerance; the injustice and the impracticality of any limitations on the liberty of commerce (internal or external) and of every tax except a direct one proportional to the net product of each piece of land—we shall see that these facts are as general and as constant as the facts of the physical order.

NOTE E.   The author's suggestion that the advance of the moral sciences will be slower than that of the physical sciences does not appear to us to be either exactly true or in accordance with what he has said. That advance has doubtless been slower. Bacon, Descartes, Galileo have preceded Locke. But after the true method of studying the moral sciences was known, their principles were developed; and in general they are far from having more real difficulties than the physical sciences. They even have one more attraction, that of serving human happiness more directly. Experience is here in agreement with reason. The progress that they have made since Locke is immense. To be convinced of this, it is only necessary to read the works of Hume, Smith, Ferguson, Rousseau, the French and Italian economists, Montesquieu, and of Beccaria. Certainly in France the remains of civil and religious intolerance, in England the respect for the opinion of the populace that prevails among men who wish to make their fortunes, in the Swiss cantons respect for aristocratic prejudices, will long prevent some of those who cultivate these sciences from doing so with the enthusiasm and perseverance necessary to discover new truths. But since these causes are not the same everywhere, it is impossible that in all the countries of Europe at the same time there should be no good minds superior to prejudices.

The author has seemed here to confuse the real progress of a science with the propagation of the truths it establishes, which it is very important to distinguish. In fact, physical truths are generally recognized as soon as they are discovered, because physicists alone are generally involved in examining and judging them. It is not the same with moral truths. Everybody believes he has the right to an opinion regarding them and the words they employ are those of ordinary language, with the result that everyone believes he can understand them without seeking to find therein the precision of scientific terms. They pertain directly to everyone's interests and it is everyone's right to judge them. Furthermore, certain classes of men arrogate to themselves the right to judge them by opposing with all their power the propagation of truths contrary to their own interests or prejudices. One has greater hope of succeeding [in these sciences] by mouthing stupidities in bad faith and by speaking at random. Prejudices are more violent in them. The greater the vested interest one has in a thing, the more dogmatically one holds to opinions concerning it. Passions are obstinate; and one holds the more firmly to one's errors, the greater one's interest in falsehood. Thus it is not true that these sciences advance more slowly; but it is certain that they spread with singular slowness, with the result that one can count the men in Europe who have cultivated them seriously. But with the help of printing, these truths will certainly be recognized in the long run; and then one will be astonished at all the intelligence, eloquence, and sophistication that was employed in combatting them and even more surprised that it was ever possible to call them into question.

NOTE F.   Certainly, there is nothing more common than the sight of a man who is very enlightened in the physical sciences, but a bad metaphysician or very uneducated in politics. Yet it is no less true that the progress of the physical sciences has greatly accelerated that of the moral sciences.

1. All the errors in the moral sciences that are either based on physical errors, or related to them, must disappear with them: for example, the religions whose founders have been inept enough to speak of physics or natural history.

2. Physical sciences, becoming an essential part of education, accustom the mind to reason more accurately, to form its own ideas and to know the methods that lead to truth.

3. One of the greatest sources of error being submission to authority, this submission—once it has become ridiculous in the physical sciences—has been unable to sustain itself in the others and can never be reestablished.

4. Governments employing their powers to perpetuate errors of certain kinds could bring back darkness and superstition. But since their own interests oblige them to foster the physical sciences, there always remains an area in which men can develop their minds and sharpen their intellect. And men once enlightened in one domain cannot be reduced to ignorance in another.

This has been proved by experience in all countries where the physical sciences have been cultivated. Barbarism in the moral sciences has been more or less dispelled; and at least errors and prejudices have disappeared.

NOTE G.   [In every science the ultimate goal is to arrive at quantitative results.] [8] Very many of the questions in the moral sciences can be only partially treated or vaguely resolved without the help of mathematical and physical knowledge. Thus, for example, the constitution of tribunals, the form and nature of legal proofs, the laws relating to missing persons, financial operations relating to loans, insurance and taxation on unequal and contingent revenues, can only be well treated by applying mathematics. The knowledge a government needs to evaluate accurately the increases or decreases in population or wealth produced by different causes also depends on all kinds of physical information. In all parts of the laws governing the disposition of things held in common (such as the water of rivers) the restrictions that must be placed upon each individual's enjoyment of his rights to liberty and property, so that it does not harm that of others, depend equally (not in terms of their principles but in terms of their detailed applications) on this same kind of knowledge.

NOTE H.   One of the most difficult moral questions that can be posed is to ask at what point it becomes permissible to trouble the public peace by opposing oppression with private force. Let us suppose two moralists, one of whom is convinced that the human race can only hope to achieve happiness by violent revolution in a country where it is oppressed, that societies tend to corruption unless legislation gives men that restless love of liberty which excites factionalism and quarrels and divides them into mutually suspicious parties, and that a peace which is not a shameful servitude, a true political death, can only subsist as the result of equilibrium between contrary efforts, each tending to break it. Then suppose another moralist convinced that the human species is indefinitely perfectible, that it can expect a durable happiness from the certain progress of reason and especially from its more extensive propagation. It is easy to see that they would decide this question according to very different principles and that their decisions would be almost always opposed in their practical applications. If the opinions of the first were adopted, the result would be disorder or general discouragement. If, on the other hand, those of the second became widespread, enlightened men would unite in peace to make those efforts whose utility they felt to be necessary and inevitable. A mathematician does not fear for geometry in the face of the league of those who would square the circle; nor does a chemist or naturalist upset himself over the ephemeral success of some systems, or the resistance sometimes excited by new truths.

NOTE I. In order to understand this passage, it is first necessary to define what is to be meant by *virtue*. We will define it here as the interior sentiment which determines a man to fulfill his duties [and perform a good action] independently of any other interest. We have said "to fulfill his duties and perform a good action" to distinguish virtue, properly defined, from the sentiment of natural commiseration which our fellows prompt in us automatically and intuitively, and from that sentiment of personal affection which links us to our children and friends. All these sentiments doubtless have a common source and they all seem to be a necessary consequence of the constitution of a sensitive and rational being. But it is necessary to distinguish them. In truth, one applies the term *virtue* more particularly to those sentiments which make us fulfill our duties against our own interests, and [if] one attaches to it an idea of courage or sacrifice, one lacks in French the terms to distinguish this particular sense from the more general one.

Here we shall take the term *virtue* in the general sense, which is apparently that meant by the author. This once established, one will easily understand how enlightenment makes the virtues easy. It informs us regarding our real and permanent interests, making us aware of the fact that it is impossible for an individual's real and permanent interests to be opposed to his duties, i.e., to his respect for the rights of others, except perhaps in a very small number of circumstances. The sentiment which brings us to fulfill our duties is developed and strengthened by reflection which makes us recognize the importance of these duties, which extends them by making us see their relationship to public order and the general good. Enlightenment must also have its effects on the courage to do good: (1) because it teaches us to understand better the real dangers to which virtue exposes us and to recognize that these dangers are less great; (2) because it shows us better the compensation for the momentary sacrifice that we must make; (3) because it teaches us to know better distant evils to which one exposes oneself in lacking virtue. . . . Will a man be less virtuous because, having discovered by reflection that the surest means of being the least unhappy is to fulfill his duties, he does so with less effort? Is an engineer who traces a drawing under the enemy's cannon no longer a man of courage because experience has taught him that the danger he runs is very small?

NOTE J. By enlightening men as to their true duties and interests, and the relationship between them; by preventing the persistent fear of death or pain from arising in their soul; by giving habit and occupation to tastes; by enlightening them as to the real advantages of wealth and power; by fortifying especially in man the sentiment of pity and the affections; by instructing him in the evil that results from actions when it is not immediately obvious, education would greatly diminish the number of criminal actions produced by fear, idleness, greed, ambition, hard-heartedness, and weaken the temptation to commit them.

With a good system of legislation, large fortunes becoming impossible, what would become of the crimes and vices produced by luxury and vanity? Once the poor man, delivered from the burden of taxation, freely enjoys the fruits of his industry, finding a more secure resource in his own labor than in devoting himself to the service of a rich man no longer able to pay him; once the rich man is limited to a mediocre fortune which he can only hope to augment gradually by his own work, the evils resulting from the laziness of the poor and the idleness of the rich will be no longer to be feared. Power will be limited to the execution of laws to which it is itself subject and which it can no longer abuse, either to oppress or to serve; and the only places to be given out will require honest labor. Will the pleasure of executing the laws then excite many men to ambition? The laws will be mild but severely executed; they will forbid only that which is forbidden by nature and condemned by public opinion. Will there then be many private crimes? Is it not smuggling, poaching, the difficulty of living from the fruits of one's labor that produces brigands? Would fanaticism commit crimes in a country where persecution alone is punished? Would hypocrisy be very common if nothing was to be gained by being a hypocrite? It is not nature, it is not society, that corrupts men: it is bad laws, and the opinions and customs that in savage societies take the place of laws. Thus if the progress of enlightenment perfects legislation and education, it will perfect the human species; and from the perfectibility that can derive from education, from the application (ever more enlightened by the physical sciences) of the common force and wealth to the common good, it will result that the perfectibility of the human species toward virtue and happiness must be as limitless as its perfectibility in the sciences.

One of the ancients said *to what avail are laws, powerless without morality?* [9] We will dare to say *to what avail is morality, powerless without [good] laws?* If manners have been almost everywhere corrupt, it is the fault of the laws; and this truth is useful because it leads us to seek to perfect the laws, which is possible and depends on the work and meditations of the philosophers.

We have already seen that luxury and inequality of wealth could have been destroyed by wise laws, and these are already among the greatest source of the corruption of manners. Idleness is another; and these same laws, combined with education, could also destroy this obstacle. Finally, a better education and wise laws would surely contribute to the establishment of good manners if they reestablished between men and women the equality that reason and justice, if not nature, must wish to subsist between them.

Has nature set some differences between men and women? Doubtless women are weaker; this is demonstrated by the fact that among all primitive peoples they have been oppressed. The physical force depends upon the muscles, upon which it is very doubtful that force of mind and spirit depends.

Women appear more sensitive than men, but (1) if they love their children more, it is because these belong to them more and affection grows in proportion to the good one does; (2) if they appear to love their husbands or lovers more passionately or with greater constancy, this might be because, according to their principles, they lose more in losing their tenderness; (3) their affections are all women have, while the majority of men exist more for their occupations than for their affections. A sentiment which occupies one for three-quarters of the day is more lively than a sentiment which only occupies one for an hour, even assuming natural sensibility to be equal.

The courage that women show in the face of pain and misfortune, the proofs of fearlessness they have given in the small number of circumstances in which they have been in a position to do so, seem to demonstrate that if they profit from the permission that common opinion gives them to abandon themselves to the first movements of fear or love, this feebleness is more the work of education than of nature.

As for intellectual qualities, it appears that in everything pertaining to subtlety of ideas or sentiments, to memory, to soundness of mind, to patience and assiduity in work, there are no other differences than those deriving from education. The only quality that no woman has ever demonstrated is genius, or the gift of discovery. There can be several possible explanations for this fact. First, one can assume that since the number of women who have devoted themselves to study has been very small, none of the few women destined for genius has been in a position to display it. One could also say that the education of women, when they have received one, is meant to teach them to develop neither their imagination nor their sentiments: such education is consistently antithetical to the development of genius. Finally, it can be observed that the gift of discovery only pertains to one thing, to the force of attention; that this force of attention is related (so far as introspection can tell) to the physical constitution of the head. There is no one who has not himself experienced the limits of this force of attention, and in this sense it might be related to the physical force of this faculty. But why should it be weaker in women? On this point we must suspend judgment until experience has demonstrated one way or the other. In any case, this inequality would not constitute an equality between the two sexes because it would show only that women are inferior to a very small number of men and are equal to all the rest. Doubtless the changes to which women are subject during the period of life in which the mind is most formed, and in that during which it makes, if not the most use, at least the most enlightened use of its resources, are an obstacle to the advance of women in the arts and sciences. But since this inferiority does not prevent them from acquiring any profound knowledge, it gives no grounds for establishing inequality.

This inequality could only be legitimate to the extent that the person in subjection was not able to acquire the knowledge necessary to fulfill social functions. Supposing then that a woman will never be able to become a great poet, a sublime mathematician, a first-rate anatomist, or a chemical discoverer, would she be less capable of raising children, managing her affairs, treating the sick, teaching the elements of the sciences, etc.?

I beg pardon of French ladies. If they read this work, they will find little gallantry. But a Swiss is obliged to speak the truth.

It is also true to say that actions of an extraordinary virtue can only be necessary in countries with bad laws. What good is courage in the face of torture in a country in which a sweet and peaceable death is the harshest punishment? Why will it be necessary to have the fortitude to brave public opinion in an enlightened country? The courage to defy oppressors, to defend the innocent at the risk of one's life and happiness, is almost useless where innocence is protected by the laws.

NOTE K. This remarkable outburst of activity began in France and spread to the rest of Europe; but it excited the clamors of opposition only in its place of birth. At first subdued, these clamors burst into full blast about 1760. Those Frenchmen who concerned themselves with the common happiness of men can be distinguished into two principal groups: the philosophes and the economists.[10] The former were concerned especially with attacking prejudices, preaching tolerance and humanity, and defending the rights of men. The latter sought particularly to develop a sound understanding of these rights and find means of perfecting them.

Foreigners have criticized the philosophes for having treated the great questions which concerned them with more wit and eloquence than profundity, and of being more interested in destroying than building. They complain that they are unable to find in the works of the philosophes any development of the true principles of tolerance: principles founded on the fact that since society is only established to preserve men's natural rights, no power has the right to violate them; and that since the liberty to do everything that is not contrary to the rights of others is one of these natural rights, no power can legitimately abridge this freedom. They claim not to find clearly or profoundly developed principles relating to the true rights of natural, civil, or political liberty, and the effects of this liberty on social happiness. They criticize the philosophes on the grounds that they sometimes appear to have mixed profound investigations into moral and political questions with metaphysical subtleties, to have introduced a kind of pyrrhonism into the political sciences, to have failed to recognize adequately that these are true sciences.

The economists, in turn, have been criticized for a language that is too obscure and scientific; for not having distinguished adequately the different degrees of proof appropriate to the various principles they have established and the opinions that form the body of their doctrine; for having attached too much importance to some of these opinions; for not having applied mathematical calculation to their researches, when necessary, with enough caution or knowledge; for having presented their science as comprising all the principles necessary for social happiness, without having demonstrated the relationship of these principles to those of justice and public law, etc.

These two groups were never either closely united or in open opposition. The economists had a low regard for the philosophes, because the latter paid only superficial attention to the principles of administration and commerce; because to them, occupied as they were with the creation of a methodical and general system of truths, even the great and luminous ideas mixed with so many errors in the works of Montesquieu himself could not compensate for the lack of order in his opinions; because, basing themselves on truer principles than those commonly adopted, they regarded themselves as having a kind of expertise. The philosophes had a low regard for the economists because of their unattractive style and their tone of enthusiasm and certainty so antithetical to philosophical doubt. Those associated with the philosophes scarcely knew the economists except as bizarre men who did not admire the great Colbert or believe that the first duty of a great minister was to give pensions to those who wrote verses in the prince's honor and his own. The liberty of thought, humanity, the rights of citizens to express an opinion in matters relating to the national interest, were common concerns of these two classes of men and brought them together. The philosophes, who attacked prejudices, intolerance, tyrannical or bizarre laws, the harshness of certain fiscal practices, frivolous distinctions of vanity, and the more dangerous pretensions of the different estates, found ranged against them the priests, the court, the magistrates, and the financiers. The economists had basically the same enemies except for the clergy, whom they had handled well—and who were beginning to relax the dictum that he who is not for me is against me.

The persecution against the philosophes was the more fierce. The majority of them were celebrated writers against whom the whole rabble of literature unleashed the hatred that is the natural result of the combination of great pride and utter mediocrity. Scarcely was it suggested that the philosophes were seditious and impious, than God and the fatherland had as defenders everyone in the literary world who was reprehensible in his conduct, his morals and his works. . . .

The preachers turned in their pulpits and tonsured heads produced condemnations signed by the bishops as pastoral letters, in which it was seriously argued that there can be no morality without religion. This proposition is belied by reason and experience, but it nevertheless serves as the foundation for the further opinion that a religion is necessary, whether it be true or false: the fundamental maxim of priests in every country, though they dare not avow it publicly.

But despite all these outbursts, only books were burned. Custom and opinion prevented the scaffolds of the sixteenth century from being rekindled and antiphilosophical writers were guilty only of the shame of having uselessly suggested legal assassinations.

The only victim of this persecution was an unfortunate young man unknown to the philosophes,[11] completely unacquainted with philosophy and much more occupied with his own pleasures, who had committed some inexpedient acts, was accused of still more, and condemned to death without it ever being possible to disguise—still less to justify—the crime of those who condemned him in terms of the text of any law. At least, none of his judges—accused of assassination in the eyes of Europe in a score of printed works—dared to justify himself; and in the researches that we have carried out in the collection of French laws known abroad, we have discovered no such law.

The persecution of the economists had no such fatal consequences. It was limited to saying that they were demented, because after all it is still less dangerous to attack financiers than priests. The only curious aspect of this persecution was the enthusiasm with which men of letters joined with the money-men to proclaim that positive knowledge was absolutely useless in politics, that this science had no principles that could be analyzed and proved, and that the height of genius was to *envelop* the principles of one's thought and follow the truth by an undulating route[12]. . . .

These two classes of men of letters were therefore two kinds of party in France for some time. But it happened by chance that one could delude oneself into seeing the destruction of some of the abuses against which these men had risen up. Thereafter, those who had followed them out of vanity separated themselves out of fear. The parties no longer existed; and there remained only a small number of men united in the search for useful truths.

NOTE L.   The author uses the expression *almost [abolished]* because in France respect for antiquity has preserved the use of torture after condemnation. However, it is clear that this practice is as barbarous as torture before condemnation—it is unjust in regard to anyone the condemned man might accuse, and equally unjust toward him since his withholding information concerning his accomplices is not a crime that deserves such punishment—and as useless in providing information regarding the crime.

The creation of a system of criminal jurisprudence would be a huge enterprise demanding time, work, and a luminous intelligence in those undertaking it, and a profound mind in the man charged with responsibility for planning and executing it.

But there would be simple means of removing the greatest inconveniences of the criminal legislation in Europe, even before such a great work were completed. It would be a question of destroying things that are contrary to the general opinion of all men of enlightenment and humanity, in the following ways:

1. By abolishing completely the use of torture.
2. By removing from the list of crimes those that are only imaginary: such as those relating to religion, which cannot be treated by any law; all actions involving private morals, excepting rape or abduction, which are crimes even in countries where relations between men and women are absolutely free. One could, in countries where divorce is not permitted, allow the continuation of a light penalty for adultery—but only admitting written proofs and excluding all evidence apart from cohabitation, leaving aside all question of the physical act constituting adultery.
3. By retaining the death penalty only for assassination; and whatever the particular nature of this crime and the manner of punishing it, limiting the punishment to simple execution without adding atrocious tortures or disgusting devices. These savage inventions are as useless in preventing crime as they are barbarous. Fixed penalties must also be established for every crime.

4. By giving the accused full information concerning all the evidence in the case and allowing him the right to counsel.
5. By admitting the right to challenge witnesses at every stage of the trial, and the right to prove the facts justifying such challenges.
6. By forbidding judges to engage in those spurious interrogations so unworthy of the august function they fulfill.
7. By granting the accused the right to challenge a fixed number of judges without being obliged to give his grounds; and protecting the right to challenge an indefinite number on stated grounds.
8. By demanding a greater plurality for the pronouncement of guilt.
9. By requiring judges to state explicitly in their sentences the individual crimes of which the accused is found guilty; and to pronounce only the sentence fixed by law for this penalty.

It is easy to see that by these means one can abolish the most dangerous abuses of the criminal laws in the indication of crimes, the punishment attached to them, the conduct of trials and the delivery of judgment. All these changes are in conformity with generally accepted principles.

EDITOR'S NOTES TO RECEPTION SPEECH

1. Here Condorcet was probably thinking principally of his two mentors, d'Alembert, who had discussed the progress of the human mind in his celebrated *Preliminary Discourse to the Encyclopedia* (1751), and Turgot, who had developed his ideas on the same subject in two discourses at the Sorbonne in 1750. See Charles Frankel, *The Faith of Reason: The Idea of Progress in the French Enlightenment* (New York, 1948); Frank Manuel, *The Prophets of Paris* (Cambridge, Mass., 1968).
2. Bernard le Bovier de Fontenelle (1657–1757) served as permanent secretary of the Academy of Sciences from 1697 to 1741. His official eulogies of deceased academicians, and the annual account he wrote of the academy's activities, were of crucial importance in developing the public image of science in eighteenth-century France.
3. The voice of Jean-Jacques Rousseau, whose First Discourse answered the prize essay question proposed by the Academy of Dijon in 1750, "Has the re-establishment of the arts and sciences contributed to the purification of morals?" Rousseau responded to this question with a profoundly disturbing negative.

4. The reference is to Captain James Cook (1728–1779), the celebrated English explorer. The accounts of Cook's three voyages were quickly translated into French.

5. The United States, with whom France signed a treaty of alliance at Versailles in 1778.

6. The first son of Louis XVI and Marie Antoinette was born in 1781 and died in 1789. On his father's side, he was descended from the first Bourbon king, Henri IV (ruled 1589–1610), who brought to an end the wars of religion in France. On his mother's side, he was descended from Leopold I, duke of Lorraine (ruled 1697–1729), whose reign marked a golden age in the history of that duchy.

7. The reference is to d'Alembert, who served as permanent secretary of the French Academy from 1772 until his death in 1783.

8. In the manuscript of these notes, this passage was subsequently crossed out by Condorcet, presumably as too radical a statement of his intellectual convictions.

9. "Quid leges sine moribus vanae proficiunt . . . ?" (Horace, *Odes*, 3.24.36.)

10. The economists here referred to are the physiocrats, who developed and propagated the economic theories propounded by François Quesnay. Physiocracy (literally, the rule of nature) made freedom of trade one of its principal slogans. In economic matters, Condorcet generally followed physiocratic thinking.

11. The chevalier de la Barre, convicted of blasphemously mutilating a crucifix in his native Abbeville, was tortured and executed in 1766. The philosophes were accused of fomenting this action, and a copy of Voltaire's *Philosophical Dictionary* was even cast into the flames with the mutilated body. The la Barre case was one of a number of instances of judicial barbarity which prompted the philosophes to campaign for reform of the French legal system (see Note L).

12. A reference to the arguments of Necker, whose book criticizing free trade in grain was violently attacked by Condorcet when it appeared in 1775.

Essay on the Application of Mathematics to the Theory of Decision-Making (1785)

The *Essai sur l'application de l'analyse à la probabilité des décisions rendues à la pluralité des voix* is Condorcet's most extensive and ambitious mathematical work. Written in 1785 to demonstrate the necessity and possibility of applying mathematical reasoning to social and political affairs, it also provided a first published statement of Condorcet's probabilistic philosophy. Convinced that the *Essay* would have little utility if its audience was limited to those technically able to follow its complex mathematical argument (which has often been denounced for its obscurity), Condorcet prefaced the work with a lengthy introduction in which he presented his analysis in nontechnical language. The following selections are taken from this introduction. Those footnotes that were merely cross-references to the text of the *Essai* proper have been omitted.

A great man, Monsieur Turgot, whose teaching and example, and above all whose friendship I shall always mourn, was convinced that the truths of the moral and political sciences are susceptible of the same certainty as those forming the system of the physical sciences, even those branches like astronomy which seem to approach mathematical certainty.

This opinion was dear to him, because it led him to the consoling hope that the human race will necessarily progress toward happiness and perfection, as it has done in the knowledge of truth.

It was for him that I undertook this work subjecting to calculation questions relating to the common utility. In doing so I attempted to prove, at least by example, the conviction he would have wished to disseminate among all those who love the truth. It was with pain that he saw among such men those convinced that one could not hope to obtain truth in these matters, those disdaining for this reason alone to concern themselves with the most important of subjects.

If humanity had not had the misfortune of losing him prematurely, a loss which will long be irreparable, this work would have been less imperfect. Enlightened by his counsel, I would have seen better or further, and I would more confidently have advanced principles that would have been his own. Deprived of such a guide, I can only offer to his memory the homage of my work, making every effort to render it less unworthy of the friendship with which he honored me.

This work would have but a very limited utility if it could only be consulted by the mathematicians, who might in any case find nothing in its methods of calculation to merit their attention. I have therefore felt it necessary to add a preliminary discourse in which, having set forth the fundamental principles of the calculus of probabilities, I seek to develop the principal questions I have attempted to resolve and the results to which calculation has led me. To judge the work, readers who are not mathematicians need only accept as true what is presented as proven by calculation.

In almost every case, the reader will find results in conformity with what the simplest reason would have dictated. But it is so easy to obscure reason with sophisms and vain subtleties that I would count myself happy merely to have based a single useful truth on the authority of a mathematical demonstration. Among the great number of important matters to which mathematical calculation can be applied, I have chosen to examine the probability of decisions taken by majority vote. This subject has been analyzed by no one, at least in the extent and detail that it deserves, and it seemed to me that it did not demand powers superior to my own, even to be treated with some utility.

When the practice of subjecting all individuals to the will of the greatest number was introduced into society, and men agreed to regard the decision of the majority as the common will of all, they did not adopt this method as a means of avoiding error and acting according to decisions based on truth. On the contrary, they found that for the sake of peace and the general utility it was necessary to place authority where the force was; that since they had to allow themselves to be led by a single will, the will of the lesser number had necessarily to be sacrificed to that of the greater number.

Reflecting on what we know of the constitutions of ancient peoples we see that they were much more concerned to counterbalance the interests and passions of the different bodies that formed part of the constitution of a state than to obtain results in their decisions that were conformable to the truth. The language of liberty and utility was more important to them than that of truth and justice; and the inter-relationship of these ideas, while it was perhaps glimpsed by some of their philosophers, was not distinctly enough known to serve as the basis of their politics.

In the modern nations, into which scholasticism introduced a spirit of reasoning and subtlety which gradually extended to all matters, one sees, even in the midst of the centuries of ignorance, some traces of the idea of giving tribunals a form enhancing the probability that their decisions would be true.

The unanimity required in England in jury decisions, the practice of demanding in France a plurality of two or three votes for condemnation, especially that of regarding a decision of the Rota[1] as irrevocable only when it had been given by three uniform judgments, and similar practices established in several Italian states: all these institutions go back to times well before the return of enlightenment. They all seem to indicate efforts to obtain decisions in conformity with reason.

Circumstances seem to demand this from us. Among the ancients— that is to say, among the Romans and the Greeks, the only peoples whose history is well known to us—important matters were decided either by the general assembly of the citizens or by bodies that had arrogated the sovereign power. Their will, whether just or unjust, founded on truth or error, necessarily had the backing of force; and to propose means of subjecting their wills to reason would have been to offer them chains and invite them to set limits to their authority or independence.

Among us, in contrast, such matters are most often decided by the decision of a body of representatives or officers, either of the nation or of the prince. Thus it is in the interest of those who dispose of the public power to employ that power only to sustain decisions that conform to the truth, and to give, to the representatives they have charged to decide on their behalf, rules which guarantee the goodness of their decisions.

In seeking to discover by reason alone the greater or lesser confidence warranted by the judgment of assemblies that are more or less numerous, assemblies subject to the requirement of larger or smaller pluralities, assemblies divided into several bodies or meeting in a single body, assemblies composed of men more or less enlightened, it can easily be seen that one would arrive only at vague results. Indeed, these results would often be so vague as to become uncertain and even to lead us into error if we accepted them without having subjected them to calculation.

Thus, for example, it would easily be seen that by requiring of a tribunal a greater plurality to condemn an accused person, one acquires a correspondingly greater assurance that an innocent person will not be sent to the gallows. But reason without calculation will not teach you the limits to which it is useful to increase this assurance; nor will it indicate how far it can be made compatible with the requirement not to allow too many guilty persons to go free.

Reason, with a little reflection, will make clear the necessity of constituting a tribunal in such a way that it is almost impossible for a single innocent person to be condemned, even over a long period of time. But it will not teach you the limits within which this probability can be defined, nor how to achieve it without multiplying the number of judges beyond a point that it is scarcely possible to exceed.

These examples are enough to demonstrate the utility and, I would almost dare to say, the necessity of applying calculation to these questions.

Before explaining my researches, it has seemed necessary for me to enter into some details concerning the principles of the calculus of probabilities.

This whole calculus, at least the entire part of it which interests us here, is based on a single general principle:

If, of a given number of possible combinations, there are a certain number of combinations that produce an event,

and another number of combinations that produce the
contrary event, the probability of each of these two events
will be equal to the number of combinations which
produce it, divided by the total number.

Thus, for example, if one takes a six-sided die, assuming that each side is equally likely to come up, since one side gives a six and the five others give other numbers, 1/6 would express the probability of throwing this side and 5/6 the probability of not throwing it.

It can be seen that the number of combinations which produce an event and the number of combinations that do not produce it are together equal to the total number of combinations, and consequently the sum of the probabilities of two contradictory events equals unity (or 1).

Now supposing that one of these probabilities is nil, the other all alone must then be equal to unity. But a probability is nil only because no combination can produce the corresponding event. The contrary event, the probability of which is 1, therefore occurs necessarily. Thus this event is certain.

It must necessarily happen that an event occurs or does not occur. It is therefore certain that one of two contradictory events will occur, and the sum of their probabilities is expressed as 1.

This is all that is meant by saying that probability is expressed by a fraction and certainty by unity.

This principle is sufficient for all cases. If one considers three events that can result from a certain number of possible combinations, the probability of the first will be equal to the number of combinations that produce it, divided by the total number of combinations; and the probability of one or the other of the two other events will be equal to the number of combinations that do not produce the first, divided by the total number.

For the same reason, the probability of the second event will be equal to the number of combinations that produce it divided by the total number.

It will be the same with the probability of the third event, and the sums of the probabilities of the three events that are alone possible will again be equal to 1.

If the combinations are not equally possible, the same principle still applies. A combination twice more possible than another is nothing else than two combinations that are equal and similar, as compared to a single combination.

Let us now examine this first principle. One sees first that if one limits oneself to understanding by the probability of an event the number of combinations in which it occurs divided by the total number of possible combinations, this principle is simply a truth of definition and the calculus based on it thus becomes rigorously true.

But one does not limit oneself to this sense alone. One understands further (1) that if one knows the number of combinations that produce an event, and the number of combinations that do not produce it, and the first is greater than the second, there is basis for believing that the event will occur rather than believing that it will not occur; (2) that this ground for belief[2] increases with the ratio of the number of favorable combinations to the total number; (3) that it increases proportionally to this ratio.

The truth of this last proposition depends on that of the two preceding. In effect, if the ground for belief becomes greater when the number of combinations increases, it can be demonstrated that if one repeats a certain number of times the judgment conforming to this opinion (i.e., the opinion that the event which has more combinations in its favor will occur rather than the other) the most probable combination of judgments is that in which the number of true judgments would be in the same proportion to the total number of judgments as the number of combinations favorable to the event to their total number. In other words, the most probable combination of judgments is that in which the ratio of the number of true judgments to the total number of judgments will be equal to what we call the probability of the event.

It can similarly be demonstrated that the greater the number of judgments, the greater the probability that these two ratios will diverge very little from one another.[3] Thus to admit that a greater probability (this word being taken in the abstract sense of the definition) is a greater ground for belief, is to admit at the same time that these grounds are proportional to the probabilities.

This posed, from the moment one admits that as soon as the number of combinations producing an event is greater than the number of combinations not producing it one has a ground for believing that the event will occur, one must admit that if the probability of another event is greater the ground for belief will also be greater.

In effect, if the probabilities are equal, the grounds for belief are equal. Suppose then a given probability, and suppose one finds by calculation that if one judges in conformity with the ground for belief that results, one will have a certain probability of not being mistaken in one's judgments more than one time out of ten. Applying the same calculation to a greater probability, one will find that in judging in conformity with the ground for credibility that results, one will have the same probability of not being mistaken more than once out of a greater number of judgments. Thus one will have in the two cases an equal probability, an equal ground for believing that one will be mistaken less in judging according to the second probability than in judging according to the first, and consequently a stronger ground for deciding to judge according to the second probability. Thus the truth of the second of these preceding propositions depends also on the truth of the first proposition. It therefore remains for us only to examine if, when the probability of an event (this word always being taken in the abstract sense) is greater than that of the contrary event, one has a ground for believing that the first event will occur.

It will be sufficient to examine this proposition in the case where the difference between these probabilities is very great. For this ground cannot exist in this case without existing, though with less force, when the difference is very small.

In fact, however small the excess of one probability over the other, one finds by calculation that if one considers a sequence of similar events, one will be able to obtain a very great probability that the event that has in its favor the greater of the two probabilities will occur more frequently than the other. It follows that one will then have a ground for believing that it will occur more frequently than the other, and consequently a ground for believing that it will occur rather than believing that it will not occur.

Let us now examine this first proposition, to which we have just reduced the two others, and which we have itself reduced to its most simple terms.

A future event is for us only an unknown event. Suppose a bag in which I know there are ninety white balls and ten black balls. Someone asks me what the probability is of drawing a white ball. Or, the ball already having been drawn but covered by a cloth, someone asks me what the probability is that a white ball has been drawn. It is clear that my reply will be the same in the two cases, and that the probability is equal. Thus I will reply that there is a greater probability of drawing a white ball; yet there is already a white ball or a black ball which is necessarily under the cloth.

Thus the ground for belief which leads me to believe that the ball is white (the probability that it is white) remains the same, even though it is sure that the ball is white, or that it is black, even though one or the other of these facts can be certain for another individual. And I have in this case an equal probability of the color of the ball being white, equal ground for believing it white, both in the case when this fact is certain and in the case when it is certainly false.

Thus there is no direct relationship between this ground for belief and the truth of the fact that is its object, nor is there one between the probability and the reality of events.

To understand the nature of this ground, it will be sufficient for us to observe that all our knowledge regarding natural events which have not struck our senses, regarding future events—that is to say, all the knowledge by which we direct our conduct and our judgments in the course of our life—are founded on these two principles: *that Nature follows invariable laws,* and *that observed phenomena have made known these laws to us.* The constant experience that the facts are in conformity with these principles is for us the only ground for believing them. Now, if one could collect together all the facts the observation of which has led us to believe these two propositions, calculation would teach us how to determine precisely the probability that they are true.

We cannot in truth collect together these facts, and we see only that calculation would lead us to a very great probability. But this difference does not change the nature of the ground for belief, which is the same in the two cases.

Thus the ground for believing that out of ten million white balls mixed with one black ball, it will not be the black ball that I draw the first time, is of the same nature as the ground for believing that the sun will not fail to come up tomorrow. These two opinions differ only in their greater or lesser probability.

If I look at two men six feet tall, one at a distance of twelve feet and the other at a distance of twenty-four, I see them as of equal height. But if I could not form any judgment on the basis of their distance, their shape, the degree of clarity or brilliance of their images, one would seem twice as large to me as the other. What is then my ground for considering them equal? It is that a constant experience has taught me that, despite the inequality of their images, bodies seen in this manner in the same circumstances were sensibly equal. Thus this judgment is based on a simple probability: the ground for belief that derives from this probability thus has enough force to become involuntary and irresistible, with the result that the judgment based on this ground is absolutely merged with the sensation itself. In this example, we see what this ground leads us to believe; and we cannot see otherwise.

If I roll a little ball between two crossed fingers, I feel two balls although there is only one. And I do so because I have constantly experienced the existence of two round bodies every time I have experienced this sensation simultaneously on two opposite sides of two fingers. Here is yet another judgment based on the probability produced by experience, which has become an involuntary sensation. Yet despite this sensation, I conclude that there is only one body by virtue of a greater probability, and this judgment prevails over the first, although habit has not had the power to change it into sensation.

The belief in the very existence of bodies is based only on a similar ground, on a mere probability. In fact, the idea of this existence is for us solely the persuasion that the system of sensation excited in us in a given instance will present itself as constantly the same in similar circumstances, or with certain differences related in a constant manner to change in the circumstances.[4] Thus this persuasion of the existence of bodies is founded only on the constancy in the order of phenomena that repeated experience has made known to us. The ground for belief in this existence is therefore absolutely of the same nature as that which derives from probability.

If it is asked at this stage what the certainty of a mathematical demonstration is, I reply that it is also of the same nature.

Suppose, for example, that I employ the binomial theorem in this demonstration. It is clear that even supposing the entire certainty of the truth of my demonstration, I am sure of the exactness of the binomial theorem only as a result of my memory of having understood and followed its demonstration. If this memory of the soundness of the demonstration is now for me a ground for belief, it is solely because experience has shown me that if I have once demonstrated a truth to myself, I will constantly rediscover this same truth every time I wish to work through the demonstration. This again is a ground for belief founded on experience of the past, and consequently on probability.[5]

Thus, strictly speaking, the only real certainty we have is that which derives from intuitive understanding of evident truths, i.e., that of the proposition whose truth we are directly conscious of; or, in a sequence of reasoning, that of the legitimacy of each consequence, the principle being supposed true, but not that of the consequence itself, since the truth of this consequence depends on propositions whose truth we have ceased to be directly conscious of. Thus the ground for believing this consequence is founded solely on probability.

There is nevertheless a difference, essential to point out, between those truths regarded as possessing an entire certainty and other truths.

In the case of the former truths, we are obliged to admit only a single supposition based on probability, namely the supposition that since the memory of having been directly conscious of the truth of a proposition has never misled us, this same memory will not mislead us on a new occasion. But in the case of other truths, the ground for belief is based first on this principle, and then on the kind of probability proper to each statement. The possibility of error depends on several causes combined. If one supposes it the same for each cause, calculation will show that it will be more than double if there are two causes, more than triple if there are three, etc. Thus we give the name mathematical certainty to probability, when it is based on the constancy of the laws observed in the operations of our understanding. We call physical certainty that probability which further supposes that same constancy in an order of phenomena independent of us, and we reserve the term probability for judgments exposed further to other sources of uncertainty.

If we now compare the ground for believing the truths we have just examined with the ground for believing a probability mathematically calculated, we will find only three differences. The first difference is that in the kinds of truths that we have examined, the probability is not assignable and is almost always so great that it would be superfluous to calculate it. The second difference is that, accustomed in the course of life to base our judgments on this probability, we form these judgments without thinking about the nature of the ground for belief that determines them, while in questions subjected to the calculus of probabilities this becomes the object of our attention. In the first case, we yield without knowing it to an involuntary inclination; in the second, we take account of the ground that determines this inclination. The third difference is that in the first case we can know only that we have greater or lesser grounds for belief, while in the second case we can express mathematically the relationship of these different grounds.

This simple analysis will be sufficient to suggest the nature of the ground for belief which results from calculated probability, and the entire extent of the utility of this calculus, since it serves us to measure with precision the grounds for our opinions in every case in which this precise measure can be useful.

PLAN OF THE WORK

In examining the probability of decisions taken by majority vote, it is necessary to distinguish two kinds of decisions. In the first kind, the decision is adopted whatever the majority reached. Thus if the number of voters is unequal, there is necessarily a decision. If the number of voters is equal, the case of an equal division of the vote is the only one in which there is no decision.

This method of decision-making seems to be applicable only to questions upon which it is necessary to take immediate action, to those in which the disadvantages of error are equal whatever the action taken, and in which these disadvantages are at the same time less serious than the disadvantages of postponing the decision.

In the second kind of decisions, they are not regarded as taken unless they have a definite majority in their favor. If this majority is not reached the decision is postponed, on the grounds that it is better to wait than to risk a bad course of action. Or, conversely, one of the two courses of action is indeed taken, either because it is considered better to risk being mistaken in taking it than to postpone the decision, or because the contrary course of action cannot be adopted with justice unless there is a great probability that it is in conformity with the truth.

Suppose, for example, that an assembly is to decide whether it is appropriate to make a new law. One can believe that since a law is useful only when it is in conformity with reason, it is necessary to require a majority such as to give a very great probability of the correctness of the decision, and it is better to make no law than to make a bad one.

One could then distinguish (and justice seems to demand it) between laws which reestablish men in the enjoyment of their natural rights, those which place shackles upon these rights, and those (at least, if any such can exist) which appear neither to augment nor diminish the exercise of natural liberty. In the first case, simple majority must suffice; a great majority necessarily seems to be required for those which set limits to the exercise of the natural rights of man, because it can never be just or legitimate to violate these rights without having a strong assurance[6] that the actual exercise of these rights would be harmful to those deprived of them. Finally, in the third case, one can find a mean between the fear of delaying useful change if one requires too great a majority and that of taking a bad course of action if one is content with too feeble a majority. We have supposed here that it could be regarded as useful in certain cases to limit the exercise of natural rights, or to continue a suspension of these rights already in effect. But this is only as a hypothesis appropriate to give an example, and not because we would accept this opinion, especially for a permanent legislation.

In general, a law which has not been voted unanimously involves subjecting men to an opinion which is not their own, or to a decision they believe contrary to their interest. It follows that a very great probability of the truth of this decision is the only reasonable and just grounds according to which one can demand such submission.

In the case of a tribunal responsible for rendering judgments in criminal matters, it is readily seen that it is impermissible to back these judgments with the full weight of the public force when they condemn an accused man, unless the form of the tribunal provides an extreme assurance that the accused is guilty, unless this assurance exists even for those who know nothing of the judgment but the constitution of the tribunal rendering it, and perhaps the majority by which the judgment was reached. The obligation imposed on every man to defend the oppressed, this obligation from which there results a veritable right to fulfill it, can yield only to the assurance that this apparent oppression is a real act of justice. . . .

There are four essential points to consider relative to the probability of decisions.

1. The probability that an assembly will not make a false decision.
2. The probability that it will make a true decision.
3. The probability that it will make a decision, true or false.
4. The probability of the decision, when one supposes it made, or when one supposes further that one knows the majority by which it was reached.

It is easy to see, first, that a form of decision-making is dangerous if it is not very probable that each vote will not result in a false decision. Second, it is clear that a form must be sought which can give a great probability of having a true decision. Otherwise the advantage of not fearing a false decision will stem simply from the fact that it is very probable that there will be no decision at all: a very great disadvantage since, depending on the matters being decided, it in large part prevents the assembly deliberating from fulfilling the purposes for which it was instituted.

The third point follows from the first two. In effect, if one has a great probability of having a true decision, and at the same time a very great probability of not having a false one, it is clear that the probability of having a decision (true or false) approaches the first probability and surpasses it.

The fourth condition requires more discussion. It is necessary, first of all, to have a great probability that the decision is in conformity with the truth, when one knows that a decision has been taken. This condition also depends on the first two; for if the probability of a true decision is great and the risk of a false one is very small, it is clear that as soon as one knows that a decision has been taken, it becomes very probable that this decision is in conformity with the truth. The probability of having a true decision must not be confused with the probability that a decision assumed to have been taken is conformable to the truth: the first is contrary not only to the probability of having a false decision, but to that of having no decision; the second is contrary only to that of having a false decision. For the first, it is necessary to compare the number of cases in which the decision is true to the number of all the possible cases; for the second, it is necessary to compare this first number only to the total number of cases in which there is a decision. To give an example, the first is the probability that an accused man who is guilty will be condemned; the second is the probability that an accused man who is condemned is guilty. Yet one must demand in addition a further condition: it is necessary that if one knows that there is a decision, and by what majority it has been taken, one have a sufficient probability of the truth of the decision. We have given the reason for this above. This assurance is necessary, for example, every time there is a question of punishing an accused man. Otherwise it might happen that a man condemned, by a majority that did not give this assurance, would be punished when there was a very low probability that he was guilty. Thus in all the cases where we have seen that it would be appropriate to fix a majority below which the opinion of the minority must be followed, or the matter regarded as undecided, it is necessary that this minimum majority be such that it result in the probability considered requisite in the decision.

It would not be enough for it simply to be very improbable that the case in which the majority is too small to give the required assurance would occur. This is so for two reasons. The first is because if this very improbable event were to occur (which is always possible) one would be obliged to act according to a decision with a low probability and recognized as such. One is doubtless exposed in all systems of majority voting to the risk of adopting a false decision, but this is when there is a great probability that it is true. But there can be no reasonable ground for submitting to a decision when it is necessary to have a real assurance of the truth of this decision to submit to it and one has, on the contrary, a very low probability. The second reason is that this disadvantage derives not from the nature of things but from the form of procedure chosen. Thus, for example, it is not unjust to punish a man although it is possible that the judges are mistaken in declaring him guilty; but it would be unjust to punish him when the majority against him was such that it did not give adequate assurance of his guilt. In the first case, there is no injustice in judging according to a probability which still exposes one to risk of error, because it is our nature to be able to judge only according to such probabilities. In the second case there is injustice, because one would have exposed oneself voluntarily to punishing a man without assurance of his guilt. In the first case one has, in punishing, a very great probability of the justice of each particular action; in the second case, one knows that in this particular action one is committing an injustice.

These principles once established, it is a question of applying calculation to different forms of decision-making and different hypothetical majorities.

For this purpose, we shall first suppose assemblies composed of voters possessing equal soundness of mind and equal enlightenment. We shall suppose that none of the voters influences the votes of others and that all express their opinion in good faith. Supposing then that one knows the probability that the opinion of each voter will be in conformity with the truth, the form of the decision, the hypothetical majority and the number of voters, one seeks to discover (1) the probability of not having a decision contrary to the truth; (2) the probability of having a true decision; (3) the probability of having any decision (true or false); (4) the probability that a decision that one knows to have been taken will be true rather than false; and, finally, the probability of this decision when the majority by which it has been taken is known. Such is the subject of the first part of this book.

In the second part, on the contrary, one supposes one of these elements known and seeks one of these three things—either the hypothetical majority, or the number of voters, or the probable truth of the opinion of each voter—regarding the two others as given.

So far we have sometimes supposed as known the probable truth of the opinion of each voter, sometimes that of the decision taken. We have said in addition that one must seek assurance (1) of not having a decision contrary to the truth; (2) of having a decision (when one knows that one has been taken) that is more likely to be true than false. We have also said that it is equally necessary to have a great probability of having a true decision; and, finally, that in a great number of circumstances it is necessary to have a sufficient assurance of the truth of the decision, even when we know that it has been taken by the smallest admissible majority.

How to know the probability of the votes of each voter, or that of the decision of a tribunal; how to determine the probability that can be regarded as a true assurance, or that which can, in other cases, be regarded as sufficient, such is the object of the third part.

I examine in the fourth part the changes introduced into the results found in the first part by inequality of enlightenment or of soundness of mind among the voters, by the supposition that the probable truth of their votes is not constant, by the influence that one of them might have upon the others, by the bad faith of some, by the practice of reducing the votes of several judges to a single vote when they are in agreement, and finally by the diminution in the probable truth of the voters' opinions that must result when a tribunal whose first decision did not reach the required majority votes again on the same question and finishes by deciding with that majority.

These last researches were necessary to be able to apply theory to practice.

The fifth part, finally, will comprise the application of the principles set forth in the preceding ones to some examples, such as the establishment of a law, an election, the judgment of an accused, a decision relating to property rights.

ANALYSIS OF THE FIRST PART

I first consider the most simple case, that in which the number of voters being unequal, the decision is made by a simple majority vote.

In this case, the probability of not having a false decision, the probability of having a true decision, the probability that the decision reached is in conformity with the truth, are all the same, since there can be no case in which there is no decision.

One finds further that if the probable truth of the vote of each voter is greater than $1/2$, that is to say if it is more probable than not that he will decide in conformity with the truth, the more the number of voters increases, the greater the probability of the truth of the decision. The limit of this probability will be certainty, from which it follows that multiplying the number of votes yields as great a probability of having a decision as desired; and this is what will be understood every time we say that the limit of probability is 1, or certainty.

If, on the contrary, the probability of the judgment of each voter is below 1/2 (i.e., if it is more probable than not that he will be mistaken) then the more the number of voters increases, the more the probability of the truth of the decision diminishes. The limit of this probability will be zero, which is to say that by multiplying the number of voters one could have a probability of the truth of the decision as small as desired, or a probability as great as desired that this decision would be erroneous.

If the probable truth of each voter's vote is 1/2, then, whatever the number of voters, that of the truth of each decision will also be 1/2.

This conclusion leads first of all to a rather important observation. A very numerous assembly cannot be composed of very enlightened men. It is even probable that those comprising such an assembly will on many matters combine great ignorance with many prejudices. Thus there will be a great number of questions upon which the probability of the truth of the vote of each voter will be below 1/2. It follows that the more numerous the assembly, the more it will be exposed to the risk of making false decisions.

Now since these prejudices and this ignorance can exist in relation to very important matters, it is clear that it can be dangerous to give a democratic constitution to an unenlightened people. A pure democracy, indeed, would only be appropriate to a people much more enlightened, much freer from prejudices than any of those known to history.

For every other nation, this form of assemblies becomes harmful, unless the assemblies are limited in the exercise of their power to decisions directly relating to the maintenance of security, liberty, and property: matters upon which a direct personal interest can adequately enlighten all minds.

One recognizes, for the same reason, to what extent it is true that the more numerous the assemblies, the less probable become useful reforms in the principles of administration and legislation; and how much the long duration of prejudices and abuses is to be feared.

Very numerous assemblies can only exercise power to advantage in the first stage of societies, where an equal ignorance renders all men more or less equal in enlightenment. One cannot hope to have a great probability of obtaining decisions in conformity with the truth; and consequently there are no legitimate grounds for restricting the number of voters, thereby subjecting the greater number to the will of the smaller. However, in the case where an assembly can be formed in such a way that there is a very great probability of its decisions being true, then there is just ground for men less enlightened than its members to submit their will to the decisions of this assembly.

Numerous assemblies would also be appropriate to a country in which, as a result of the progress of enlightenment, there was a great equality between minds, as to the soundness of their judgments and the truth of the principles according to which they governed their conduct; and this is the only case in which either wise laws or the reform of bad ones can be expected from very numerous assemblies. . . .

[Condorcet then proceeds to discuss various hypothetical conditions of decision-making, e.g., the requirement of a constant or proportional majority, the combination of the votes of a number of separate assemblies, or the institution of superior and inferior deliberative bodies.]

Thus it can be seen that the form most appropriate to fulfill all the conditions required is at the same time the simplest one: that in which a single assembly, composed of enlightened men, alone pronounces a judgment by a majority large enough to give adequate assurance of the truth of the judgment, even when the majority is the minimum required. It is also necessary that the number of voters be large enough to yield a great probability of obtaining a decision.

Enlightened voters and a simple form of decision-making are the means of uniting the greatest number of advantages. Complicated forms do not remedy the lack of enlightenment of the voters, or remedy it only imperfectly, or even involve disadvantages greater than those one has been attempting to avoid.

So far it has been assumed that there could only be two opinions in a decision, i.e., that one was deliberating on the truth of a simple proposition or its opposite. It remains to examine the circumstances in which the choice cannot be reduced to two contradictory opinions. . . .

When there are only two opinions and it is a question of pronouncing between two contradictory propositions, one of which is true and the other false, if one knows the probability that each voter will decide in favor of the truth rather than error, one knows the probability that the decision at a given majority will be in favor of the truth, or that there will not be an erroneous decision, or that there will be a decision, or that a decision taken will be true rather than false.

To apply the same theory now to more complicated propositions, it is necessary to observe first of all that every complex proposition is reducible to a system of simple propositions, and that all the opinions that can be formed in deliberating upon this proposition are equal in number to the combinations that one can make of these propositions and those contradicting them.

Thus, for example, if the complex proposition that one is examining is formed of two simple propositions, there are four possible opinions; if it is formed of three simple propositions there are eight possible opinions; if four propositions, then sixteen possible opinions, and so on. . . .

[It follows from the preceding argument:]

1. that to have a majority decision that merits confidence, it is absolutely necessary to reduce all opinions in such a way that they represent in a distinct manner the different combinations that can arise from a system of simple propositions and their opposites;
2. that then counting separately all the votes given in favor of each of these propositions or its opposite, it is necessary to take that proposition from each pair which has the majority, and to form from all these propositions the opinion that must prevail;
3. that it is indifferent in this case to take the votes on the whole system, or to take them successively on each proposition.

It is useless to enter into any detail as to the manner of fixing the majority. In effect, it is evident that it is necessary to be sure, both for each particular proposition and for the system of propositions as a whole, that the conditions necessary for all kinds of decisions have been fulfilled.

The more complicated the question, the more simple propositions it will involve; the more difficult it will also be to fulfill these conditions and to have a sufficient probability of obtaining a true decision, and of the decision obtained being true. Furthermore, the need to entrust the decision only to men enlightened enough that the probable truth of the vote of each voter is very great, is still more indispensable here than in the case where it is a question of pronouncing upon a simple proposition.

If the propositions which are combined to form the various opinions were invariably such that none of their combinations mathematically possible implied a contradiction, we would have nothing to add here. But that generally occurs only when the propositions are independent one of another.

If they are related one to another, there can be combinations that involve contradictions in terms. . . .

[At this point, Condorcet analyzes several examples of decisions yielding a contradiction in terms, the most important of which is the case of an election between three candidates, A, B, and C. He begins by showing that if the candidates are compared one against another there are eight possible combinations ranking the candidates. Using the notation $>$ to indicate the preferability (or, as Condorcet would have it, the superiority) of one candidate as compared to another, this can be shown as follows:

    (I) $A > B, A > C, B > C$ (A is preferred)
    (II) $A > B, A > C, C > B$ (A is preferred)
    (III) $A > B, C > A, B > C$ (contradictory)
    (IV) $A > B, C > A, C > B$ (C is preferred)
    (V) $B > A, A > C, B > C$ (B is preferred)
    (VI) $B > A, A > C, C > B$ (contradictory)
    (VII) $B > A, C > A, B > C$ (B is preferred)
    (VIII) $B > A, C > A, C > B$ (C is preferred).

Of these eight combinations, six yield a clear statement of preference for one candidate. The remaining two give contradictory results.]

This posed, it is easy to see, first of all, that the method usually employed in elections is defective. In effect, each voter is limited to designating the candidate he prefers. Thus in the example of three candidates, a voter casting his vote for A does not express his preference as between B and C, and so on. Now this manner of voting can result in a decision really contrary to the opinion of the majority.

Suppose 60 voters, for example, of whom 23 vote in favor of A, 19 in favor of B, and 18 in favor of C. Suppose, further, that the 23 voting for A have decided unanimously that C is better than B; that the 19 voting for B have decided that C is better than A; and, finally, that of the 18 voting for C, 16 have decided that B is better than A and only 2 that A is better than B.

One would then have

1. 35 votes for the proposition *B is better than A,* and 23 for the opposite proposition, *A is better than B;*
2. 37 votes for the proposition *C is better than A,* and 23 for the opposite proposition, *A is better than C;*
3. 41 votes for the proposition *C is better than B,* and 19 for the opposite proposition, *B is better than C.*

We would then have the system of the three propositions which enjoy a majority, formed of three propositions (B > A, C > A, C > B) which imply a judgment in favor of C.

Moreover, we would have the two propositions forming the opinion in favor of C (C > A, C > B) decided, one by a majority of 37 to 23, the other by a majority of 41 to 19. The two propositions which form the opinion in favor of B(B > A, B > C) would be decided, one by a majority of 35 to 25, the other by a minority of 19 to 41. Finally, the two propositions which form a judgment in favor of A (A > B, B > C) would be decided by a minority, one of 25 to 35, the other of 23 to 37.

Thus the candidate really enjoying the vote of the majority would be precisely the one who would have had the least votes according to the ordinary method of election. And A, the candidate who would have had the most votes according to the ordinary form of election, is found, on the contrary, to be the candidate who would in reality have been furthest from enjoying the confidence of the majority.

Thus it can already be seen that the form of election generally adopted must be rejected. If it had to be preserved, this could only be in cases where there was no necessity to elect immediately and where there could be a requirement that no one be elected who had not received more than half of the votes. Even in this case, this form still has the disadvantage that it is open to the risk of a candidate who had really gained a very great majority being regarded as not elected.

In general, one should therefore substitute for this form of election that in which each voter, expressing the order in which he ranks the candidates, would pronounce at the same time upon the respective preference he accords them.

From this order would be taken the three propositions which must form each opinion, if there are three candidates; the six propositions which must form each opinion, if there are four candidates; the ten propositions if there are five candidates, etc. This would be done by comparing the votes in favor of each of these propositions or of its opposite.

By this means one would arrive at the system of propositions which would be formed by the majority among the eight possible systems for three candidates, the 64 possible systems for four candidates, the 1024 possible systems for five candidates. And if one considered only those systems which do not imply a contradiction, there would be only six possible for three candidates, 24 for four candidates, 120 for five candidates, and so on.

We can now ask whether the majority can occur in favor of one of these contradictory systems and we find that this is possible.

Suppose that in the example already chosen, in which there are 23 votes for A, 19 for B, 18 for C, the 23 votes for A are for the proposition *B is better than C*. This latter proposition will then have a majority of 42 to 18. Suppose, further, that of the 19 votes in favor of B there are 17 for the proposition *C is better than A,* and 2 for the proposition *A is better than C*. The proposition *C is better than A* will have a majority of 35 to 25. Suppose, finally, that of the 18 votes for C, 10 are for the proposition *A is better than B,* and 8 for the contrary proposition, *B is better than A*. We will then have a majority of 33 to 27 in favor of the proposition, *A is better than B*.

The system which obtains the majority will then be composed of the three propositions, A > B, C > A, B > C. This system is the third of the eight previously discussed. And it is one of those that implies a contradiction. We will therefore examine the result of this form of election, 1) without regard for the contradictory propositions; 2) with regard for them.

We have seen that of the six systems really possible there are two in favor of A, two in favor of B, and two in favor of C. Thus in one of the preceding examples, where we have supposed that out of 60 votes the proposition *A is better than B* obtained 25 votes to 35, the proposition *A is better than C* obtained 23 votes to 37, and the proposition *B is better than C* obtained 19 votes to 41, the majority is in favor of system VIII, formed of the three propositions, B > A, C > A, C > B. The first of these propositions has a majority of 35 to 25, the second of 37 to 23, the third of 41 to 19.

The probability that this system is in conformity with the truth will then be derived from the probability of the truth of each voter's opinion. . . .

Suppose now that the three propositions which have the majority form one of the two contradictory systems. If there is no necessity to elect, the decision will be regarded as null and void. But if there is a necessity to elect, that decision will be followed which results from the two most probable propositions. For it is easy to see (as we have noted), that any two of the three propositions then form a decision contradicting the third. Thus, for example, in system III (formed of the three propositions, A > B, C > A, B > C) the first two propositions give an opinion in favor of C, the first and the third give an opinion in favor of A, and the second and third give an opinion in favor of B. Now let the proposition B > C have a lesser probability, and the proposition A > B have a greater. It is clear that these two propositions, B > C, B > A, each have a lesser probability than the two propositions A > B, A > C. B must therefore be excluded. But, as between A and C, C must be preferred because the proposition C > A has the majority.

If it is the proposition C > A which has the greatest majority, one will find that in the combinations C > A, C > B, B > C, B > A, the two propositions that form the first combination each have a greater majority or a lesser minority than those forming the second. Thus C must be preferred to B; but as between C and A, C must be preferred. Thus the vote must be interpreted as favoring C.

Let us observe finally that these contradictory systems cannot occur without indicating uncertainty in the opinions; and they will not occur if one of the candidates has more than half of the votes cast in the ordinary manner of voting, or if a majority of a third is required for the acceptance of the propositions forming the decision.

The preceding reflections suggest this general rule: that whenever it is essential to make the election, it is necessary to take successively all the propositions that have a majority, beginning with those possessing the largest. As soon as these first propositions produce a result, it should be taken as the decision, without regard for the less probable decisions that follow.

If this procedure does not yield the result least subject to error, or to a result that has a probability over $1/2$ and is formed from two propositions more probable than their opposites, at least it will give a decision that avoids the least probable propositions and involves a lesser injustice between the candidates, taken two by two. We shall return to this question in the fifth part of this book.

This discussion has presented only an imperfect sketch of the theory of decision-making on complicated propositions and of the theory of elections. But it shows that the following requirements are necessary to secure the two conditions essential to every decision, i.e., the probability of reaching a decision, and the probability of the decision reached being true:

1. In the case of decisions on complicated questions, it is necessary for the system of simple propositions involved in such questions to be rigorously worked out, for each possible opinion to be clearly stated, for each voter to express his judgment on each of the propositions forming this opinion and not simply on the general result. The manner in which the question is put to the vote is therefore very important; and the business of establishing this form is one of the most delicate and difficult responsibilities that the body charged to decide, or those who have established it, can confer. Yet among the ancients, and even among the moderns, it has been almost everywhere left to chance, or given as a power or right attached to a particular office, rather than imposed as a duty that demands wisdom and precision.

2. It is necessary, furthermore, that voters be enlightened; and that they be the more enlightened, the more complicated the question

upon which they decide. Otherwise, while one will indeed find a form of decision-making to prevent a false decision, this will at the same time render any decision almost impossible. It will therefore be a means only of perpetuating abuses and bad laws.

Thus the form of the assemblies which decide men's lot is much less important for their happiness than the enlightenment of those who sit in these assemblies; and the progress of reason will contribute more to the happiness of peoples than the form of political constitutions.

ANALYSIS OF THE THIRD PART

[In this part, Condorcet turns to the problem of evaluating the degree of assurance of the truth of a decision that will be adequate to oblige acceptance of the decision by those who have not directly participated in making it. Having established that different degrees of assurance are necessary for different kinds of decisions, he proceeds to analyze the particular case of the establishment of a new law.]

. . . When it is a question of establishing a new law, it seems at first glance that one should above all seek assurance of not having a false decision, not only because of the importance of the consequences that a bad law inevitably entails, but also because of the difficulty of reforming such a law once its error has been discovered. This has even been the only object apparently regarded as essential in the majority of constitutions; and the hope of reforming the vices of the constitution and of remedying abuses has often been sacrificed to this consideration.

This principle of putting obstacles in the way of the destruction of bad laws, to avoid the risk either of frequent innovations or of bad new laws, has three different causes. The first is the very old and almost general opinion that the human race, far from gaining in wisdom, degenerates with time and can only be restored to the same point of wisdom, virtue, and happiness by violent upheavals. It is evident that once this opinion is adopted any procedure that avoids change, even through lack of the majority necessary to form a decision, must appear advantageous. If it is very probable that the old law is good, it is necessary, in order to reform it, to have a much greater probability of the truth of the decision which (by substituting another law for it) declares that the first law is bad.

But this opinion must be regarded as a prejudice based on the dissatisfaction that men have with their lot. It is strengthened by the envy men feel toward their contemporaries; by the authority almost everywhere exercised over opinion by the aged, who are naturally regretful of the time of their youth; and, finally, by ignorance of antiquity, which is judged according to the enthusiasm of those who wish to take pride in having studied it.

The second cause of this principle is the opinion (no less widespread) according to which laws are regarded not as necessary consequences of the nature of men and of their rights, but as sacrifices of these rights required by considerations of common utility. Thus if one regards a new law as one more violation of natural liberty, it is very simple to seek means of ensuring that no laws will be established, except in the case where pressing necessity makes its establishment almost generally desired. This opinion could have been excusable in the beginning of political societies, where even a part of the laws necessary for their maintenance were lacking, and where men had an often exaggerated opinion of the rights of natural liberty in the social state.

But it is not the same in long-established societies, where there has rather been cause for complaint of the excessive number of laws; where new laws must almost invariably involve the destruction or correction of an old law established in the time of ignorance and prejudices; where the concern must be not to restrict the rights of primitive liberty but to restore them to men deprived of them by considerations of a false and limited politics.

The third cause of this principle is the fear of very frequent innovation which (it is claimed) would enfeeble the respect for the laws. It is true that when the laws are not the consequences of fixed principles and real, well-proven truths, this respect is then founded on habit and not on reason. The older the laws, the stronger this respect accordingly becomes. But since it is a question here of establishing laws formed in accordance with truth and justice, it is precisely with substituting the empire of reason for that of habit that one must be concerned.

It is therefore just as important to make sure that a good law will not be rejected for lack of the required majority as it is to be assured that no bad law will have the majority. And one must seek assurance that a new law will be rejected only because it is bad, and not because there has been no decision on this law.

Finally it is necessary, when a law is adopted by the minimum majority required, to have an adequate assurance that this law is good.

Now it is easy to see from the formulae produced by calculation that if one first has this adequate assurance for the case of the minimum majority, and then in addition has an equal assurance of having a true decision rather than a false one, the risk of having a false decision will be so small that it is useless to concern oneself particularly with the means of fulfilling the first condition.

Thus our principal task here is to discover the probability that gives assurance of the validity of a law passed by the smallest possible majority, such that one can believe that it is not unjust to subject others to this law and that it is useful to submit oneself to it. Then the person responsible for employing the public force for the maintenance of this law would have an adequate assurance that he is only doing so justly. Then, too, the citizen obeying this same law would feel that while he is obliged as a necessary condition of the social order not to conduct himself in a certain category of actions simply according to his own reason, he at least has the advantage of following only those opinions which, setting his own judgment aside, he must regard as possessing a degree of probability sufficient to direct his conduct. Consequently, each individual would be obliged to conduct himself only according to the kind of assurance permitted him by the very nature of things.

Every man has the right to conduct himself according to his own reason. But when he enters into a society, he agrees to submit to the common reason those of his actions which must be governed for all according to the same principles. His own reason prescribes this submission; and thus it is still according to his own reason that he acts, even in renouncing the right to make use of it. Thus when he submits to a law contrary to his personal opinion, he must say to himself:

> *It is not a question of myself alone, but of everyone.*
> *Thus I must not act according to what I myself believe to*

> *be reasonable, but according to that which everyone–like*
> *me, setting aside his own opinion–must regard as in*
> *conformity with reason and truth.*

It is a question now of seeking to determine this necessary assurance, that is to say (as we have already observed) of discovering a probability below which one cannot act without injustice or imprudence. We will suppose here that the risk of error must be such that we neglect a similar risk even when it is a question of our own life. . . .

[Condorcet proposes that it would be justifiable to discount the risk of an unwise law provided that the probability of passing such a law were no greater than a risk of death regarded by most men as negligible. Arguing that a man of thirty-seven has no more fear of sudden death (i.e., death from an illness lasting less than a week) than a man of forty-seven, he estimates that the risk of sudden death increases between these two ages by $1/144768$.]

We conclude that $144767/144768$ can be taken as expressing the probability that must be regarded as giving an adequate assurance, when it is a matter of pronouncing upon a new law, that a decision passed by the minimum majority required will be true, or that a true decision will be obtained at the required majority. This probability will perhaps appear very great; and one might imagine that it would be very difficult to secure it. But calculation shows that an assembly of sixty-one voters with a majority of nine votes required would fulfill these conditions, provided that the probability of the truth of each voter's opinions were equal to $4/5$ (that is to say, that one assumed that each voter would be mistaken only once in every five votes). If one assumed that each voter would be mistaken only once in every ten votes, then it would be sufficient to require a majority of six votes in an assembly of forty-four voters.

The more the probable truth of the voter's opinion diminishes, the more the majority required must increase, as must the number of voters; and this number increases with great rapidity when the probable truth of the voters' opinions is very small. It follows that in a country in which enlightenment is far from widespread, but where there are a certain number of enlightened men, it can be possible to satisfy the two conditions required by delegating the decision to a small assembly, while it would be impossible (or at least very difficult) to satisfy them if one were obliged to entrust it to a numerous assembly.

Thus one sees that the advantage of entrusting the responsibility for pronouncing upon the laws to a more or less numerous assembly of representatives depends upon the manner in which enlightenment is distributed in each country; and that there can be cases in which it would be disadvantageous to increase the number of these trustees of the general reason. . . .

ANALYSIS OF THE FIFTH PART

[In the course of the fifth part, Condorcet takes up the question of numerous assemblies in which the increased size of the assemblies means the admission of many voters whose opinions have a low probability of being true. He argues that in such assemblies it will often be impossible to satisfy the conditions necessary to give adequate assurance of a true decision.]

But it can be observed that in the majority of matters submitted to the decision of an assembly, the same voters whose opinions have such a small probability of being true can be enlightened enough—certainly not to pronounce with some probability of truth as to which man among a great number has the most merit—but to choose, as the most enlightened, one of those whose opinions will have a large enough probability of being true. Thus a numerous assembly composed of voters who are not very enlightened could be usefully employed only to choose the members of a less numerous assembly to which the decision on other matters would then be entrusted. One would then easily be able to fulfill for this latter decision all the conditions that justice and the general interest require. If one remembers especially that it is almost never a matter in decision-making of a simple proposition, and rarely even of an isolated decision, but of a system of interrelated decisions in which a single false decision can destroy the harmony of the whole, it will be seen that this last form is the only one that can have some hope of fulfilling the conditions it is necessary to observe.

What we have said concerning the disadvantages of a too numerous assembly applies even more forcefully to the case where the probable truth of the opinions of a certain number of voters falls below $1/2$. But it is necessary to observe in this case that one cannot even hope to remedy this disadvantage by charging this numerous assembly with the choice of those to whom the decision will then be delegated.

In effect, when the probability of the truth of a voter's opinion falls below $1/2$, there must be a reason why he decides less well than one would at random. This reason can only be found in the prejudices to which this voter is subject. Now it is probable that this same voter will give his preference to men who share these prejudices, that is to say, to men whose opinions, in a great number of decisions, will have a probable truth of less than $1/2$.

Thus, provided a society possesses a large number of enlightened men, free from prejudice; and provided that the right of the great number lacking sufficient enlightenment is limited to choosing those whom it considers wisest and best informed, to whom the citizens consequently entrust their right to decide on questions beyond their competence, an adequate assurance of decisions conformable to truth and reason can be attained.

But this is not true if those who pass for being enlightened in the public opinion are subject to prejudices. For every question the examination of which can be influenced by these prejudices, election can give no assurance of voters who are free from prejudices, and whose votes have a sufficient probability of being true. On the contrary, it will only be a means of ensuring that those to whom the decisions are entrusted will be subject themselves to these prejudices, and will have a probability below $1/2$ of their decisions being true. It follows that it would be more advantageous in this case to rely on a small number of men taken at random from among the class of those in whom some education can be supposed.

We are thus brought here to a conclusion similar to that of the first part, namely that the form that one can give to the assemblies pronouncing upon a law (or any other matter) cannot yield any means of obtaining the assurance that one must seek, unless one can be assured of composing these assemblies of enlightened men.

We find in addition that if the men who pass for being educated share the popular opinions, this last condition cannot be fulfilled. Thus one can only regard majority decisions as appropriate to make known that which is true and useful in a case where a great part of the society is enlightened, and where the men who are educated, who have cultivated their intellect and exercised their reason, are not subject to prejudices. Then, in effect, it is enough that the direction of affairs be entrusted to those who, in the common opinion, pass as being capable and enlightened; and one can have the assurance of this in some constitutions, and a fairly great hope of it in almost all.

CONCLUSION

The reader of this book has doubtless noticed that I have only sketched the solution of several important questions, and that it must be regarded as a simple essay, less fit to enlighten those who will read it than to inspire in them the desire to see the multiplication of the applications of calculation to these same questions.[7] I have not believed myself able to offer a good book. I have hoped simply to produce a book fit to stimulate better ones. To extend important discoveries and place them within the grasp of the greatest number, to attempt to direct the attention and labors of learned men towards a goal that one believes useful: such must be the ambition of the majority of authors. Too few men can pretend to the glory of contributing, by the discovery of new truths, to the happiness of their fellows.

When one sees that on almost every point calculation only gives the result that reason would at least have made one suspect, one might be tempted to regard it as useless. But it is easy to observe (1) that calculation at least has the advantage of rendering the advance of reason more certain and of offering it stronger weapons against subtleties and sophisms; (2) that calculation becomes necessary every time that the truth or falsehood of opinions depends upon a certain precision in the values involved. For example, every time that the conclusion of a course of reasoning will remain the same provided that a certain probability is greater than another, reason alone will lead us to this conclusion in a great number of questions. But if one must draw opposite conclusions according to whether the value of the probability is contained, or not contained, within more narrow limits, it can easily be seen that reason alone cannot lead us with any certainty to the conclusion which must be preferred. Reason is sufficient provided one needs only vague observation of events; calculation becomes necessary as soon as the truth depends upon exact and precise observations.

The reasons that we have already set forth at the beginning of this preliminary discourse are not the only ones. There is no one who has not observed in his own experience that he has changed his mind on certain matters, according to age, circumstances, or events, without however being able to say that this change was founded on new grounds, and without being able to assign any other cause than the more or less strong impression of the same objects. Now, if instead of judging according to this impression, which multiplies or exaggerates a part of the objects while it attenuates or prevents one from seeing others, one could count or evaluate them by calculation, our reason would cease to be the slave of our impressions.

This last consideration is the more important in that our opinion decides not only upon our own interests, but upon those of other men. In this latter case, simply to believe in an opinion is not enough to be just; it is necessary in addition to have grounds for believing that opinion, and to have grounds that can be regarded as true proofs. Thus one must not regard as indifferent the means of evaluating whenever possible the degrees of the probability which determines our decisions and of ensuring by this method the justice of our judgments and our actions.

We will dare to add that the application of calculation to the discussion of a great number of questions affecting men's interests would be one of the best means of bringing them to recognize the value of knowledge. The number of those who doubt its utility, or who pretend that it would be dangerous to spread it, is very small in our day, if one wishes to count only those who in good faith hold an opinion so degrading for human nature.

One knows too well today that the ignorant man has no other interest than his independence. Force can enchain him, servitude can brutalize him, superstition can lead him. But if he breaks his chains, if he escapes from his stupid indifference, if his guide goes astray, then his instinct reappears in all its force and he becomes more terrible even than the savage. Indeed, he becomes similar to those ferocious animals whom man has subjected, who once freed from their chains recover all their fury, and have lost only the kind of generosity which they owed to their independence.

The enlightened man, on the contrary, in knowing his rights, also learns to know their limits. He knows when he must sacrifice his wishes, and sometimes even his true rights, to his own happiness or to that of others. In knowing the entire extent of his duties, he learns that respect for the well-being and peace of others is one of the most important and most sacred. He sees himself presented with more than one source of happiness, more than one means of doing good; and he will choose that which is easiest, that which he can be sure of obtaining at least cost.

But cannot the light of knowledge dazzle men rather than enlighten them? Can truth be the prize of men's first efforts? Can it not happen that one substitutes for primitive errors those which are more subtle and more dangerous, because they will be more difficult to destroy? Will not enthusiasm, which carries to the extreme the opinions based on prejudices, exaggerate also the half-truths that reason will make known? Will the human mind be the less exposed to the risk of going astray, because the space it has opened for itself is more extensive?

Such are the objections that can still, in an enlightened century, be opposed to the utility of the advance of knowledge. When philosophy unites only with eloquence and literature these objections must appear plausible; perhaps, even, they are not without some foundation. But they lose all their force when philosophy unites with the sciences, and especially with the mathematical sciences. Then obliged to follow their always certain and measured march, it will have neither enthusiasm nor error to fear. Accustomed to precise results, it will recognize all the uncertainty that a vague result necessarily bears with it; and it will know the danger of uncritically accepting the consequences that seem to follow necessarily from it, but which become more and more uncertain the further they are developed.

The precision of results, and their certainty, would mark a well-defined limit between specious opinions which are only the hasty outcome of a first glance, and those opinions which deserve to be placed in the ranks of truths to be followed in practice. One would have the double advantage that those who seek useful truths would have surer truths and less risk of going astray, while those who feared the effects of such truths would no longer be able to oppose them so successfully with sophisms and prejudices. This eternal conflict between error and truth would be more peaceful, and success would depend less on chance or on the skill of the combatants.

Finally, this application of the sciences to philosophy is a means not only of extending knowledge and of making it surer, but also of multiplying its utility, since it cannot fail to be extended successively to a greater or lesser number of new objects and of important questions which today would seem very far from being solvable by such methods. Now in multiplying the means of doing good, in extending them to a greater number of objects, one would teach men more tranquilly to forego those advantages an uncertain hope of which they would recognize as too dearly to be bought. In thus opening a vaster field of endeavor to minds dominated by the love of good, one would assure the utility of their efforts, and prevent their enthusiasm from being dangerous; and this is perhaps the surest means of reconciling two things that have almost everywhere been separated up to now—namely, activity for the public good and tranquillity.

One would be mistaken, in fact, if one regarded these applications as necessarily limited to a small number of objects. The precise knowledge of everything relating to the duration of human life, and to the influences upon it of climate, habit, diet, manner of life, different occupations, laws themselves, and governments; a knowledge no less exact of all the details relating to the productions of the earth and human consumption; a nonarbitrary evaluation of the real utility of public works or national institutions, of the salutary or deleterious effects of a great part of the laws of administration; the method of ensuring by calculation the precision of results, of deducing certain consequences from them, of knowing by this means the truth or falsehood of a great number of opinions; the resources to be drawn from these applications for the advancement of our knowledge of man as a physical and moral being: all these objects are at once of the greatest importance and the greatest extent. One is very far from exhausting the knowledge of this kind that seems immediately to offer itself. And when this knowledge is exhausted, why in this part of the sciences as in every other should there not then open before us a field of inquiry far more vast even than that already traversed?

Here, as in the physical sciences, there is perhaps an infinity of objects which will always resist calculation, but one can also respond that in each of these areas the number of matters to which calculation can be applied is equally inexhaustible.

Ridiculous applications of calculation to political questions have doubtless been made. How many equally ridiculous applications have not been made in all parts of the physical sciences? But it would be gratuitous for us to stop to prove a truth that no man who has studied philosophy and the mathematical sciences equally could ever cast in doubt.

We will finish this preliminary discourse with a reflection that can be useful. We have seen above that all the certainty we can attain is founded on a natural tendency to regard as constant that which we have seen to be repeated a great many times. Must not this same inclination lead us equally to believe the constancy and the reality of the things that we hear repeated without contradiction? Will we not be in this regard in the same situation as the man whom one has made to feel two balls by placing a single ball between two crossed fingers; and who, if he does not reflect upon the circumstances surrounding this phenomenon, will believe himself certain of the existence of two balls?

The obscurity, the very incomprehensibility of the ideas that words pronounced before us give rise to in our minds, does not enfeeble this tendency in those who have not acquired the habit of forming precise ideas for themselves. An astronomer who calculates an eclipse can be without conscious knowledge of the truth of the theory upon which the method he uses is based; although he uses logarithms, for example, it is not necessary that he have at that very moment a clear and precise idea of what a logarithm is. If the astronomer differs from someone who believes a proposition that he does not understand, but by which he is nevertheless struck, it is because the astronomer recalls that he has at some other time done, according to a demonstration that appeared to him certain, what he today does mechanically, while the belief of the other man has always been equally mechanical. Thus the prejudiced man perfectly resembles an arithmetician whom one has made learn by heart a method of calculating eclipses and the theory of this method without explaining them, and who calculates eclipses by routine. It is easy to see that it would not occur to this man to doubt the truth of these propositions that he does not understand, and according to which he calculates, and that he would even believe them very firmly. Those who claim to square the circle are another example of the same truth. They would not believe the absurd proposition to which they are so dogmatically attached if they had a clear idea of the terms of this proposition. Thus this tendency to believe what one has believed, which has the same origin as the tendency to believe constant that which one has seen uniformly repeated, can actually be extended to the most incomprehensible things.

Reason and calculation tell us that probability increases progressively with the number of constant observations that are the basis of our belief. But does not the force of the natural tendency which leads us to believe depend at least as much on the force of the impression that these objects make upon us? Thus if our reason does not come to our help, our opinions will really be the work of our sensibility and our passions. Now observation seems to prove that this tendency to believe constant and real that which has constantly occurred depends uniquely on a purely passive impression and not on reasoning, since reason can give us no ground for believing that this tendency will not deceive us.

This manner of explaining the source of our errors and our dogmatism can lead to useful consequences for the means of rescuing from their baleful influence the two classes of humanity whom it is most important to preserve from error and who are the most exposed to it: namely, children and the people.

Such are the results of the questions we have discussed in this *Essay*, and the reflections to which these results have led us. May this work be of some utility. And may those who will deign to read it judge that I have not profaned the memory of a great man in dedicating to him this feeble work, and in daring to speak in public of the friendship that united us.

NOTES TO "ESSAY ON THE APPLICATION
OF MATHEMATICS TO THE THEORY
OF DECISION-MAKING"

1. The Rota was traditionally the supreme tribunal of the Holy See.
2. Here, as elsewhere in this translation of the *Essay*, the term "ground for belief" is used to translate Condorcet's phrase *"motif de croire."* There is, however, an ambiguity in the term that is essential to explain. In French, the term "motif" can have both a logical and a psychological dimension: hence "motif de croire" implies not only the rational ground for belief but the psychological force of the conviction with which we believe. The case of a ball rolled between two crossed fingers, Condorcet suggests (p. 41), illustrates the way in which these two aspects can be confused: in this case, I do not simply *conclude* erroneously that there are two balls; I actually *feel* the two balls. Condorcet developed the implications of this analysis in his later *Eléments du calcul des probabilités* [Elements of the Calculus of Probabilities]. There he distinguished between the ground for belief—the greater or lesser frequency of the experiences involved in any given case—and the force of the sentiment of belief, which leads us to regard as constant any event that has been often repeated. The force of this sentiment naturally increases with the frequency of the experiences involved; but it also increases, Condorcet argued (following Hume in *A Treatise of Human Nature*), with the intensity or force of particular experiences (or impressions) upon the mind. Since the intensity of particular experiences has no relation to the probability of their recurrence, however, a disparity develops between the strength of the sentiment of belief and the weight of the rational ground for it. Correct reasoning therefore consists, Condorcet concluded, in evaluating the rational ground for belief through the application of the calculus of probabilities, thereby escaping the often misleading and erroneous influence of the sentiment of belief.
3. "For these two demonstrations, see the third part of Jakob Bernoulli's *Ars conjectandi* [The Art of Conjecturing], a work of genius, and one of those that makes it most regrettable that this great man commenced his mathematical career so late and that death interrupted it so soon" [Condorcet's note]. The *Ars conjectandi* was published in 1713, eight years after the death of its author, the Swiss mathematician Jakob Bernoulli (1654–1705). Although unfinished, the work established the mathematical foundations of the classic theory of probabilities and laid the basis for its applications to statistics.
4. "See the article "Existence" in the *Encyclopedia*, where this matter is treated profoundly and with great clarity" [Condorcet's note]. The author of this article was Turgot.
5. See above, p. 18, where Condorcet first develops the argument that even the truths of mathematics, often regarded as the very paradigm of certain knowledge, ultimately enjoy only a kind of psychological probability. For the most forceful statement of this argument in eighteenth-century thought, see Hume, *A Treatise of Human Nature*, edited by L.A. Selby-Bigge (Oxford, 1888), pp. 180–181.

6. "We will use the term *assurance* in the rest of this discourse, to designate that kind of probability that is called *moral certainty* in the schools, in order to avoid the ambiguities of the word certainty" [Condorcet's note].

7. "The first mathematician to conceive of the application of calculation to political questions was the celebrated Johan de Witt [1625–1672], Grand Pensionary of Holland. His wise and courageous conduct in this important position, his virtues, his patriotism, his tragic death, have rendered his name dear to all those who love their country and are touched by virtue. There were greater names in the last century; yet perhaps none could be cited as more worthy of respect.

Johan de Witt had been the disciple of Descartes, and one of his best disciples. Before becoming Grand Pensionary, he had published a work on the theory of curves containing original and ingenious views. He was the first to attempt to fix the rates for life annuities on the basis of the probabilities of life as given by mortality tables. On politics, on the true interests of nations, on the liberty of trade, he had ideas far superior to those of his century. His premature death was a misfortune for Europe as for his native country" [Condorcet's note]. See p. 205, note 1.

On the Influence of the American
Revolution on Europe
(1786)

Like many liberal Frenchmen, Condorcet followed the events of the American Revolution closely. Enthusiastic in his support, he followed the process by which Americans gave constitutional form to their new nation with a keen, but by no means uncritical, eye. This essay, published anonymously and dedicated to Lafayette by "an obscure inhabitant of the Old World," first appeared in 1786. It was reprinted two years later with an appendix containing a translation of the Federal Constitution of 1787 and a commentary upon it.

The introduction and first chapter of this essay, printed below, provide a succinct statement of Condorcet's understanding of the rights of man before the French Revolution.

[INTRODUCTION]

The path of truth, the poet Sadi has said, is narrow and lies between two precipices. At the least false step, we slip to the bottom. Stunned, we pick ourselves up from the fall. Painfully we clamber up the approach to the summit. We think we have reached it; we make one last effort—and we fall again on the other side.

America had scarcely declared its independence and our politicians already saw clearly that England's ruin and France's prosperity must be the necessary consequence of this happy revolution. This independence once recognized and assured, they seem to view it with indifference; and they think only of doubting their predictions at the very instant that events begin to validate the latter part of them.

I have considered this moment, when opinion seems to be going off in the contrary direction, as precisely the time at which it could be useful to discuss calmly the consequences of this great event. I shall attempt to be a restrained prophet.

The prize-essay question proposed by the abbé Raynal, on the good or evil consequences for Europe of the discovery of the New World, excited my interest.[1] I dared to undertake an answer to this question. But sensing that this endeavor was beyond my powers, I have saved from the flames only the chapter in which I examine the effects of American independence on humanity, on Europe, on France in particular, and summarize the principles according to which I attempt to find a method of measuring the different degrees of public happiness.

A nation taken as a body is an abstract entity; it can be neither happy nor unhappy. Thus when one speaks of the happiness of a nation taken collectively, only two things can be understood. Either this refers to a kind of mean value, regarded as the result of the happiness or unhappiness of individuals. Or it refers to the general means to happiness: i.e., the tranquillity and well-being that the soil, the laws, industry, relations with foreign nations, can provide for the general mass of citizens. A sense of justice is all that is necessary to recognize that this latter meaning is the one that should be understood.

Otherwise, it would be necessary to adopt the maxim all too common among republicans, ancient and modern, that the lesser number can be sacrificed to the greater. This is a maxim that places society in a perpetual state of war, subjecting to the empire of force that which should be ruled by reason and justice.

The general means of happiness for man in society can be divided into two classes. The first comprises everything which assures and extends the free enjoyment of man's natural rights. The second includes the means of diminishing the number of evils to which humanity is subjected by nature, of providing for our essential needs more surely and with less labor, of procuring for us a greater number of enjoyments by the employment of our powers and the legitimate use of our industries. The means of augmenting our powers and our industry must consequently be placed in this same category.

The rights of man are:

1. Security of person, which includes the assurance that one will not be disturbed by any violence, either within one's family or in the use of one's faculties, the independent and free exercise of which must be preserved in everything which is not contrary to the rights of another.
2. Security and free enjoyment of property.
3. Since in society there are certain actions which must be subject to common rules; since it is necessary to establish punishments for violations by an individual of the rights of others (whether by violence or fraud), man also has the right to be subject in all these matters only to general laws extending to the entire body of citizens. The interpretation of these laws may not be arbitrary; and their execution must be entrusted to impartial hands.
4. Finally, the right to contribute, either directly or through representatives, to the making of these laws and to all actions taken in the name of society at large, is a necessary consequence of the natural and primitive equality of man, and its equal enjoyment by each man using his reason must be regarded as the ultimate goal. Until this goal has been attained, it cannot be said that citizens enjoy this right in its entire extent.

There are no rights of man that cannot be easily deduced from those to which we have just attempted to reduce them. And it would even be easy to prove that all the principles of the civil and criminal law—like those of the laws relating to administration, commerce, and police powers—are a consequence of the obligation to respect the rights comprised in the first three categories.

The happiness of a society is greater, the more extensively these rights are enjoyed by the members of the state. But the enjoyment of each of these same rights is not equally important for the common happiness. I have listed them here in the order in which I think they contribute to this happiness; and I will even add that in a populous society the last of these rights must, of necessity, be virtually negligible for the majority of the inhabitants.

Zealous republicans have regarded this right as the most fundamental of all. And it is certainly true that in an enlightened nation free from superstition, where it would really belong to every citizen who could or would exercise it, the enjoyment of this right would ensure the enjoyment of all the others. But it loses its most precious advantages if prejudices divert those who must exercise it from the narrow paths traced for them by the immutable laws of justice; and, in terms of public happiness, a republic with tyrannical laws can fall far short of a monarchy.

In adopting this order, it is nevertheless recognized that the very frequent or very grave violation of a less essential right can do greater harm to the common happiness than the minor or very rare violation of a more important right. Thus, for example, a procedure in the criminal legislation that would expose innocent men to the danger of condemnation by ignorant or prejudiced judges can do more harm to a country than a law commanding capital punishment for an imaginary crime which is very rarely invoked in the place where this punishment is established. Fiscal laws, or laws restricting commerce, can be more harmful than the arbitrary power to imprison when it is rarely used.

These principles are simple. But the manner of evaluating the degrees of evil or good produced by these different violations of natural rights, or by the destruction of abuses contrary to these rights, begins to be difficult. It is not enough to know precisely the effects of each unjust law and each useful reform. It is also necessary to have a common measure to which they can be compared.

As for the second category of means of happiness, it is easy to see that they also depend in great part on the freer and more extensive exercise of natural rights. After this, they can be reduced, first to the enjoyment of a durable and secure peace with foreign powers; then to the augmentation of the means of procuring more enjoyments with an equal labor, whether by the growth of knowledge or the development of industry, by the extension of relations with other peoples or, above all, by a greater equality in the distribution of these means among the members of society. In effect, since the population is necessarily proportional to the means of subsistence produced in a normal year, it can easily be seen that the mass of enjoyments for the plurality of citizens can never be very great, at least in any constant and enduring way. Thus it is in the more equal distribution of these enjoyments that one must seek the public happiness. All the civil laws and all the laws relating to commerce must lead to the maintenance or re-establishment of this equality among members of a nation, without infringing the right of property or restricting the legitimate exercise of freedom.

It results from these same principles that a people's happiness, far from being increased by the misfortune or weakening of its neighbors, must (on the contrary) grow with the prosperity of other peoples. For it will then receive from them the example of good laws or the destruction of abuses; the demonstration of new techniques in industry; all the advantages, in short, of the communication of knowledge. And it is evident at the same time that the mass of common enjoyments, and the ability to distribute them more equally, are the necessary effect for all peoples of the progress of each of them.

The only exception to this general law is the case of a people led astray by a false policy ultimately carried out at its own expense, which wearies its neighbors by its ambition and seeks (by war, by monopolies, or by restrictive commercial laws) to render its power dangerous to them and its prosperity useless.

Such are the principles according to which I shall try to show what influence the American revolution must have.

Readers will perhaps grant the author of these reflections only one merit, that of dreaming even more grandly than the abbé Saint-Pierre.[2] He will reply, like the abbé, as follows: "I shall easily console myself for having passed my whole life as a dreamer, if I can hope that, a century after me, the execution of one of my ideas can do some good."

This is even too much to demand. In seeking to spread some truths isolated and sterile in themselves, one can in the long run facilitate combinations of ideas that are more felicitous and more fertile. Is it not also being useful to help draw the attention of good minds to an important matter, to inspire in them the desire to make such a matter the object of their reflections and investigations? One would have no right to the glory they might merit, but one would at least experience the pleasure of having been the cause of some good. Would a slight sacrifice of pride, the humiliation of being mistaken in good faith, or of having enunciated trivial or common truths on great matters, be too high a price to pay for this pleasure?

CHAPTER ONE. *INFLUENCE OF THE AMERICAN REVOLUTION ON THE OPINIONS AND LEGISLATION OF EUROPE*

The human race had lost its rights. Montesquieu found them and restored them to us (Voltaire). It is not enough, however, that these rights be written in the philosophers' works and engraved in the heart of virtuous men. It is also necessary that the ignorant or feeble man be able to read them in the example of a great people.

America has given us this example. Its Declaration of Independence is a simple and sublime exposition of these rights, so sacred and so long forgotten. Among no nation have they been so well known, or preserved in such perfect integrity.

It is true that Negro slavery still exists in some of the United States; but all enlightened men feel its shame, and its danger, and this blemish will not long continue to sully the purity of the American laws.

These wise republicans, still attached to some remnants of English prejudices, have not recognized clearly enough that prohibitive laws, commercial regulations, and indirect taxes are veritable infringements upon the right of property; that, since one does not truly possess what one cannot freely dispose of, they interfere with the free exercise of this right. In establishing a more extensive toleration than any other nation, they have accepted some limitations demanded by the people which are nevertheless contrary, if not to the exercise of personal freedom, at least to the right of every man to suffer no privation for believing what his reason has obliged him to believe. One could also, perhaps, find in the laws of some of the states feeble evidence of a fanaticism too embittered by long persecutions to yield to the first efforts of philosophy. But if one compares these infringements upon the natural rights of man to all those an enlightened man could discover in the laws of the wisest peoples (especially in those of the ancient nations, who are so much admired and so little known) it will be recognized that our opinion of American laws is not the fruit of an exaggerated enthusiasm, either for that nation or for our own age.

Moreover, if one can reasonably reproach the Americans, it is only for particular errors or for ancient abuses which circumstances have not permitted them to correct. They need only be consistent to remedy them all. They are the only people among whom one finds neither maxims of Machiavellism erected into political principles, nor leaders who declare their belief (sincere or feigned) in the impossibility of perfecting the social order and reconciling public prosperity with justice.

The spectacle of a great people among whom the rights of man are respected is useful to all other peoples, despite the differences of climate, customs, and constitutions. It teaches them that these rights are everywhere the same; that with the exception of a single right which the virtuous citizen must know how to renounce in certain constitutions, for the sake of public tranquillity,[3] there is no state in which man cannot enjoy all his other rights in their entirety.

This spectacle demonstrates the effect of the enjoyment of those rights on the common prosperity, in showing that the man who has never feared outrages against his person acquires a more elevated and compassionate soul; that the individual whose property is always assured finds probity easy; that the citizen who depends only on the laws has more patriotism and courage.

This example, so useful to all the nations who can contemplate it, was about to be lost to the human race. Great nations disdain the example of little peoples, and England, which had given an imposing example for a century, would only have lent credence by its fall to the opinion (so widespread, so dangerous, and so false) that laws can have only a passing empire over peoples, and that political bodies are condemned to dissolution after a few moments of a more or less brilliant life. If America had succumbed to English arms, despotism would soon have forged there the chains of the mother country, and the English would have experienced the fate of all republics who have ceased to be free in wishing to have subjects rather than only citizens.

Now England would have lost its laws in losing its liberty. It can doubtless happen that in a peaceful monarchy a wise legislator respects the rights of man enough to make the proud republican envious of the lot of his happy subjects. We know that this truth, important for the tranquillity of these constitutions, was proved by the French philosophes precisely at the same time as they were being accused in the journals, in episcopal letters to the faithful, and in prosecutors' briefs, of preaching sedition. But violence alone can subject the man who has once enjoyed liberty; and for the citizen to consent to subjection it is necessary to strip him of his very dignity as a man.

By a necessary consequence of the respect of the American laws for the natural rights of humanity, every man, whatever his religion, his opinions, his principles, is sure of finding asylum there. In vain did England offer the same advantages, at least to Protestants. The industriousness of its inhabitants leaves no resource to that of the foreigner; its wealth repulses the poor man; little place remains on a soil where commerce and industry have multiplied men. Even its climate is suited only to the peoples of a small part of Europe. America, on the contrary, offers industriousness seductive hopes. The poor man finds there an easy subsistence. An assured property, sufficient to his needs, can there become the prize of his labor. Its more varied climate suits men of all lands.

But, at the same time, America is separated from the peoples of Europe by a vast expanse of ocean. To bring oneself to cross it, other motives are necessary than a simple desire to enhance one's well-being. Only the oppressed could have the will to surmount this obstacle. Thus Europe, without having great emigrations to fear, will find in America a useful restraint upon ministers tempted to govern too badly. Oppression must become more timid here, when it knows that there remains an asylum for those marked out as its victims; and that they can both escape it and punish it by forcing it to appear with them before the tribunal of public opinion.

Liberty of the press is established in America. With just reason, the right to say and to hear the truths one believes useful has been regarded as one of the most sacred rights of humanity.

In a country where the willow was a sacred tree, and where it was forbidden, under penalty of death, to break a branch from it to save a drowning man, could it be said that the law admits no violation of the liberty or the security of citizens? If the absurdity of laws against the liberty of the press does not seem equally obvious to us, this is unfortunately because habit has the fatal power to familiarize feeble human reason with that which must revolt it.

The mere example of all the good that liberty of the press has done and will continue to do in America will be that much more the useful to Europe in that it is more fit than the example of England to reassure against the pretended disadvantages of that liberty. We have already witnessed more than once the sight of the American peacefully submitting to laws the principles or effects of which he has passionately attacked. We have seen him respectfully obeying those entrusted with the public power, without renouncing the right to seek to enlighten them and to denounce to the nation their faults or their errors. We have seen public discussions destroy prejudices and prepare the support of public opinion for the wise views of these newborn laws.

We have seen this liberty, far from favoring intrigue, dissipate self-interested associations and prevent those who had been led by personal views from forming parties. We have been able to conclude that declamations and libels are dangerous only insofar as the severity of the laws obliges them to circulate clandestinely.

We have seen, finally, that opinion, easily and promptly spread throughout an immense land by means of printing, offers the government, in difficult circumstances, an arm often more powerful than the laws. I shall cite only one example. Desertion had occurred in a part of the militia; it had not been possible to enact the most severe penalties because the hope of impunity would have robbed them of all their force. It was proposed to publish the names of the guilty in the newspaper of their region, and the fear of this punishment was more effective than fear of death. It is clear that this noble and generous manner of restoring citizens to the path of duty must owe all its success to the right that the accused would have to protest with equal publicity against an unjust charge.

In England, the practice of eluding by often ridiculous subtleties the laws still existing against the liberty of the press, the scandal of libels, the venality of political writers, the false passion of a patriotism not really felt, have prevented recognition of the fact that it is more to the liberty of the press than to its constitution that this country owes the maintenance of the laws and the preservation of respect for that portion of the rights of humanity which opinion has consecrated there.

Far from exciting troubles in America, the most extensive toleration yet enjoyed by any people is making peace and fraternity flourish. With such an example in sight, will the governments of the countries where intolerance still reigns continue to believe it necessary to the calm of states and not finally learn that they can without danger obey the voice of justice and humanity? Once upon a time, fanaticism dared to show itself openly, demanding the blood of men in the name of God. Reason has forced it to conceal itself; it has taken the mask of political expediency, and it is for the sake of peace that it demands still to be left with the means of troubling that peace. But America has proven that a land can be happy, although it has in its midst neither persecutors nor hypocrites. And the politicians who would have had difficulty in believing this on the authority of the wise would doubtless believe it on the authority of this example.

In observing how the Americans have based their peace and happiness on a small number of maxims which seem to be the simple expression of what good sense could have dictated to all men, one will cease to laud these overcomplicated machines in which the multitude of springs make the working violent, irregular, and troublesome; in which so many counterweights, supposed in theory to balance one another, combine in reality to weigh upon the people.[4] Perhaps one will recognize the unimportance, or rather the danger, of these political subtleties which have been too long admired, of these systems according to which the laws (and consequently truth, reason, and justice, their immutable bases) are supposed to change with the temperature and adapt to the forms of government, to the practices that superstition has consecrated, and even to the stupidities adopted by each people, as if it would not have been more human, more just, and more noble to seek in a reasonable legislation the means of disabusing peoples of them.[5]

It will be seen that it is possible to have brave warriors, obedient soldiers, disciplined troops, without recourse to the harshness of the military administrations of several European nations, where subordinates are judged on the basis of the secret reports of their superiors, condemned without having been heard, and punished without having been able to defend themselves; where it is a new crime to demand to prove one's innocence, and a greater crime still to declare in print that one is not guilty. It is necessary however, to acknowledge that it is not to corruption, to calculated injustice, to a tyrannical harshness, that we must attribute this system of secret oppression which violates at once the rights of citizens and those of nations. Still less is it attributable to necessity, for it is at once as useless and as dangerous to discipline and to the security of the state, as it can be unjust. What then is to be blamed? Alas! It is only that invincible ignorance of the natural right which excuses the offense; and the example of a free people submitting peacefully to military, as to civil, laws will doubtless have the power to cure us of it.

The spectacle of the equality that reigns in the United States, and which assures its peace and prosperity, can also be useful to Europe. We no longer believe here, in truth, that nature has divided the human race into three or four orders, like the class of Solipeds, and that one of these orders is also condemned to work much and eat little. We have been told so much of the advantages of commerce and of circulation, that the noble is beginning to regard a banker and a merchant almost as his equal, provided he is very rich. But our philosophy goes no further; and we still declared in print not long ago that the people is in certain countries subject to taxation (in money and labor) by its very nature.[6]

We said, not so very long ago, that the sentiment of honor can exist in all its force only in certain states and that it is necessary to degrade the greatest part of a nation in order to give the remainder a little more pride.[7]

But this is what one will be able to read in the history of America. A young French general,[8] charged to defend Virginia against a superior army, saw that the soldiers who had been taken from their regiments to form his body of troops were abandoning it. To stop this kind of desertion, he declared that, wishing to have with him only chosen men, he would return all those whose valor, fidelity, or intelligence he suspected. From that moment, no one thought of leaving. A soldier whom he wished to entrust with a particular mission demanded of him the promise that, if he perished in executing it, it would be printed in the newspaper of his region that he had left the detachment only on the general's orders. Another, unable to march because of his wounds, rented a wagon at his own expense to keep up with the army. Thus one will be forced to agree that the sentiment of honor is the same in all constitutions, that it acts with equal force upon men of all conditions, provided none of these conditions is degraded by an unjust opinion or oppressed by bad laws.

Such are the benefits that humanity as a whole must expect from the American example, and we should be surprised if these advantages are regarded as chimerical because they do not have an immediate physical influence upon the lot of individuals. This would be to ignore that the happiness of man in society depends almost uniquely upon good laws. It would be to ignore that if men owe their first homage to the legislator who unites the wisdom to conceive such laws with the will and the power to prescribe them, the first benefactors of peoples after him are those who by their example and their teaching indicate to each legislator the laws he must make.

NOTES TO ''ON THE INFLUENCE OF THE AMERICAN REVOLUTION''

1. Guillaume-Thomas-François de Raynal (1713–1796), was the principal author of perhaps the most influential French work of the two decades prior to the Revolution. His *Philosophical and Political History of the Establishments and Commerce of the Europeans in the Two Indies* (1770), a history of European colonization to which Diderot and others also contributed, went through many editions and became more pointed in its political and social criticism as it did so. In 1780, Raynal established a prize-essay competition at the Academy of Lyon, proposing the question "Has the discovery of America been harmful or useful to the human race?"

2. Charles-Irenée Castel de Saint-Pierre (1658–1743), was the author of a number of wide-ranging reform schemes. His most ambitious project, a scheme to secure perpetual peace at a time when war had been virtually endemic in Europe for a century, made his name practically synonymous with unrealistic utopianism.

3. Condorcet is here again referring to possible limitations upon the right to vote, the fourth of the rights of man enuniciated in the introduction to this essay. See above, pp. 73–74.

4. This criticism of the theory of the balance of powers was to become a common theme in Condorcet's thinking. See below, pp. 86–87, 155–56.

5. An attack upon the relativism of Montesquieu's *The Spirit of the Laws*, which Condorcet repudiated on the grounds that a good law must ultimately be the same for all men.

6. This is a reference to the remonstrance of the Parlement of Paris against Turgot's proposal to replace the forced labor of the *corvée* (used to build and maintain roads) with free labor to be paid for by the proceeds of a tax on all property owners. This proposal, the magistrates insisted, contravened the fundamental principle that the clergy and nobility were exempt from the *corvée* and the *taille*, the burden of which naturally fell upon the lower order of the people.

7. Another critical reference to *The Spirit of the Laws*, this time attacking Montesquieu's emphasis on honor as the moving principle of monarchical states.

8. This is, of course, a reference to Lafayette, to whom this essay was dedicated. The incident, reported in slightly different terms in Lafayette's memoirs and in his correspondence with Washington, occurred in April 1787. See Louis Gottschalk, *Lafayette and the Close of the American Revolution* (Chicago, 1942), pp. 216–217.

Essay on the Constitution and Functions of the Provincial Assemblies (Postscript) (1788)

While many liberals supported the demands of the parlements for the convocation of the Estates-General, Condorcet was convinced that this was a reactionary and anarchical campaign designed chiefly to sabotage the government policy of national regeneration through the institution of provincial assemblies. The *Essay on the Constitution and Functions of the Provincial Assemblies*, his most comprehensive treatise on politics, was an elaborate discussion of the constitutional forms that would render the provincial assemblies truly representative of the nation as a whole and truly expressive of the public reason. Ultimately, Condorcet insisted, these provincial assemblies could be linked to a national assembly composed of representatives elected from them without distinction of order and Estate: the result would be a more truly representative body than the antiquated Estates-General. Before the *Essay* had left the printer, however, Brienne was forced (8 August 1788) to announce the definite convocation of the Estates-General in 1789. Belatedly, Condorcet added a postscript, full of foreboding, to the proofs of a work already outstripped by events.

When this work was sent to the printer, there was reason to believe that the meeting of the Estates-General would not occur in the near future. The simplest means of re-establishing the nation in the exercise of its rights, and citizens in the enjoyment of those they received from nature, was to seek first to perfect the constitution of the different orders of assemblies in each province; and then to link them to the constitution of a national assembly in which representation would be equal and real. Such is the object of the first part of this work.

Events upon which it is not yet time to render judgment have accelerated the calling of the national assembly. It would doubtless have been desirable for the nation to have had the time to enlighten itself as to its rights and true interests; for the citizens destined to serve as its representatives to have been able, by following the work of the provincial assemblies, to acquire local information concerning the details of administration. Our instruction as to the constitution of states is limited, in general, to a few maxims taken from the *Spirit of the Laws* that are more ingenious than solid, more dangerous than useful, and an admiration for the English constitution that is more passionate than enlightened.[1] How could the nation be truly enlightened on matters which the absence of freedom of the press has prevented it from discussing, and on the details of an administration that hides the true reasons and results of its operations in the dust of its bureaux?

A national assembly prepared for its task by public instruction would have inspired only hope. Its calling would have been a time of sure restoration for the nation, rather than a crisis the outcome of which is uncertain.

Today, scarcely a few months remain to dissipate that immense cloud of errors that the ignorance, habits, and prejudices of several centuries have amassed, to destroy the sophistical arguments upon which passions and particular interests have based their errors. And after this short space of time . . . ?

What man accustomed to reflect upon these questions will not be frightened by the sight before us: on the one hand, a multitude of arrangements that would render the good impossible for a long series of generations, by setting up obstacles to progress greater than those we now bewail; on the other hand, such a small number of ways in which it would be possible, without sacrificing any of the benefits attainable today, to prepare greater ones for the future rather than thwarting them? How frightened would he be to see, at the same time, such dangerous opinions repeated in every mouth, fermenting in every head, while everything that would be truly useful is unknown or disregarded?

How easy it is to make men regard the mere distribution of authority as a barrier against it; to confuse liberty with prerogatives that only combine together and multiply the number of those to whom abuses are useful; to believe that one is defending the people when one is defending only prejudices, pretensions, and pride!

Let us dare to present here to our fellow citizens certain principles which we deem sufficient to preserve them from the errors of their own judgment, and from those into which another's cunning could lead them.

It is first necessary to acquire a thorough knowledge of the natural rights of man in all their extent: the rights of liberty, the rights of property, the rights of equality (still so misunderstood among all the nations who dare to boast of their freedom). Certainly, one should not abandon oneself to the hope of restoring these rights in their entirety all at once; but neither should one allow any re-establishment of an antiquated practice, or any novelty that can cause the slightest violation of these rights.

Nature has made only men and citizens. Every prerogative implies a duty; it must be only a means of better fulfilling that duty, for the greatest utility of those who are merely men and citizens. Whoever professes or practices other maxims, whatever mask he borrows, is an enemy of liberty.

In every law it is necessary to ask first what is just, and then what is the best means of ensuring that the just is observed. Reason alone can teach us what justice consists in, and how to make public order conform to it. But reason can only have a general influence if it is perfectly free. Only in this century has it begun to appear among men; and everything that bears the imprint of time must inspire distrust much more than respect.

Truth and justice are the same in all countries and for all men. What is good in one province could not be bad in another. Uniformity in all the objects of public order is an additional bond among men; every difference is a seed of discord.

Every power has been established for the good of him who obeys it. It is absurd to suppose that men must raise one excessive power over them in order to counterbalance another equally excessive. Each power must be given only the extent necessary for it to be useful. Man did not put himself into society to be jostled between opposing powers, becoming equally the victim of their unity or of their quarrels. He entered into society in order to enjoy all his rights in peace, under the direction of an authority solely instituted to maintain them, an authority which, never having the power to violate these rights, can have no need of being counterbalanced by another power.

In a country happy enough to have particular assemblies in each district (as in a great number of French provinces), a declaration of the rights of man and the citizen drawn up by enlightened men is the true barrier against every power, the only barrier that does not threaten the public tranquillity or individual security.

Any assembly that does not keep good faith in its engagements, regarding respect for the rights of individuals as a sacred duty; any assembly that believes itself free of the obligation to observe justice simply because it represents the general body of citizens, is more dangerous for liberty than if an equal power were united in the hands of a single man.

Happy the nation if its choice falls on men imbued with these maxims; if it prefers men who reason to those who merely declaim, those with knowledge to those with prestige or wealth, those (finally) who are patriotic to those who simply make a show of patriotism.

NOTE TO ''ESSAY ON THE CONSTITUTION AND FUNCTIONS OF THE PROVINCIAL ASSEMBLIES (POSTSCRIPT)''

1. Condorcet consistently opposed the theory of the balanced constitution his contemporaries found developed by Montesquieu in *The Spirit of the Laws* and exemplified in the English government of their day. See pp. 80, 86–87, 155–56.

II *The Philosophe during the French Revolution*

On the Society of 1789
(1790)

The Society of 1789 was founded early in 1790 by a group of moderates closely associated with Lafayette, in an attempt to counterbalance the more radical influences developing within the Jacobin Club. Its goal was the restoration of order and the achievement of peaceful constitutional change in accordance (as its name implied) with the principles of 1789. This was to be accomplished, as Condorcet explained in the prospectus of the *Journal of the Society of 1789* (of which he became the principal editor), by the development of the rational principles underlying the "social art," and their application to the debate over the constitution. In short, the Society of 1789 was to be part political club, part academy of political and social science.

As the year progressed, however, the Society of 1789 lost influence. The more liberal members drifted away and the remaining members became more conservative. In this pamphlet, Condorcet explained the goals of the society, as he understood them, and sought to answer its critics.

You wish, Sir, to know the origin and principles of this Society of 1789. Your esteem for some of its members has prompted your interest, by which the society is honored.

You wish to know by what fatality in its writings—the style and principles of which announce so clearly to what class of readers corruption or malignity destine them—a society is accused of being hostile to liberty, when it brings together men who were the most zealous, vigorous, and enlightened apostles of liberty in those times when it had so few devotees among us. You do not suspect them of having changed; you believe in reason and virtue. I shall satisfy your questions.

In October 1789, some citizens (the majority of whom had not waited for the calling of the Estates-General to reflect upon the principles of the moral and political sciences) formed a society devoted to considering the means of reestablishing order, preserving the peace, and giving the French laws all the perfection that the progress of the social art permitted them to attain.[1] For there is at each level of civilization a real perfection (as there is at each level of enlightenment an ideal perfection) which we are destined by nature to approach indefinitely without ever being able to attain.

It was soon realized that, at a time when the urgency of public affairs left no one the free disposition of his time, a small society could have no vigor. It was therefore resolved to form, according to an extensive plan, a large society whose object would be to investigate, develop, and spread the principles of a free constitution; and, more generally, to seek means of perfecting the social art in all its extent.

This new association took the name, *Society of 1789.*

You know that there exist two ways of considering political matters. The first consists in following the course of events, taking (as each question presents itself) the course of action that seems most expedient, and then looking for principles one can appear to invoke in defense of a policy one has decided upon in advance. An opinion is not adopted because it is true, but because it favors the success of projects already formed. One attempts not to prove truths (still less to discover new ones), but to impress other minds and rally opinion in one's favor. And far from wasting time in undeceiving men and enlightening them, one observes the way their opinions are tending and accelerates their movement in that direction. One assumes their prejudices in order to lead them more surely where one desires.

The other method is very different. Those who follow this method seek unalterable and universal principles in the eternal nature of man and things. If they stop to discuss questions raised by events, it is always to bring the discussion back to these general principles. They see the future in the present, and consider each particular law in the context of the entire system of the social order. They regard prejudices as enemies to be destroyed, and not as instruments the use of which it is good to reserve to oneself. They search for what is true and just, and are sure of having found what is useful.

This method is yours, Sir, and it is the one that the Society of 1789 has wished to adopt. We have regarded the social art as a true science founded, like all other sciences, on facts, experiment, reasoning, and calculation; susceptible, like all the others, of an indefinite progress and development, and becoming more useful the more widely its true principles are spread. And we have concluded that it would be good for a society of men free in their opinions and independent in their conduct to occupy themselves in accelerating the progress of this science, hastening its development, and disseminating its truths.

Thus there is an essential difference between the Society of 1789 and those associations that citizens might form with the purpose of uniting their forces to secure a reform in the constitution or legislation of their country. Such societies are doubtless useful; but they are not the only useful ones.

It is necessary for a society like ours to remain isolated in order to preserve a complete independence. This does not exclude a fraternal relationship or a regular exchange of correspondence, of the kind that exists among the learned societies of Europe. These learned societies send one another their works; academicians who travel are admitted to the sessions of foreign societies; they consult one another, and it sometimes even happens that they cooperate in important researches.

But a more intimate association among societies concerned with political matters in the same country could only be dangerous, especially if one of them affected a kind of superiority over the others. This would be to create a nation within a nation; to substitute the sectarian spirit for the spirit of analysis and research; to establish a real aristocracy. For is aristocracy (at least that not established by the laws) anything else than the existence of a particular body more united than the rest of the citizens because it is less numerous, which with this advantage opposes its force to their scattered forces and thereby disposes more or less exclusively of laws, positions, and reputations? They would become in the political body what the Jesuits were in the Roman church, and soon they would be accusing someone of being the enemy of liberty, just as the Jesuits accused Arnauld of being the enemy of the faith.[2]

A society that is more philosophical even than political must especially profess a tolerance offensive to restless and violent spirits. Consecrated to the defense of the principles of a free constitution, and to the perfection of the social art, it must doubtless proscribe opinions evidently inconsistent with its liberty as with the existence of a well-ordered society. But this inconsistency must be evident to the general body of enlightened men. That intolerance which regards those who do not share its opinion as criminals or corrupt men, factious spirits or slaves, has all the foolishness and danger of religious intolerance without the excuse of supernatural revelation, which at least gives a right to claim the indulgence of reason.

If tolerance is necessary within a society, ready admission would be fatal. It is necessary to have a form of admission corresponding to that compatibility in the manner of thinking without which all discussion degenerates into dispute. The incompatibility which prevents men from enlightening each other, because it prevents them from listening to each other, is not limited to an opposition of principles on the ordinary matters of discussion. When this division takes on a sectarian character, it extends to disagreements on other matters. Suppose that in Germany the Protestant theologians had wished to institute a series of conferences with the intention of enlightening themselves as to the means of refuting the Catholic controversialists; or that the French priests had decided to get together to discuss the means of resolving the difficulties posed for them by the Protestants. Can one believe that, if Lutherans and sacramentalists had been gathered together in the same room, or Jansenists and Molinists,[3] they would have sacrificed the hate that separated them to the interest of the common defense? Even at the time when public opinion was so excited by the quarrel over French and Italian music, can one believe that it would have been possible to institute a useful discussion of matters completely unrelated among men of the two parties?[4]

The exaggeration of opinions is another danger from which every society must take care to preserve itself. It is easier to exaggerate someone else's opinion than to form an opinion of one's own. And when one can acquire a reputation for patriotism and courage by this easy means, many men are tempted to employ it. A society in which a certain number of men resorted to this tactic by inclination or because they were powerless to find any better, would make no progress along the road to reason. On the contrary, it would finish by deviating from this road at every instant.

In a free and independent society, every member must be equal. It must never recognize a head. To wish to make personal opinions dominate is to affect tyranny in a republic. Knowledge and talent must certainly attain the power that nature has given them; but this power must only be exercised by the use of talents and knowledge. It is especially against intriguing mediocrity that one must have recourse to ostracism: against men who wish to be head of a party because they can never be a leader of opinion, men aiming to govern by cunning those whom they cannot command in the name of reason. The despotism of genius is always milder; and men of that quality, if they were conscious for a moment of the pleasure of dominating, would soon sacrifice it for the pleasure of producing.

Finally, such a society must reserve the right, even after the laws have received the approval of the public power, to discuss them, to point out their defects and demonstrate their disadvantages. For it is the principle of a free constitution that this society must develop or spread, and not the laws of a particular constitution. Authority in politics is the first step toward slavery. And men who would like to see liberty only in respect of the opinions adopted in the legislation they had established, would resemble those priests who pretend that one cannot be an honest man unless one offers sacrifice in their temple.

Such, Sir, are the principles that have directed the Society of 1789 in its establishment, regulations, and action. It has considered itself obliged to open its sessions to deputies of the National Assembly who cannot belong to the society as ordinary members because they are not permanently resident in Paris. It has made its first object of discussion, in its own assemblies, the questions that must be discussed in the legislature. This was a means of rendering its activities more immediately useful. But it has limited itself wisely to broad questions essentially related to general legislation. Particular protests have been studiously set aside.

NOTES TO "ON THE SOCIETY OF 1789"

1. This group was probably the "friends of peace," alarmed by the anarchy that threatened France in the last months of 1789, for whom Condorcet wrote his *Réflexions sur ce qui a été fait, et sur ce qui reste à faire, lues dans une société d'amis de la paix* (*Reflections on what has been done, and what remains to be done, read to a society of friends of peace*) (*Oeuvres*, 9:443–68). In addition to Condorcet himself, the group included Lafayette and his associates, the liberal nobles La Rochefoucauld and Liancourt, and the economic publicist and administrative adviser, Dupont de Nemours. On the Society of 1789, see K.M. Baker, "Politics and Social Science in Eighteenth-Century France," in J.F. Bosher, ed., *French Government and Society (1500–1850). Essays in Memory of Alfred Cobban* (London, 1973), pp. 108–30.

2. Antoine Arnauld (1612–1694) became the leading figure of French Jansenism in the mid-seventeenth century. Attacked by the Jesuits for his unorthodox views on grace and free will (to which attacks he replied in polemical kind) he was expelled from the Faculty of Theology of the Sorbonne and eventually driven into exile for the last years of his life. In addition to his theological writings, Arnauld was the author of a number of philosophical works, including the influential textbook on logic known as the *Port-Royal Logic*.

3. Jansenism, so called after the Dutch theologian, Cornelius Otto Jansen (1585–1638), was a movement within Catholicism which stressed the radical corruption of human nature and the weakness of the unredeemed will, together with the corresponding necessity for (and power of) grace as the arbitrary gift of God. Molinism, named after the Spanish theologian Luis de Molina (1535–1600), represented a tendency in the opposite direction. Both of these movements were opposed by the Jesuits as unorthodox and subversive of traditional doctrine. With attempts to suppress it in France, the issue of Jansenism took on political dimensions and remained a source of constitutional conflict until the mid-eighteenth century.

4. In the 1750's, the so-called *guerre des bouffons* divided Parisian society into two opposing camps, the partisans of French opera (particularly the music of Rameau) and those of Italian opera. Pamphlets issued on all sides; and the author of one of the more noisy pro-Italian tracts, Jean-Jacques Rousseau, was burned in effigy by the actors and musicians of the Paris Opera. A similar conflict, no less acrimonious, occurred in Paris twenty years later, between the supporters of the German composer, Gluck (who transformed the tradition of French opera) and those of the Italian composer, Piccini.

On the Admission of Women to the Rights of Citizenship (1790)

This article, an attempt to enlighten the representatives of the national assembly in accordance with the aims of the Society of 1789, appeared in the *Journal of the Society of 1789* on 3 July 1790. It provides Condorcet's clearest statement on the rights of women. A translation was first published in England in 1912 as part of the campaign for women's suffrage (*The First Essay on the Political Rights of Women*, translated by Dr. Alice Drysdale Vickery [Letchworth, 1912]). A revised version of that translation is reprinted here.

Custom can familiarize mankind with the violation of its natural rights to such an extent that, even among those who have lost these rights, no one thinks of reclaiming them or is even conscious of any injustice.

Certain of these violations have even escaped the notice of the philosophers and legislators most zealously concerning themselves to establish the common rights of individuals of the human race and to lay the foundation of political institutions on the basis of these principles.

For example, have they not all violated the principle of the equality of rights in calmly depriving half of the human race of the right of taking part in the formation of laws by the exclusion of women from the rights of citizenship? Is there a stronger proof of the power of habit, even among enlightened men, than to hear the principle of equality invoked in favor of 300 or 400 men deprived of their rights by an absurd prejudice and forgotten in the case of some 12 million women?

This exclusion must be an act of tyranny, unless it can be proved either that the natural rights of women are not absolutely the same as those of men, or that women are not capable of exercising these rights.

Now the rights of men result simply from the fact that they are sentient beings, capable of acquiring moral ideas and of reasoning concerning these ideas. Women, having these same qualities, must necessarily possess equal rights. Either no individual of the human species has any true rights, or all have the same. And he who votes against the rights of another, of whatever religion, color, or sex, has thereby abjured his own.

It would be difficult to prove that women are incapable of exercising the rights of citizenship. Why should individuals exposed to pregnancies and other passing indispositions be unable to exercise rights which no one has dreamed of withholding from persons who have the gout all winter or catch cold quickly? Admitting for the moment that men possess a superiority of mind which is not the necessary result of their different education (this is by no means proved, and it should be before women can be deprived of a natural right without injustice), this inferiority can consist only in two points. It is said that no woman has made any important discovery in the sciences, or has given any proof of the possession of genius in the arts, literature, etc.; but it is not pretended that the rights of citizenship should be accorded only to men of genius. It is added that no woman has the same extent of knowledge, the same power of reasoning as certain men. But that only proves that, with the exception of a limited number of exceptionally enlightened men, there is absolute equality between women and the remainder of the men; that this smaller class of men apart, inferiority and superiority are equally divided between the two sexes. Since it would be completely absurd to restrict to this superior class the rights of citizenship and the eligibility for public functions, why should women be excluded from them any more than those men who are inferior to a great number of women?

Will it be said, further, that there exists in the minds and hearts of women certain qualities which ought to exclude them from the enjoyment of their natural rights? Let us first interrogate the facts.

Elizabeth of England, Maria Theresa, the two Catherines of Russia, have shown that women lack neither force of character nor strength of mind.

Elizabeth possessed all the pettiness of women. Did these failings do more harm during her reign than resulted from the pettiness of men during the reign of her father, Henry VIII, or her successor, James I? Have the lovers of certain empresses exercised a more dangerous influence than the mistresses of Louis XIV, or even Henry IV?

Will it be maintained that Mistress Macaulay would not have expressed her opinions in the House of Commons better than many representatives of the British nation? [1] In dealing with the question of liberty of conscience, would she not have expressed more elevated principles than those of Pitt, as well as more powerful reasoning? Although as enthusiastic for liberty as Mr. Burke could be for tyranny, would she, in defending the French Constitution, have approached the absurd and offensive nonsense with which this celebrated rhetorician attacked it? Would not the rights of citizens in France have been better defended, in 1614, by the adoptive daughter of Montaigne than by the counsellor Courtin, who was a believer in magic and occult powers? [2] Was not the Princesse des Ursins superior to Chamillard? [3] Could not the Marquise du Châtelet have written a despatch as well as M. Rouillé? [4] Would Mme. de Lambert have made laws as absurd and as barbarous as those of the Keeper of the Seals, d'Armenonville, against Protestants, robbers, smugglers, and negroes? [5] In looking back over the list of those who have governed the world, men have no right to be so proud.

Women are superior to men in the gentle and domestic virtues. Like men, they know how to love liberty, although they do not share all its advantages; and in republics they have often been known to sacrifice themselves for it. They have demonstrated the virtues of citizens whenever chance or civil troubles have brought them upon a scene from which the pride and the tyranny of men have excluded them in all nations.

It has been said that women, in spite of much ability, much sagacity, and a power of reasoning carried to a degree equalling that of subtle dialecticians, are never governed by what is called reason.

This observation is not correct. Women are not governed, it is true, by the reason of men. But they are governed by their own reason. Their interests not being the same as those of men through the fault of the laws, the same things not having the same importance for them as for us, they can (without lacking reason) govern themselves by different principles and seek a different goal. It is as reasonable for a woman to concern herself with her personal attractions as it was for Demosthenes to cultivate his voice and his gestures.

It has been said that women, although superior in some respects to men—more gentle, more sensitive, less subject to those vices which proceed from egotism and hardness of heart—do not really possess the sentiment of justice; that they obey their feelings rather than their conscience. This observation is more correct, but it proves nothing. It is not nature, but education, and social existence, that causes this difference. Neither the one nor the other has accustomed women to the idea of what is just. Instead, they have taught women what is "proper." They are excluded from public affairs, from all that is decided according to rigorous ideas of justice or positive laws. The things with which they are occupied and upon which they act are precisely those which are regulated by natural propriety and sentiment. It is therefore unjust to allege, as an excuse for continuing to refuse women the enjoyment of their natural rights, grounds which only have a kind of reality because women do not exercise these rights.

If reasons such as these were admitted against women, it would also be necessary to deprive of the rights of citizenship that portion of the people who, because they are occupied in constant labor, can neither acquire knowledge nor exercise their reason. Soon, little by little, only persons who had taken a course in public law would be permitted to be citizens. If such principles are admitted, we must, as a natural consequence, renounce any idea of a free constitution. The various aristocracies have had nothing but similar pretexts as their foundation or excuse; the very etymology of the word is proof of this.

Neither can the dependence of wives upon their husbands be alleged against their claims, since it would be possible at the same time to destroy this tyranny imposed by civil law. The existence of one injustice can never be grounds for committing another.

There remain, then, only two objections to discuss. In truth, these only oppose the admission of women to civic rights on grounds of utility, which cannot outweigh a true right. The contrary maxim has only too often served as the pretext and excuse of tyrants. It is in the name of utility that commerce and industry groan in chains and that the African remains afflicted with slavery; it was in the name of public utility that the Bastille was filled to overflowing, that the censorship of the press was instituted, that accused persons were denied a public trial and subjected to torture. Nevertheless we will discuss these objections, in order to leave no argument unanswered.

There would be danger, we are told, of the influence exercised by women over men. We reply at once that this influence, like any other, is much more to be feared in secret than in a public discussion; that, whatever influence may be peculiar to women would be lessened, in that if it extends beyond a single individual it cannot last once it is made known. Moreover, since women have not up to this time been admitted in any country to absolute equality, since their empire has nonetheless existed everywhere (and the more women have been degraded by the laws, the more dangerous their influence has been), it does not appear that this remedy ought to inspire us with much confidence. Is it not probable, on the contrary, that this empire would diminish if women had less interest in preserving it; if it ceased to be their sole means of defense, and of escape from persecution?

If politeness does not permit the majority of men to maintain their opinions against women in society, this politeness stems largely from pride: we yield a victory of no importance; defeat does not humiliate because it is regarded as voluntary. Can one seriously believe that it would be the same in a public discussion of an important matter? Does politeness forbid the bringing of a case against a woman?

But, it would be said, this change would be contrary to the general utility, because it would take women away from those duties that nature seems to have reserved for them. This objection does not seem to me to be well founded. Whatever form of constitution may be established, it is certain that in the present state of civilization among European nations there will never be more than a very small number of citizens able to occupy themselves with public affairs. Women would be torn from their homes no longer than agricultural laborers from their plows, or artisans from their workshops. Among the richer classes, we nowhere see women giving themselves up so persistently to domestic affairs that we should fear to distract their attention: a really serious occupation would divert their interest much less than the frivolous pleasures to which idleness and a bad education condemn them.

The principal cause of this fear is the idea that every person admitted to the rights of citizenship immediately thinks of nothing but governing others. This may be true to a certain extent, at a time when a constitution is being established, but the feeling can scarcely prove durable. And so it is unnecessary to believe that because women could become members of national assemblies, they would immediately abandon their children, their homes, and their needles. They would be only the better fitted to educate their children and to rear men. It is natural for a woman to suckle her children and watch over their early years. Detained in the home by these cares, and less strong than the man, it is also natural that she should lead a more retiring, more domestic life. These women would be in the same position as men obliged by their position in life to engage in several hours work a day. This may be a reason for not giving them the preference in elections, but it cannot be the reason for excluding them by law. Gallantry would doubtless lose by the change, but domestic relations would be improved by equality in this as in other things.

Up to this time the manners of all known peoples have been brutal or corrupt. I only know of one exception, and that is in favor of the Americans of the United States, who are spread few in number over a wide territory. Up to this time, among all peoples, legal inequality has existed between men and women; and it would not be difficult to prove that, in these two equally general phenomena, the second is one of the principal causes of the first. For inequality necessarily introduces corruption, and is its most common (if not even its sole) cause.

I now demand that these arguments be refuted by other methods than derision and declamation; that, above all, someone show me a natural difference between men and women which may legitimately serve as foundation for the deprivation of a right.

The equality of rights established among men in our new constitution has brought down upon us eloquent declamations and never-ending derision. But up until now, no one has been able to counter it with a single reason, and this is certainly neither from lack of talent nor lack of zeal. I dare to believe that it will be the same with regard to equality of rights between the two sexes. It is odd that, in a great number of countries, women have been judged incapable of all public functions, yet worthy of royalty; that in France a woman has been able to be regent, and yet up to 1776 she could not be a milliner or dressmaker in Paris;[6] and that, lastly, in our elective assemblies we accorded to the right of feudal property what we refused to the right of nature.[7] Several of our noble deputies owe to ladies the honor of sitting among the representatives of the nation. Why, instead of denying this right to women who are owners of noble estates, did we not extend it to all those who possess properties or are heads of households? Why, if it be found absurd to exercise the right of citizenship by proxy, deprive women of this right rather than leave them the liberty of exercising it in person?

NOTES TO ''ON THE ADMISSION OF WOMEN''

1. Mrs. Catharine Macaulay (1731–1791), described by Mary Wollstonecraft as "the woman of the greatest abilities that this country [England] has ever produced," was the author of a multi-volume history of England that enjoyed considerable popularity. In the 1770's she visited Paris, where she was well received in philosophical circles; and in 1784 she set out for America, where she visited George Washington at Mount Vernon. Radical in her opinions, unorthodox in her private life, Mrs. Macaulay was the target of much satire in her native country.

2. Marie de Jars de Gournay (1566–1645), regarded by the philosopher Montaigne as his adoptive daughter, was a celebrated literary figure in her own right. Editor of Montaigne's *Essays*, she was the author of several works on the rights of women.

3. Marie-Anne de Trémouille, princesse des Ursins (1642–1722), was a powerful French noblewoman who, after a rather complicated early life, came to exercise great influence over the policy of the Spanish court in the period of the War of the Spanish Succession (1701–1714). During much of the same period, Louis XIV's principal minister in France was Michel de Chamillard (1651–1721), who was reputed to have won the king's favor by his skill at billiards. A weak minister, blamed for the social and economic hardships that afflicted the French in the early years of the eighteenth century, Chamillard was relieved of his offices in 1709.

4. Gabrielle-Emilie le Tonnelier de Breteuil, marquise du Châtelet (1706–1749), mathematician and natural philosopher, was a woman of powerful intellect and extensive scientific accomplishment. She translated Newton's *Principia* into French and exercised an important influence on Voltaire. Pierre Rouillé (1657–1712), an intelligent and respected French diplomat, was charged with several important missions by Louis XIV during the War of the Spanish Succession.

5. Anne-Thérèse de Marguenat de Courcelles, marquise de Lambert (1647–1733), was one of the most accomplished literary hostesses of Paris in the early decades of the eighteenth century. Her salon was a favorite meeting place of leading men of letters and the elite of Parisian society. She was the author of numerous works on moral subjects and the condition of women. Joseph-Jean-Baptiste Fleuriau d'Armenonville was Keeper of the Seals (*Garde des sceaux*) from 1722 to 1727.

6. "Before the suppression of the guilds [by Turgot] in 1776, a woman could not become a master milliner or dress maker, or acquire a mastership in one of the other occupations in which women were engaged, unless she was married or a man lent or sold her his name in order to acquire a *privilège*. See the preamble to the edict of 1776" [Condorcet's note].

7. In the elections to the Estates-General, the right to a vote in the electoral assemblies of the nobility was extended to women who held possession of noble properties (*fiefs*), but they were only allowed to exercise this right by proxy.

The Nature and Purpose of Public Instruction (1791)

In the course of 1791, Condorcet published a series of five articles on public instruction in the *Bibliothèque de l'homme public* (The Public Man's Library), a journal offering a compendium of writings on the science of politics. These articles presented a comprehensive statement of the educational views he was to bring before the Legislative Assembly in 1792, in an influential plan for public education. The first, printed below, reveals the importance of public instruction in Condorcet's liberal political theory.

I

A. SOCIETY HAS AN OBLIGATION TO PROVIDE THE PEOPLE WITH PUBLIC INSTRUCTION.

1. As a means of making equality of rights an actuality.

Public instruction is an obligation of society toward its citizens. It would be vain to declare that all men enjoy equal rights, vain for the laws to respect the first principle of eternal justice, if the inequality in men's mental faculties were to prevent the greatest number from enjoying these rights to their fullest extent.

Social existence necessarily diminishes natural inequality by bringing common resources to bear upon the well-being of individuals. But the individual becomes at the same time more dependent for his well-being on his relationship with his fellow men. It follows that the effects of inequality would increase in proportion to that dependence, if the inequality arising from mental differences were not mitigated and its consequences for the common happiness and the exercise of common rights not reduced to a minimum.

THIS OBLIGATION CONSISTS IN NOT PERMITTING ANY INEQUALITY TO SUBSIST WHICH ENTAILS DEPENDENCY.

It is impossible for instruction, even when equal, not to increase the superiority of those whom nature has endowed more favorably.

But to maintain equality of rights, it is enough that this superiority entail no real dependence: that each individual be sufficiently instructed to exercise for himself the rights guaranteed him under the law, without subjecting himself blindly to the reason of another. In such a situation, the superiority of a few—far from being an evil for those who have not received the same advantages—will contribute to the good of all. Their talents and enlightenment will become the common patrimony of society.

Thus, for example, the man who does not know how to read, write, and do arithmetic really depends upon the more literate man to whom he must constantly have recourse. He is not the equal of those to whom education has given this knowledge; he cannot exercise the same rights to the same extent and with the same independence. Similarly, the man who has not been instructed in the basic laws governing the rights of property does not enjoy these rights in the same way as the one who has: in discussions arising between them, they do not engage on equal terms. But the man who knows the rules of arithmetic necessary in everyday life is not in a state of dependence upon the scholar who possesses the highest degree of genius in mathematics; and the scholar's talent will have a real utility for such a man without ever hindering him in the exercise of his rights. Similarly, the man who has been instructed in the elements of civil law is not dependent upon the most enlightened jurist, whose knowledge can only help but not enslave him.

INEQUALITY OF INSTRUCTION IS ONE OF THE PRINCIPAL SOURCES OF
TYRANNY.

During the centuries of ignorance, the tyranny of force was joined by
that of feeble and uncertain knowledge concentrated exclusively in a
few small classes. Priests, jurists, men who possessed the secret of
commercial operations, even doctors trained in a few schools, were no
less masters of the world than fully armed warriors. Indeed, the
hereditary despotism of these warriors was itself based upon the
technical superiority conferred, before the invention of gunpowder, by
an exclusive apprenticeship in the art of bearing arms.

Thus, among the Egyptians and the Indians, certain castes who had
reserved to themselves the knowledge of the mysteries of religion, and
of the secrets of nature, succeeded in exercising over these unfortunate
peoples the most absolute despotism conceivable to human imagination.
Thus, at Constantinople, even the military despotism of the sultans was
forced to bow before the authority of the privileged interpreters of the
laws of the Koran. Certainly, today, we need not fear these same
dangers in the rest of Europe, where knowledge cannot be concentrated
in any hereditary caste, or exclusive corporation. Occult or sacred
doctrines which create an immense interval between two portions of the
same people can no longer exist. But the degree of ignorance which
makes man the plaything of the charlatan who seeks to seduce him, and
obliges him, since he cannot defend his own interests, to trust himself
blindly to guides whom he can neither judge nor choose: this, with the
state of servile dependence in which it results, still exists among almost
all peoples. For the majority among them "liberty" and "equality" can
only be words which they hear read in their codes and not rights which
they know how to enjoy.

*2. To diminish the inequality which arises from a difference in moral
sentiment.*

There is yet another inequality for which general instruction, equally
distributed, is the sole remedy. When the law has rendered all men
equal, the only distinction separating them into various classes is that
which derives from their education. This distinction is due not only to
disparity in knowledge, but to the differences in opinions, tastes and

sentiments which are its inevitable consequence. The son of a rich man will not belong to the same class as the son of a poor man unless there is a system of public instruction to close the gap between them. The class which receives better instruction will necessarily have gentler manners, a more refined sense of integrity, a more scrupulous honesty. Its virtues will be purer; its vices, on the other hand, less repulsive; its corruption less revolting, barbaric, and incurable. There will then exist a real distinction beyond the power of the laws to destroy. By establishing a veritable separation between those who have knowledge and those who are deprived of it, this distinction will necessarily make knowledge an instrument of power for some rather than a means of happiness for all.

The duty of society, relative to its obligation to extend the actual equality of rights as much as possible, therefore consists in providing each individual with the instruction necessary to exercise his common functions—and to recognize his responsibilities—as a man, as father of a family, and as a citizen.

3. To increase the amount of useful knowledge in society.

The more men are prepared by education to reason correctly, to understand the truths presented to them and to reject the errors intended to victimize them—the more a nation sees its enlightenment increasing and extending over a greater number of individuals—the greater hope must there be of obtaining and maintaining good laws, a wise administration, and a truly free constitution.

It is therefore incumbent upon society to offer each and every man the means of acquiring an education commensurate with his mental capacities and the time he can devote to his instruction. No doubt, a greater difference will result in favor of those endowed with greater talent and those to whom an independent fortune allows the liberty to devote a larger number of years to study. But if this inequality does not subject one man to another, if it strengthens the weakest citizen without giving him a master, it is neither wrong nor unjust. It would indeed be a fatal love of equality that feared to extend the class of enlightened men and to increase their enlightenment.

B. SOCIETY HAS AN OBLIGATION TO PROVIDE PUBLIC INSTRUCTION RELATIVE TO THE VARIOUS OCCUPATIONS.

1. To maintain a greater degree of equality among those practicing them.

In the current state of society, men are divided into various occupations, each of which requires specialized knowledge.

The progress of these occupations contributes to the common good. Real equality is also promoted by opening access to them to those individuals, so destined by their tastes and abilities, who for lack of public instruction might nevertheless be absolutely excluded from them by their poverty or, if admitted, condemned to mediocrity and hence to a condition of dependence. The public authority must therefore include among its obligations the duty of assuring, facilitating, and multiplying the means of acquiring this knowledge. This obligation is not limited to instruction relative to occupations that can be regarded as a kind of public service. It also applies to those that men practice for individual advantage, without thinking of their effects on the common prosperity.

2. To make these occupations more equally useful.

This equality of instruction would contribute to the perfection of the arts. Not only would it eliminate the inequality which differences in wealth produce among those who wish to practice them, but it would also establish another more general form of equality, namely equality of well-being. It is irrelevant to the general happiness that a few men enjoy more elaborate pleasures as a result of their wealth, provided that men can satisfy their needs with facility, attaining in their housing, their dress, their food, in all the habits of their daily life, a measure of health and cleanliness, and even of comfort and attractiveness. Now the only means of attaining this goal is to perfect the products of technology, even the most common ones. Thus a greater degree of beauty, elegance, or refinement in those destined only for the wealthy few, far from being an evil for those who do not enjoy them, even contributes to their advantage by favoring the progress of the industry animated by competition. This benefit would not exist, however, if leading places in the technical occupations were the unique prerogative of a few men who had been able to secure a more extensive education, rather than a superiority achieved by natural talent in a situation of educational equality. The workman who is ignorant simply produces defective products; but the one who is inferior because of his lesser talents can withstand competition in all matters which do not require the ultimate perfection of his trade. The first is bad; the second is merely less good.

3. To diminish the danger to which some occupations are exposed.

The advantage of rendering the various occupations less unhealthy can be regarded as yet another consequence of general instruction. The means of preventing the illnesses associated with a large number of them are more simple and better known than generally imagined. The greatest difficulty is to get these measures adopted by men familiar only with the routine of their occupation, who are disconcerted by the slightest change and lack the adaptability which only thoughtful practice can give. Compelled to choose between a loss of time decreasing their profit and a precaution that would safeguard their life, they prefer a remote and uncertain danger to a present hardship.

4. To accelerate their progress.

General instruction would also serve to liberate men who practice the various occupations, and those who employ them, from that multitude of petty secrets infecting the practice of almost all the technical trades, hindering their progress, and supplying endless opportunity for bad faith and quackery.

In fact, if the most important practical discoveries are generally the result of theoretical developments in the sciences governing these arts, there are many particular inventions which only the practitioners of particular arts can even think of seeking, because they alone realize the need for them and recognize their advantages. The instruction they will receive will facilitate this search for new inventions; and, above all, it will save many would-be inventors from fruitless projects. Lacking this instruction, those artisans endowed by nature with the talent for invention, far from being able to regard it as a blessing, will often find it to be only the cause of their ruin. Instead of seeing their fortune increase as a result of their discoveries, they waste it in futile researches. Taking wrong roads, the dangers of which they are prevented by ignorance from recognizing, they end by falling into madness and misery.

C. Society also has an obligation to provide public instruction
as a means of perfecting the human race.

1. By affording all men born with genius the opportunity to develop it.

By successive discoveries of truths of every kind, civilized nations
have escaped from barbarism and from all the evils stemming from
ignorance and prejudice. By the discovery of new truths, the human
race will continue its advance toward perfection. Since there is no
discovery which does not provide a means of proceeding to another;
since each step provides us with greater strength, even as it brings us to
obstacles yet more difficult to overcome, it is impossible to assign any
limit to this advance.

It is therefore a real duty of society to promote the discovery of
speculative truths as the sole means of advancing the human race to the
successive degrees of perfection, and consequently of happiness, to
which nature permits us to aspire. This duty is all the more important
because the good can endure only as long as progress is made toward the
better. We must either continue toward perfection or run the risk of
being dragged back by the constant and inevitable pressure of passions,
errors, and events.

So far, only a very small number of individuals receive a childhood
education permitting them to develop all their natural faculties. Scarcely
one child in a hundred can pride himself on possession of this advantage.
Moreover, among those to whom fortune denies it, experience has
shown that those individuals who through force of genius (aided by
some happy chance) come to attain an education nevertheless fall short
of the full measure of their potential. Nothing can compensate for the
lack of this elementary education. It alone can inculcate the habit of
method, and impart the variety of knowledge, so necessary to achieve in
any branch of knowledge the full stature to which one might naturally
aspire.

It is therefore important to establish a system of public instruction
that allows no talent to go unnoticed, offering it all the help heretofore
reserved for the children of the wealthy. This was realized even during
the centuries of ignorance. Hence those numerous foundations for the
education of the poor. But these institutions, tainted by the prejudices of

the times in which they were founded, were not restricted in any way to individuals whose education could benefit the public good. They became merely a kind of lottery offering a few privileged individuals the uncertain advantage of rising to a superior class. They did very little for the happiness of those they favored and nothing for the common good.

Considering what genius was able to accomplish in spite of all obstacles, we can judge what progress the human mind would have made, had a better organized system of instruction increased the number of inventors at least a hundredfold.

It is true that ten men, starting from the same point, will not make ten times as many discoveries in any given science; nor of course will they advance ten times further than one man alone. But real progress in the sciences is not limited to intensive steps forward. It also consists in extensive advance, in assembling a great number of truths discovered by the same methods and derived from the same principles. Often it is only after having exhausted these truths that it is possible to go beyond them. From this point of view, the number of these minor discoveries leads to real progress.

It must also be noted that increasing the number of men occupied in the same field of research strengthens the hope of discovering new truths. Since different minds respond more easily to different difficulties, chance—so often a factor in influencing the choice of subjects (and even of methods) for research—must then produce more favorable combinations. Moreover, the number of men of genius destined to create methods, to open up a new field, is much smaller than the number of talented men from whom discoveries in detail can be expected. The succession of geniuses, instead of being frequently interrupted, will become the more rapid, the greater the number of young minds given the means of fulfilling their destiny. Meanwhile, these discoveries in detail are useful especially in their applications. Between the genius who invents and the practical man who applies these discoveries to the common good, there always remains a gap; often it cannot be closed without discoveries of an inferior order.

Thus part of this instruction would place ordinary men in a position to profit from the works of genius and to utilize them for their needs or for their happiness. Another part would seek to stimulate the talents vouchsafed by nature, removing obstacles and fostering their development.

2. By preparing new generations through the culture of those preceding them.

The kind of perfection to be expected from more equally distributed instruction is perhaps not limited to fulfilling the full potential of individuals born with natural faculties that are always equal. It is also not as chimerical as it might seem at first glance to believe that culture can improve whole generations and that the improvement of individual faculties can be transmitted to their descendants. Indeed, experience seems to have proved this. Peoples whom civilization has passed by, even though surrounded by enlightened nations, do not seem to rise to their level at the very moment that equal means of instruction are available to them. Observation of domesticated animals seems to offer an analogy consonant with this opinion. The way these breeds have been raised not only changes their size, shape, and purely physical characteristics; it also seems to affect their natural traits and their character.

It is therefore simple enough to believe that if several generations of men receive an education directed toward a constant goal, if each of the individuals comprising them cultivates his mind by study, succeeding generations will be born with a greater propensity for acquiring knowledge and a greater aptitude to profit from it. Whatever opinion one may have concerning the nature of the soul, whatever skepticism one may have adopted, it would be difficult to deny the existence of intermediate intellectual organs, necessary even for the thoughts apparently most removed from things of the senses. Among those who have devoted themselves to profound speculations, there is none to whom the existence of these organs has not been manifested, often by the fatigue they feel. Their degree of strength or flexibility, albeit not independent of the physical constitution as a whole, is not in proportion to the health or vigor of the body or the senses. Thus, the intensity of our faculties is associated, at least in part, with the perfection of the intellectual organs; and it is natural to believe that this perfection is not independent of the state in which they are found in the persons from whom we inherit our existence.

The immense mass of truths accumulated by a long succession of centuries must not be regarded as an obstacle to this indefinite improvement. The methods of reducing them to general truths, of organizing them into a simple system, of expressing them in more precise formulae, are also susceptible of the same progress. The more truths the human spirit has discovered, the more capable will it be of retaining and organizing them in greater number.

If this indefinite improvement of our species is a general law of nature, as I believe, man must no longer consider himself as a being bound to a fleeting and isolated existence, destined to vanish after an alternation of happiness and sorrow for himself, of good and evil for those whom chance has made his neighbors. He becomes an active part of a great whole, a co-worker in an eternal creation. In a momentary existence on a speck in space, he can by his efforts encompass all places, bind himself to all centuries, and still act long after his memory has disappeared from the earth.

We pride ourselves on our enlightenment. But can we observe the present state of societies without discovering that our beliefs, our habits, bear the traces of the prejudices of twenty forgotten peoples whose errors alone have escaped the ravages of time and survived revolutions? I could cite the example of nations in which philosophers and clockmakers exist, where institutions introduced out of necessity, at a time when the art of writing was not yet born, are nevertheless revered as masterpieces of human wisdom; where the first means that presented themselves to savage peoples are still used to measure time in a public document. Is it possible not to feel the immense distance separating us from the goal of perfection which we already perceive in the distant future, a goal toward which genius has opened up and smoothed the way, constantly drawing us onward by its indefatigable activity, even while a space still more vast must reveal itself before the eyes of our descendants? Is it possible not to be equally amazed by all that remains to be destroyed and by all that the future—even the near future—offers to our hopes?

D. PUBLIC INSTRUCTION IS ALSO NECESSARY TO PREPARE NATIONS FOR THE CHANGES TIME MUST BRING.

Changes in the climate of a country or in the nature of its soil, caused either by the general laws of nature or the effects of continuous cultivation over a long period of time; new agricultural methods, or the discovery of new techniques in the arts and crafts; the introduction of machines which require less labor, compelling workers to change their occupations; the increase or decrease in population: all these factors necessarily produce greater or lesser revolutions in the relationship among citizens, or that between one nation and another. The result can be new benefits for which one must be prepared in order to profit, or misfortunes which one must know how to remedy, turn aside, or prevent. It is therefore necessary to be able to anticipate these changes and be ready in advance to make changes in habitual ways of doing things. A nation always governed by the same maxims, a nation not prepared by its institutions to adapt to the changes that are the inevitable result of the revolutions brought by time, would see its ruin springing from the same opinion and practices that had assured its prosperity in the past. Only an excess of wrongs can cure a nation given over to routine. On the other hand, a nation prepared by general instruction to obey the voice of reason, escaping the iron yoke which habit imposes upon stupidity, will profit by the first lessons of experience and at times even anticipate them. For just as the individual obliged to leave his place of birth must acquire more ideas than the one who stays behind, mastering further resources the further afield he goes, so nations advancing through the centuries require an education that is constantly being renewed and corrected—following the march of time, sometimes anticipating it, but never opposing it.

The revolutions brought about by the general advance of the human race toward perfection must certainly lead to reason and happiness. But how many passing misfortunes would be necessary to pay for it, if general instruction did not draw men closer together? How far would that epoch recede if the progress of an enlightenment that was never equally distributed fed an eternal war of greed and treachery among nations, as among the various classes within them, rather than uniting them in that fraternal exchange of needs and services that is the foundation of a common happiness?

II. DIVISION OF PUBLIC INSTRUCTION
INTO THREE PARTS

These reflections suggest the necessity for three very distinct kinds of instruction.

The first is a common instruction with the following purposes:

1. to teach each individual, according to his capabilities and the length of time at his disposal, the knowledge that is good for all to possess whatever their occupation and aptitudes;
2. to ensure means of knowing the particulars of each subject, in order to be able to profit from them for the common good;
3. to prepare pupils for the knowledge required in the occupations for which they are destined.

The second category of instruction must be concerned with the studies related to the various occupations that it is useful to perfect, either for the common good or for the particular benefit of those who pursue them.

The third category is purely scientific. It must train those individuals destined by nature to advance the human race through new discoveries, thereby facilitating, accelerating, and multiplying these discoveries.

A. THE NEED TO DISTINGUISH IN EACH OF THESE CATEGORIES BETWEEN THE INSTRUCTION OF THE CHILD AND OF THE ADULT.

These three categories of instruction are further divided into two parts. Of course, it is first necessary to teach children what it will be useful for them to know when they enter into the full possession of their rights and when they exercise in an independent manner the occupation for which they are destined. But there is also another kind of education that must continue over the entire span of life. Experience has shown that there is no middle ground between making progress and losing ground. The man who did not continue to improve his reason after his formal education is over, strengthening the knowledge he has acquired with new ideas, correcting the errors or rectifying the incomplete notions he may have received, would soon see all the fruit of his early years vanish. Time would erase the traces of those early impressions not renewed by further knowledge; losing the habit of application, his mind would also lose its flexibility and its force. Even in the case of those whom an occupation necessary for their livelihood leaves least liberty, the time of formal education is nowhere near all that they can permit themselves for self-instruction. The discovery of new truths, the development or application of truths already known, the passage of events, changes in the laws and institutions, must bring about circumstances in which it becomes useful and even imperative to add new knowledge to that learned at school. Thus it is not enough for education to form men. It is also necessary for education to maintain and perfect those it has formed, enlightening them, safeguarding them from error, preventing them from relapsing into ignorance. The gates of the temple of truth must be open to all ages. Once the wisdom of parents has prepared the mind of children to listen to its oracles, they must always be able to recognize its voice, never falling into the trap of confusing it with the sophisms of imposture. Society must therefore provide easy and simple means of instruction for all those otherwise deprived of it through inadequate financial resources, and whose elementary education has not prepared them to seek and distinguish for themselves the truths it would be useful for them to know.

B. THE NEED TO DIVIDE INSTRUCTION INTO SEVERAL LEVELS, ACCORDING TO THE NATURAL ABILITY OF THE CHILD AND THE TIME HE CAN DEVOTE TO HIS EDUCATION.

According to the means of their parents, the circumstances of their family, the profession for which they are destined, children can devote a greater or lesser amount of time to their education. All individuals are not born with equal capacities; nor, taught by the same methods for the same number of years, will they learn the same things. By attempting to make children with less ability and talent learn more, one would increase the effects of this inequality rather than decrease them. It is not what we have learned that is useful, but what we have retained and, above all, what we have made our own either by reflection or habit.

The sum of knowledge which it is fitting to give each individual must therefore be in proportion not only to the time he may devote to his studies, but to his power of attention, the extent and duration of his memory, the facility and precision of his intelligence. The same observations can be applied equally to instruction relative to certain professions, and even to truly scientific studies.

Now public instruction is necessarily the same for all individuals receiving it at the same time. These differences can therefore only be dealt with by establishing different courses of instruction graduated according to these views. In this manner, each student will complete a greater or lesser number of grades according to the amount of time at his disposal and the extent of his ability to learn. Three orders of establishment would seem to be adequate for general instruction; and two for instruction relating to the various occupations, or to the sciences.

Each of these orders of establishment can also lend themselves to different levels of instruction, given the possibility of restricting the number or scope of the subjects it offers. Thus a wise father (or whoever acts *in loco parentis*) could adapt this common instruction to the diverse talents of the child and to the goal of his education, according to his natural ability and his desire or interest in learning. In the educational institutions established for adults, each could similarly find instruction proportional to his needs. An education which equity must necessarily provide for all would then no longer be devised for the small number of men favored by nature or fortune.

C. Reasons for establishing several levels of elementary education.

1. To make citizens capable of fulfilling public functions, so that these do not become an exclusive occupation.

I find three main reasons for multiplying the number of levels of elementary education.

The common utility requires that private occupations, in which the practitioners have profit or fame as their goal, and occupations in which contact with others are always on an individual basis, become increasingly specialized since the more limited an occupation, the better it can be practiced with equal capacity and the same work. Such is not the case, however, with occupations directly related to society as a whole. These are real public functions.

When the making of laws, the tasks of administration, and judicial functions become private occupations reserved for those who have prepared for them through specialized study, it can no longer be said that real liberty exists. There necessarily forms in such a nation a kind of aristocracy, not of talent and knowledge, but of occupations. Thus it is that in England the profession of law has succeeded in concentrating almost all real power among its members. The freest country is that in which the greatest number of public functions can be exercised by individuals who have received only an elementary education. Thus it is essential that the laws seek to simplify the exercise of these functions. At the same time, a wisely organized system of education must extend this elementary instruction as far as necessary to render individuals who have been able to profit from it worthy of exercising their functions.

2. To prevent occupational specialization from reducing the people to stupidity.

[Adam] Smith has remarked that the more specialized the mechanical occupations become, the greater the danger that the people will contract that stupidity which is natural to men limited to a small number of ideas, all of the same kind. Instruction is the only remedy for this evil, which is all the more dangerous in a state to the extent that the laws have established greater equality. In fact, if this equality extends beyond purely personal rights, the fate of the nation then depends in part on men incapable of acting in accordance with their reason and of forming a will of their own. Laws decree equality of rights; but public instruction alone can make this equality real. Equality established by laws is ordained by justice; but education alone can guarantee that this principle of justice is not in contradiction with the principle prescribing that men be granted only those rights whose exercise in conformity with reason and the common interest does not infringe upon the rights of other members of the social order. It is therefore necessary that one of the levels of the common instruction enable men of merely average ability to fulfill all public functions well. Another must require as little time for study as can be spared by the individual destined for the most restricted branch of a mechanical occupation, in order to save him from stupidity—not by the extent, but by the discrimination and the soundness of the notions he will receive.

Without this, we would introduce a very real inequality by making power the exclusive patrimony of individuals who had purchased it by devoting themselves to particular occupations; or we would abandon men to the authority of ignorance, which is always unjust and cruel, always subject to the corrupt will of some hypocritical tyrant. This deceptive appearance of equality could only be maintained by sacrificing property, liberty, and security to the whims of ferocious agitators at the head of a misguided and stupid multitude.

3. To diminish vanity and ambition by means of general instruction.

One of the great evils of a populous society is the turbulent greed with which men who do not spend all their time providing for their subsistence, or enriching themselves, seek positions that give them power or flatter their vanity. Scarcely has a man been able to acquire a few half-truths than he already aspires to govern his town or enlighten it. A citizen is regarded as leading a useless and almost a shameful life if he busies himself with his own affairs, remains quietly in the bosom of his family to prepare his children's happiness, cultivate friendship, exercise charity, and fortify his mind with new knowledge and his soul with new virtues. However, it is difficult to hope that a nation can enjoy a peaceful liberty, and perfect its institutions and its laws, without the increase of that class of men, whose impartiality, disinterestedness, and enlightenment must ultimately direct public opinion. They alone can set up a barrier against charlatanism and hypocrisy, which would lay hold of all offices without their useful resistance. Men summoned by their talents or virtues to these positions could not, without their help, combat intrigue successfully. Indeed, a natural instinct will always inspire in men with little knowledge a sort of mistrust of those who seek to obtain their votes. Unable to judge on the basis of their own knowledge, will they accept the candidates' view of themselves or that of their rivals? Will they not mistrust the candidates' opinions, suspecting a hidden interest all the more readily in that, were this motive to exist, they would not be able to distinguish it? It is therefore essential that the confidence of the common run of citizens can rest upon men who aspire to nothing, and who are in a position to guide their choice.

This class of men, however, can exist only in a country in which public education offers a great number of individuals the possibility of acquiring that knowledge which consoles and embellishes life, relieving for us the weight of time and the fatigue of repose. In such a country, these noble friends of truth can multiply enough to become useful, finding in the society of their equals an encouragement of their modest and peaceable career. Only there, where ordinary knowledge offers ambition no seductive hopes, is common virtue alone necessary for individuals to accept the mere title of honest man and enlightened citizen.

What we have just said concerning the education of children applies also to that of adults. Their education must be proportional to their natural capacity, to the extent of their elementary instruction, and to the amount of time they are willing or able to devote to it. It must seek to establish all the equality that can exist between things necessarily unequal, thereby eliminating dependence without excluding superiority.

Under a constitution founded upon unjust principles—in which an adroit mixture of monarchy or aristocracy ensured the tranquillity and well-being of the people whose liberty it destroyed—general public instruction would doubtless be useful. However, such a state could maintain peace, and even a sort of prosperity, without it. But a truly free constitution, in which all classes of society enjoy the same rights, cannot subsist if the ignorance of some of its citizens prevents them from understanding the nature and limits of these rights, and obliges them to pronounce on what they do not know, choosing when they cannot judge. Such a constitution would destroy itself after a few convulsions, degenerating into one of those forms of government that can preserve peace in the midst of an ignorant and corrupt people.

D. The need to examine separately each division and each level of instruction.

For each of the numerous divisions just established, we must examine: (1) what the objects of instruction must be, and at what point it should stop; (2) what books should serve for each subject and what further means of instruction would be useful; (3) what the teaching methods should be; (4) what teachers should be chosen, by whom and by what means.

In fact, these various questions should not be resolved in the same manner for each of the divisions just established. The truly systematic spirit does not consist in extending the applications of the same rule haphazardly, but in deriving from the same principles the rules appropriate to each question. It is the ability to compare, under all their aspects, all the just and true ideas which offer themselves to meditation, eliciting the new or profound combinations hidden therein. It is not the art of generalizing the combinations formed by chance from the small number of ideas that present themselves first to the mind. Thus in the system of the world, the stars (subject by a common law to a reciprocal dependence) move each in a different orbit, follow diverse directions; carried along at speeds changing at every moment, they present an inexhaustible variety of appearances and movements as a result of one and the same principle.

III. PRELIMINARY QUESTIONS

But before entering into these details, several preliminary questions must be resolved. We must determine: (1) whether public education instituted by government should be limited to instruction; (2) to what point the rights of the public authority extend over this instruction; (3) should this instruction be the same for both sexes or should separate institutions be established for each.

A. PUBLIC EDUCATION MUST BE LIMITED TO INSTRUCTION.

1. Because the necessary differences in occupations and incomes preclude anything beyond this.

Must public education be limited to instruction? Among the ancients we find several examples of a common education in which all young citizens were considered children of the republic and raised for it, rather than for their families or themselves. Similar institutions have been sketched out by several philosophers, who believed that they had discovered therein a means of preserving the freedom and the republican virtues they saw constantly disappearing after a few generations from countries in which they had shone with the greatest splendor. But these principles cannot be applied to modern nations. That absolute equality in education can only exist among peoples for whom the work of society is performed by slaves. It was always by supposing one nation abased that the ancients sought means of elevating another nation to all the virtues of which human nature is capable. Since the equality they wished to establish among the citizens was constantly founded upon the monstrous inequality of slave and master, all their principles of liberty and justice were based upon inequality and servitude. Thus they were never able to escape the just vengeance of outraged nature. They ceased everywhere to be free, because they would not suffer others to be as free as they.

Their indomitable love of liberty was not a generous passion for independence and equality, but the fever of ambition and pride. A mixture of harshness and injustice corrupted their most noble virtues. How could a peaceful liberty—the only kind that can endure—have belonged to men who could be independent only by exercising domination, who could live as brothers with their fellow-citizens only by treating all other men as enemies? Yet let those today who boast of loving freedom, even while they condemn to slavery human beings whom nature has created their equals, not claim even these tarnished virtues of the nations of antiquity. They no longer have as excuse either the prejudice of necessity, or the invincible error of a universal custom. The vile man whose greed extracts a shameful profit from the blood and suffering of his fellows is in subjection, no less than the slave he sells, to the master who is his prospective customer.

Among us the burdensome tasks of society are allotted to free men obliged to work in order to satisfy their needs. These men are nevertheless the equals of those whom wealth has dispensed from such tasks, and they enjoy the same rights. A great proportion of the children of citizens are destined for arduous occupations to which they must be apprenticed and devote their full time at an early age. Their labor becomes part of the family resources even before they have completely left childhood behind them. At the same time, there are a great number of children from families comfortable enough to permit them more time (and even to pay the costs) for a more extensive education. Such children accordingly prepare themselves by their education for the more lucrative occupations. Finally there are children born independently wealthy, for whom the sole purpose of education is to assure them the means of living happily and acquiring the wealth or the consideration that position, service, or talents confer.

It is therefore impossible to subject to a rigorously identical education men whose destinies are so different. If such an education were established to cater to those who have less time to devote to their instruction, society would be forced to sacrifice all the advantages to be expected from the progress of knowledge. If, on the other hand, it were planned specifically for those able to devote their entire youth to their instruction, either it would be necessary to renounce the advantages of an educational system embracing the general mass of citizens, or there would be insurmountable obstacles to it. In neither case would children be educated for themselves, for their country, for the needs they would have to satisfy, or for the duties they would have to assume.

A common education cannot be differentiated in the same way as a system of instruction. It must be complete, or it is worthless and even harmful.

2. Because otherwise it would infringe upon the rights of parents.

Another motive compels us to limit public education to instruction alone, namely that it is impossible to go beyond instruction without violating rights that the state must respect.

Men have come together in society only to obtain the most complete, peaceful, and assured enjoyment of their natural rights. These certainly include the right to watch over the early years of one's children, making up for their lack of understanding, supporting their feeble efforts, guiding their budding reason, and preparing them for happiness. This is a duty imposed by nature; it entails a right that paternal tenderness cannot abandon. Thus it would be a fundamental act of injustice to give the real majority of heads of families—or, even worse, the majority among their representatives—the power to oblige fathers to renounce the right of raising their families themselves. Such an institution would break the bonds of nature, destroy domestic happiness, weaken or even annihilate those sentiments of filial gratitude that are the first germ of all the virtues. It would condemn the society that adopted it to a merely conventional happiness and factitious virtues, creating a nation of warriors or a society of tyrants; but it could never create a nation of men and a people of brothers.

3. Because a system of public education would be contrary to the freedom of opinion.

Education, furthermore, to take the term in its fullest sense, is not limited only to positive instruction, to the teaching of truths of fact and calculation. It embraces all political, moral, or religious opinions. Liberty of opinion in these matters would be merely an illusion if society laid hold of each generation of children to dictate what they must believe. The individual who enters society with opinions inculcated by his education is no longer a free man; he is the slave of his teachers. His chains are all the more difficult to break because he himself does not feel them; he thinks he is obeying his own reason when in fact he is only submitting to that of others. It might be objected that he will be no more free, in effect, if he accepts the opinions of his family. But then these opinions are not shared by all citizens. Each individual soon perceives that his belief is not universal; he becomes aware that he must mistrust it; it no longer has in his eyes the character of an accepted truth. His error, should he persist in it, is merely voluntary. Experience has demonstrated how the power of these early ideas weakens as soon as objections are raised against them; how the vanity of rejecting them often prevails over the vanity of refusing to change them. Even were these opinions originally more or less common among all families, they would soon diverge if an error of the public authority did not offer them a focus for uniformity. All the danger would disappear with their uniformity. Moreover, the prejudices acquired by family upbringing are the result of the natural order of societies: they are remedied by wise instruction, disseminating enlightenment. Prejudices instilled by public authority, on the other hand, constitute a veritable tyranny: an attack against one of the most precious aspects of natural liberty.

The ancients had no conception of this kind of liberty. Indeed, it seems as if the only goal of their institutions was to annihilate it. They would have permitted men only such ideas and sentiments as entered into the scheme of the legislator. Nature had created mere machines, to be regulated in their motives and directed in their action by the law alone. No doubt, this system was pardonable in developing societies, in which one was everywhere surrounded by prejudice and error; and during a period in which a small number of truths, suspected rather than known, divined rather than discovered, were the lot of a few privileged men, themselves even forced to conceal them. Then one could believe that it was necessary to base the happiness of society on errors; and consequently to preserve the opinions considered proper to insure it by safeguarding them from every dangerous examination.

But today it is recognized that truth alone can be the foundation of an enduring prosperity; that constantly increasing enlightenment no longer permits error to arrogate an eternal empire. It follows that the aim of education can no longer be to consecrate established opinions but, on the contrary, to subject them to free examination by succeeding generations that will be progressively more enlightened.

Finally, a complete education would apply to religious beliefs. Thus the public authority would be obliged to establish as many different kinds of education as there were old or new religions professed in its territory; or else it would force citizens of diverse creeds to adopt a common belief for their children, or to limit themselves to choosing from among the small number it would be agreed to encourage. It is well known that in these matters the majority of men adopt the beliefs they have accepted since their childhood and that it rarely occurs to them to examine them. Thus if these matters form part of public education, they cease to be the free choice of the citizens and become a yoke imposed upon them by an illegitimate power. In a word, it is equally impossible to admit religious instruction into a system of public education or to exclude it, without violating the conscience of parents who regard an exclusive religion as necessary, or even as useful to morality and to the happiness of an after-life. It is therefore essential that the public authority limit itself to organizing instruction, leaving the rest of a child's education to his family.

B. THE RIGHTS OF PUBLIC AUTHORITY OVER INSTRUCTION ARE LIMITED.

1. Public authority has no right to link the teaching of ethics to the teaching of religion.

In this respect, indeed, its action must be neither arbitrary nor universal. We have already seen that religious opinions cannot form part of the common instruction since they must be the choice of an independent conscience. No authority has the right to prefer one over another. It follows that it is necessary to make the teaching of ethics strictly independent of these opinions.

2. Public authority has no right to authorize the teaching of opinions as truths.

Regardless of the subject, the public authority can have no right to authorize the teaching of opinions as truths; it must impose no beliefs. If it regards some opinions as dangerous errors, it must not combat or prevent them by ordering that the contrary opinions be taught. Instead, this should be done by eliminating these opinions from public instruction, not by means of the law, but by a wise choice of teachers and teaching methods. Above all, it should be done by assuring good minds the means of avoiding these errors and recognizing all their dangers.

The duty of the public authority is to arm the full force of truth against error, which is always a public evil. But it does not have the right to decide where truth resides or where error is to be found. In the same way, the function of ministers of religion is to encourage men to fulfill their duties; but the claim to decide exclusively what these duties are, would be the most dangerous of clerical usurpations.

3. Consequently, the public authority must not entrust teaching to perpetual bodies.

It is therefore of the utmost importance that the public authority avoid entrusting the task of instruction to self-recruiting teaching bodies. Their history is the story of the efforts they have made to perpetuate vain opinions long since relegated by enlightened men to the category of errors; it is the story of their attempts to impose upon human minds a yoke by means of which they hoped to prolong their influence or extend their wealth. Whether these bodies are monastic orders, semi-monastic congregations, universities, or simple corporations, the danger remains the same. The instruction they give will always be intended not to advance the progress of knowledge but to increase their power; not to teach the truth, but to perpetuate prejudices useful to their ambition and beliefs which serve their vanity. Moreover, even if these corporations were not the covert apostles of opinion useful to them, hereditary ideas would establish themselves among them. All the passions of pride would combine to perpetuate the system of a head who had governed them, or of a famous brother whose glory they had been stupid enough to appropriate to themselves. Even in the very art of seeking the truth, one would see the introduction of consecrated habits, the most dangerous threat to its progress.

Certainly, we need no longer fear the return of those great errors which afflicted the human mind with a long sterility, which enslaved entire nations to the capricious fancies of a few learned doctors to whom they seemed to have delegated the right to think for them. But by how many petty prejudices could not these teaching bodies still obstruct or suspend the progress of the truth?

So skillful are they in following with an indefatigable dogmatism their system of domination, who knows whether they could not retard the progress of truth long enough to rivet upon us the new chains they have destined for us, and to do so before we were warned by their very weight to cast them off? Who knows whether the rest of the nation, betrayed at one and the same time by its teachers and by the public authority which should have protected it, would be able to discover their schemes soon enough to frustrate or prevent them? Create teaching bodies and you may be certain that you have created tyrants or the instruments of tyranny.

4. The public authority cannot establish a body of doctrine to be taught exclusively.

It is clear that opinions will be unavoidably intermixed with the truths that must be the object of instruction. If the truths of the mathematical sciences are never susceptible to confusion with error, the choice of demonstrations and methods must nevertheless vary according to their progress and according to the number and nature of their usual applications. Thus if in this branch—and in this branch alone—a dogmatism in teaching would not lead to error, it would still be antithetical to any kind of progress. In the natural sciences, the facts are constant. But some facts, after having presented a complete uniformity, soon display differences and modifications in the light of more sustained examination or more comprehensive observation. And others, at first regarded as general, cease to be so because time or more careful research reveals exceptions. In the moral and political sciences, the facts are not as constant as they are in the natural sciences, or at least they do not appear to be so to those who observe them. The more obstacles interest, prejudice, and passion place in the path of truth, the less can we flatter ourselves on having found it; and the more presumptuous it would be to wish to impose upon others the opinions we regard as true. It is especially in these sciences that there exists an immense gap between recognized truths and those which have escaped our researches, a gap which opinion alone can fill. Superior minds have bridged this gap with truths that enable them to advance with sure step and even to leap beyond its limits. But for the rest of mankind, these same truths are still confused with opinions, and no individual has the right to distinguish them for another and to say *This is what I order you to believe and what I cannot prove to you.*

Generally recognized truths based upon certain proof are the only ones that must be regarded as immutable, and one cannot but be alarmed at their limited number. Those believed to be the most universally accepted—those against which one would assume that there would never be objections—often owe this advantage to chance, which has left them free of the attention of the great number. But let these truths once become the subject of discussion, and we would soon see uncertainty spring up, and opinion long divided and uncertain.

However, since these sciences have more influence on the happiness of mankind, it is all the more important that the public authority not dictate the common doctrine of the moment as eternal truths, lest it turn public instruction into a means of consecrating prejudices useful to it, transforming into an instrument of power that which must be the surest barrier against its unjust abuse.

5. *It is all the more important that the public authority not impose its opinions as the basis of instruction, in that it cannot be regarded as having attained the level of enlightenment of the century in which it is exercised.*

Those entrusted with public power will always lag more or less far behind the point attained by the minds destined to increase the stock of knowledge and enlightenment. Even if a few men of genius were to be found among those who exercise power, they would never be able to attain a preponderance that would enable them to implement the results of their meditations in practice. Confidence in a profound reason whose steps one cannot follow, voluntary submission to talent, homage to renown—the characteristics that alone would make such a preponderance possible—these cost personal pride so dearly that it will be a long time before they become habitual sentiments, and not a kind of obedience forced by imperious circumstances and reserved for times of danger and trouble. Moreover, the real limits of knowledge at every epoch are marked not by the particular reason of some man of genius, who can also have his personal prejudices, but by the common reason of enlightened men. It is necessary for instruction to approach these limits more closely than the public power is able to do. For the object of instruction is not to perpetuate the knowledge that has become general in a nation, but to improve and extend it.

What if the public authority, rather than following the progress of enlightenment, even at a distance, were itself enslaved to prejudices? What if, for example, instead of recognizing the absolute separation between political power (which governs actions) and religious authority (which can only influence the conscience), it prostituted the majesty of the laws to the point of using them to establish the bigoted principles of an obscure sect, dangerous in its dark fanaticism and dedicated to ridicule by sixty years of convulsions. What if, under the influence of the mercantile spirit, it used the laws to establish a system of prohibitions favoring the projects spawned by greed and the routine fostered by ignorance; or if, submissive to the voice of some zealot purveyors of occult doctrines, it ordered that the illusions of interior illumination be preferred to the light of reason? What if, misled by avaricious profiteers who consider themselves at liberty to buy and sell men simply because this traffic yields one percent more than other commerce, deceived by barbaric planters who count as nothing the blood and tears of their brethren provided they can convert them into gold, and dominated by vile hypocrites, the public authority were to legitimize by an act of shameful contradiction the most flagrant violation of the rights it has itself established? To what extent could it order the teaching of these offensive maxims, or of principles directly contrary to its own laws? What would become of instruction in a nation in which public law and political economy changed with the opinions of the legislators; in which it was not permitted to establish truths condemning their conduct; in which, not content with deceiving or oppressing their contemporaries, the legislators extended their chains to succeeding generations, whom they condemned to the eternal shame of sharing their corruption or their prejudices?

6. *The duty and the right of the public authority is therefore limited to establishing the object of instruction and ensuring that it will be well carried out.*

After having determined the object and the extent of each subject of instruction, the public authority must make certain that the choice of teachers, books, or methods is in accord with the reason of enlightened men of the time, and leave all else to their influence.

7. *The constitution of each nation must only form part of instruction as a matter of fact.*

It has been said that the teaching of the constitution of each country must form part of national instruction. This statement is no doubt correct, provided the constitution is regarded simply as a matter of fact; provided one is content to explain it and develop it; and provided its teaching is limited to saying: *Such is the constitution established in the State, which all citizens must obey.* But if we are to understand by this statement that it is necessary to teach the constitution as a doctrine conforming to the principles of universal reason, or to excite in its favor a blind enthusiasm which renders the citizens incapable of judging it—if one is to say to them: *This is what you must adore and believe*—then it is essentially the creation of a kind of political religion that is being advocated. This amounts to preparing a chain for the human mind; to violating the most sacred rights of liberty under the pretext of learning to cherish them. The goal of instruction is not to make men admire legislation that is fully completed, but to render them capable of evaluating and correcting it. It is not concerned with subjecting each generation to the opinions and the will of that preceding it, but to enlighten successive generations more and more, so that each becomes more and more worthy to govern itself by its own reason.

It is possible for the constitution of a country to include laws that are absolutely contrary to good sense or justice. Such laws may have escaped the attention of legislators in times of trouble; they may have been wrested from them by the influence of an orator or a faction, or under the pressure of popular unrest. Some may have been inspired by corruption, others by erroneous views of local and ephemeral utility. It can happen, indeed it will often happen, that the men responsible for these laws did not realize in what way they were contrary to the principles of reason; that they intended not to violate these principles but merely to suspend their application for a limited time. It would therefore be absurd to teach the established laws in any other way than as the current will of the public authority, to which citizens are obliged to submit. Any other policy would be open to the ridicule of authorizing the teaching of contradictory principles under the guise of truth.

8. These reflections must also apply to the instruction of adults.

What has been said regarding instruction during childhood applies equally well to that which must embrace the rest of life. Its object must not be to propagate particular opinions, to inculcate principles useful to certain views, but to instruct men in the facts it is important for them to know, to acquaint them with the issues that affect their rights or their happiness, and to offer them the help that is necessary to enable them to decide for themselves.

Without a doubt, those who exercise public authority must enlighten the citizen concerning the reasons for the laws they require them to obey. It is therefore necessary to beware of proscribing these explanations of the laws, these expositions of their reasons and purposes, which are an homage to those in whom the actual power resides, those on whose behalf the legislators act merely as interpreters. But beyond the explanations necessary for the law to be understood and executed, these legislative preambles or commentaries must be regarded less as a kind of instruction than as an account rendered by the depositaries of power to the people from whom they have received it. Above all, we must beware of believing that such explanations are adequate to fulfill the duty of the legislators with regard to public instruction. It is not enough for them simply to refrain from placing obstacles in the way of the enlightenment that could lead the citizens to truths contrary to their own opinions. It is also necessary for them to have the generosity, or rather the fairness of mind, to foster this enlightenment themselves.

In arbitrary governments, great care is taken to organize education in such a way that it fosters a blind obedience to the established power, and then to censor speech and publications in such a way that the citizens never learn anything which is not appropriate to confirm them in the opinions their masters have wished to inspire in them. In a free constitution, power is in the hands of men chosen by the citizens, and frequently renewed. Yet although this power seems consequently to be identified with the general will or the common opinion, it is all the more necessary that it not seek to extend over minds the control that the laws must exercise only over actions. Otherwise it would enslave itself, obeying for centuries the errors it had once established. Let the example of England therefore serve as a lesson to other nations. In that country a superstitious respect for the constitution (or for certain laws to which it has become the custom to attribute national prosperity) and a servile cult of a few maxims consecrated by the interests of the rich and powerful classes are incorporated into the educational system. They are maintained in the interests of all those who aspire to wealth or power; and they have become a sort of political religion which renders almost impossible any progress toward the improvement of the constitution and the laws.

This opinion is completely contrary to that of those so-called philosophers who want even truths to be accepted by the people as prejudices; who propose to lay hold of the first moments of an individual's existence to indoctrinate him with ideas that time will be unable to destroy, to attach him to the laws and constitution of his country by a blind sentiment, and to lead him to reason only by playing on the marvels of the imagination and the turmoil of the passions. But I ask them how they can be so certain that what they believe is, or always will be, the truth? Who has given them the right to decide where the truth may be found? By what prerogative do they enjoy that infallibility which alone can authorize a man to impose his opinion as a rule for the mind of another? Are they more certain of their political truths than the fanatics of all sects believe themselves to be of their religious chimeras? Yet the right is the same; and the motive is similar. To permit men to be dazzled instead of enlightened, to seduce them into believing the truth by inculcating it as a prejudice, is to authorize and sanction all the follies of enthusiasm and all the tricks of proselytism.

C. INSTRUCTION MUST BE THE SAME FOR WOMEN AS IT IS FOR MEN.

We have proved that public education must be limited to instruction; we have also demonstrated that various levels of instruction must be established. There is therefore nothing that prevents it from being the same for women and men. Indeed, since all instruction should be limited to setting forth truths and developing their proofs, it is difficult to see why the difference between the sexes would require any difference in the choice of these truths or in the manner of proving them. The complete system of common instruction has as its function to teach individual members of the human race what they must know to be able to enjoy their rights and fulfill their duties. If this system seems too extensive in its entirety for women who are not called upon to exercise any public function, their instruction can be limited to the elementary levels. But this should be done without closing the higher levels to those women fortunate enough to be endowed with natural aptitudes which their families wish them to cultivate. In the case of a profession exclusively reserved for men, women would not be admitted to the specialized instruction it might require. But it would be absurd to exclude them from instruction relating to professions in which they must be competitive.

1. Women must not be excluded from instruction in the sciences, since they can make themselves useful to scientific progress either by carrying out observations or by writing elementary textbooks.

As for the sciences, why should their pursuit be forbidden to women? Even though they might not be able to contribute to scientific progress by their discoveries (and even this might only be true in terms of discoveries of the first order, which require prolonged study and extraordinary force of mind) why should not those women whose life must not be filled by the exercise of a gainful profession, and cannot be completely filled by domestic occupations, work usefully for the advancement of knowledge by occupying themselves with those observations that demand an almost minute accuracy, great patience, and a sedentary, well-regulated life? Perhaps women would even be more suitable than men to impart method and clarity to elementary books, more disposed by their amiable flexibility to adapt themselves to the minds of the children they have observed at a less advanced age, and whose development they have followed with a more tender interest? An elementary textbook can only be well written by those who have acquired far more knowledge than it contains: we explain badly what we know, when we are stopped at each step by the limits of our knowledge.

2. It is necessary that women share the instruction given to men:

SO THAT THEY CAN WATCH OVER THE INSTRUCTION OF THEIR CHILDREN.
To be worthy of the name, public instruction must extend to the general mass of citizens. It is impossible for children to profit from this instruction if, limited to the lessons they receive from a common schoolmaster, they have no teacher at home to supervise their studies in the interval between lessons, to prepare them to listen to these lessons and help them to understand them, and to make up what might have been lost in a moment of absence or distraction. From whom could children of poor citizens receive this help if not from their mothers? For mothers seem called upon to fulfill this duty by the fact that they devote themselves to the care of their family or engage in sedentary occupations, while men's work (which almost always takes them away from home) does not permit them to undertake it. Thus it would be impossible to establish the equality of instruction necessary to maintain the rights of man, unless women were put in a position to watch over the instruction of their children by attending at least the first levels of the common educational system. And without this equality of

instruction it would not even be legitimate to support public instruction through revenues from national properties, or with any part of the revenues derived from taxes.

BECAUSE LACK OF INSTRUCTION FOR WOMEN WOULD INTRODUCE INTO THE FAMILY AN INEQUALITY DETRIMENTAL TO ITS HAPPINESS.

Moreover, instruction could not be established for men alone without introducing a clear inequality, not only between husband and wife, but between brother and sister, and even between mother and son. Nothing would be more detrimental to the purity and happiness of domestic life. Equality is everywhere the primary element of happiness, peace, and virtue, but this is especially true in families. What authority could maternal tenderness possess if ignorance destined mothers to become the object of the ridicule or scorn of their children? It will perhaps be said that I am exaggerating this danger; that the young are now being taught things that not only their mothers but even their fathers do not know, without anyone being struck by the resulting disadvantages. But it must be observed, first of all, that since many of these things are regarded as useless by the parents and often by the children themselves, they do not give the latter any superiority in their own eyes. It is the teaching of really useful knowledge that is currently at issue. Moreover it is a matter of general education, and the disadvantages of such superiority would be far more striking in that context than in the case of an education reserved for the classes in which politeness of manners and the advantages that parents derive from their wealth prevent children from taking too much pride in their burgeoning knowledge. Those who have been able to observe youths from poor families who by some chance have enjoyed a cultivated education will easily recognize this fear as well founded.

BECAUSE IT IS A MEANS OF PRESERVING IN MEN THE KNOWLEDGE THEY HAVE ACQUIRED IN THEIR YOUTH.

I shall add further that men who have profited from public instruction will retain its advantages much more easily if they find that their wives have had a more or less equal instruction; if they can share with their wives in the reading necessary to keep up their knowledge; if the instruction prepared for them during the interval which separates their childhood from their establishment in their own homes is also offered to members of the other sex to whom they are naturally attracted.

BECAUSE WOMEN HAVE THE SAME RIGHT TO PUBLIC INSTRUCTION AS MEN.

Finally, women have the same rights as men. They therefore have a right to the same opportunities to acquire the knowledge that alone confers the effective means to exercise these rights with the same independence and to the same extent.

3. Instruction must be given in common and women must not be excluded from teaching.

Since instruction must be generally the same for men and for women, teaching must be in common. It must also be entrusted to a schoolteacher chosen from either sex.

WOMEN HAVE TAUGHT IN ITALY AT TIMES WITH SUCCESS.

Several women have occupied chairs in the most famous Italian universities. They have fulfilled with distinction the duties of professors in the most elevated sciences without causing the slightest inconvenience or encountering the slightest opposition—without even being the butt of humor—in a country which can scarcely be regarded as free from prejudices or characterized by a simplicity or purity of manners.[1]

IT IS NECESSARY FOR MEN AND WOMEN TO SHARE INSTRUCTION FOR THE SAKE OF ECONOMY AND CONVENIENCE.

Teaching children of both sexes in the same school is almost essential for primary education. It would be difficult to establish two schools in each village and to find enough teachers, especially in the beginning, if the choice were limited to only one sex.

THIS IS ALSO CONDUCIVE TO MORALITY, RATHER THAN DANGEROUS TO IT.

Moreover, bringing together members of the two sexes, in public and under the eyes of the teacher, is far from being dangerous to morality. On the contrary, it would serve to preserve it against the various kinds of corruption that are principally caused by the separation of the sexes in the years of late childhood and early adolescence. At that age the senses mislead the imagination—too often misleading it beyond return—if a sweet hope does not direct it toward more legitimate objects. These degrading and dangerous habits almost always have their origin in the errors of a youth deceived in its desires, condemned to corruption out of boredom, and extinguishing in false pleasure a sensibility that torments its sad and solitary servitude.

WE MUST NOT ESTABLISH A SEPARATION WHICH WOULD BE REAL ONLY FOR THE WEALTHY CLASSES.

It would not be legitimate, under a free and equal constitution, to establish a separation purely illusory for the great majority of families. This separation can never be real outside the schools, either for the inhabitants of the countryside or for those citizens of the towns who are less than wealthy. Thus, bringing together both sexes in the school would only diminish the inconveniences of an interaction that cannot be avoided by these classes in everyday life, where however it is neither open to the scrutiny of the peer group nor subject to the vigilance of a teacher. Rousseau, who attached a perhaps exaggerated importance to the purity of morals, thought this purity would be preserved if the sexes mingled during their games. Would there be a greater danger in bringing them together for more serious occupations?

THE PRINCIPAL CAUSE OF THE SEPARATION OF THE SEXES IS GREED AND PRIDE.

Let no one be deceived. These ideas of a strict separation should not be attributed solely to the severity of religious morality, to that ruse invented by sacerdotal politics in order to dominate the mind. Pride and greed are at least as important: it is to these vices that hypocritical moralists have wished to pay their self-seeking homage. We owe the generality of these austere opinions on the one hand to the fear of unequal alliances, and on the other to the fear of the consequences of refusing to sanction unions based on personal relationships. Far from upholding them, it is therefore necessary to combat them in countries which desire legislation enjoining the citizens merely to follow nature, obey reason, and uphold justice. In the institutions of a free nation everything must foster equality, not only because it is also a human right, but because the maintenance of order and peace makes it imperative. A constitution which establishes political equality will never be durable or peaceful if it is intermingled with institutions that maintain prejudices fostering inequality.

IT WOULD BE DANGEROUS TO PRESERVE THE SPIRIT OF INEQUALITY AMONG WOMEN. THIS WOULD PREVENT ITS DESTRUCTION AMONG MEN.

The danger would be much greater if, while a common education accustomed children of one sex to consider themselves as equals, the impossibility of establishing a similar one for those of the other sex relegated them to a solitary education in the home. The spirit of inequality thereby maintained among one sex would soon extend to both. The result would resemble what has happened up to now to the equality found in our *collèges*,[2] which disappears forever as soon as the schoolboy believes himself a man.

CO-EDUCATION IS FAVORABLE TO EMULATION. IT FOSTERS A SENSE OF COMPETITION BASED ON FEELINGS OF BENEVOLENCE AND NOT ON THE PERSONAL RIVALRIES FOSTERED IN THE *COLLÈGES*.

Some might fear that instruction necessarily continued beyond childhood will suffer from too many distractions afflicting individuals occupied with more pressing and touching interests. But this fear has little foundation. If these distractions are an evil, there will be ample compensation in the competition that will be inspired by the desire to merit the esteem of the loved one, or to earn that of her family. Such a spirit of competition would be more generally useful than that inspired by love of glory, or rather by pride. For the true love of glory is neither a childhood emotion nor a sentiment destined to become general among the human race. To wish to inspire it in mediocre men (for mediocre men can, indeed, obtain first prizes in their class) is to condemn them to envy. This last kind of emulation arouses passions of hatred and inspires in children the ridiculous sentiment of self-importance, thereby causing more harm than the benefit it can produce by stimulating intellectual activities.

Human life is not a struggle in which rivals contend for prizes. It is a voyage that brothers make together: where each employs his forces for the good of all and is rewarded by the sweetness of mutual benevolence, by the pleasure that comes with the sentiment of having earned the gratitude or the esteem of others. A spirit of emulation motivated by the desire to be loved, or to be valued for essential qualities and not for one's superiority over others, could also become very powerful. It would have the advantage of developing and strengthening those sentiments the habit of which is useful to acquire. By contrast, the crowns bestowed in our *collèges*—which induce the schoolboy to believe himself already a great man—only arouse a childish vanity from which a wise system of instruction would seek to preserve us if, by misfortune, its origin lay in our nature and not in our blundering institutions. The habit of striving for first place is either ridiculous or unfortunate for the individual in whom it has been inculcated. It is a real calamity for those whom fate condemns to live with him. The need to deserve esteem, on the other hand, leads to that inner peace which alone makes happiness possible and virtue easy.

CONCLUSION

Generous friends of equality and liberty, unite to obtain from the public authority a system of instruction that will make reason popular— or fear for the early loss of all the fruits of your noble efforts. Do not imagine that the best devised laws can make an ignorant man the equal of a clever one, or form a free man from the slave of prejudice. The more the laws respect the rights of personal independence and natural equality, the easier and more terrible will they make the tyranny that ruse exercises over ignorance, turning it at one and the same time into its instrument and its victim. If the laws have destroyed all unjust power, guile will soon find a way to create even more dangerous ones. Suppose, for example, that in the capital of a country subject to a free constitution a troop of audacious hypocrites succeeds in forming an association of accomplices and dupes. Suppose that in five hundred other towns little societies receive from the first their opinions, their will, and their movement; that they exercise the actions they are directed to carry out over a people whose ignorance makes them prey to the phantoms of fear and defenseless before the snares of calumny. Is it not evident that such an association will rapidly draw ambitious mediocrity and dishonored talents under its flag; that it will find docile satellites among that multitude of men with no other occupation but their vices, condemned by public scorn to infamy and want? Soon, laying hold of all powers, governing the people by seduction and public men by terror, it will exercise under the mask of liberty the most shameful and ferocious of all tyrannies. Yet how would your laws respecting the rights of man prevent the progress of such a conspiracy? Do you recognize how feeble and limited are the means of honest men when it comes to leading an ignorant populace, as compared with the shameful wiles of audacity and imposture? Doubtless, it would be sufficient to tear the perfidious mask from the face of these leaders; but could you do it? You count on the force of truth; but truth is all-powerful only over minds accustomed to recognize it and cherish its noble accents.

Moreover, do you not see corruption stealing into the midst of the wisest laws and poisoning its very springs? You have granted the people the right to elect; but corruption, preceded by calumny, will present its list to the people and dictate its choices. You have safeguarded judgments from partiality and interest; but corruption will be able to give them over to credulity, which it is already sure of its power to seduce. For corruption, the most just institutions and the purest virtues are merely instruments that are more difficult to handle, but more certain and powerful. But is not all its power based on ignorance? What then would it do if the reason of the people, once developed, could defend it against the charlatans paid to deceive it; if error no longer bound a docile herd of stupid proselytes to the voice of the skillful cheat; if the prejudices which spread a treacherous veil over all truth did not surrender control of public opinion to sophistical cunning? Would cheats be hired, if dupes were no longer to be found? Let the people know how to distinguish the voice of reason from that of corruption, and it will soon see the golden chains that corruption has prepared for it fall at its feet. Otherwise, the people itself will hold out to corruption its troubled hands, submissively offering to pay the very seducers delivering it over to its tyrants. It is by spreading enlightenment and reducing corruption to shameful impotence that you will give birth to those public virtues that alone can bring strength and honor to the eternal reign of a peaceful liberty.

NOTES TO "THE NATURE AND PURPOSE
OF PUBLIC INSTRUCTION"

1. Laura Bassi (1711–1778) was professor of anatomy and Françoise Agnesi (1618–1699) professor of mathematics at the University of Bologna [Condorcet's note].
2. The *collèges* to which Condorcet is here referring were the secondary schools of the old regime, frequently run by clerical teaching orders, especially the Jesuits. The predominantly classical and religious education offered in these schools had been under increasingly vigorous attack since the middle years of the eighteenth century. The expulsion of the Jesuits from France in 1762, intimately related to dissatisfaction with the teaching in their schools, also prompted considerable interest in educational reform along secular lines. For an informative glimpse into the world of the *collèges* during this period, see R. R. Palmer, ed., *The School of the French Revolution. A Documentary History of the College of Louis-le-Grand . . . (1762–1814)* (Princeton, 1975).

On the Principles of the Constitutional Plan Presented to the National Convention (1793)

Condorcet presented his constitutional plan to the Convention, on behalf of its Committee on the Constitution, on 15–16 February 1793. Although his political views were here doubtless limited by current political exigencies and modified by committee debate, there is little doubt that the plan remained largely his own work. The speech he gave presenting the plan to the assembly (published here in part) is the authentic expression of his life-long concern to establish a rational system of political decision-making.

Quickly enmeshed in the struggle between the Girondins and the Jacobins for control of the Convention, Condorcet's constitutional plan was never adopted.

To form, for a territory of 27,000 square leagues inhabited by 25 million persons, a constitution founded wholly on the principles of reason and justice and securing each citizen in the enjoyment of his rights; to integrate the various parts of this constitution in such a way that the necessity for obedience to the law, and for the submission of individual wills to the general will, shall leave popular sovereignty, civic equality, and the exercise of natural freedom unimpaired: this is the problem we were given to solve.

Never before has a people freer from prejudices and more liberated from the yoke of ancient institutions presented a greater opportunity for the creation of its laws in firm accordance with general principles consecrated by reason. Never before, however, have the upheavals caused by a more complete revolution, the passions aroused by a more rapid movement of ideas, the burden of a more dangerous war, and greater difficulties in the state of public affairs seemed to present greater obstacles to the establishment of a constitution.

It is necessary that the new constitution be appropriate for a people in the midst of a revolution; and that it be equally good for a people entirely at peace. Calming agitation without enfeebling the public spirit, it must permit this agitation to subside without rendering it more dangerous through repression, and without perpetuating it by ill-conceived and uncertain measures that would change this temporarily useful passion into a spirit of disorganization and anarchy.

All hereditary prerogative is at once an evident violation of natural equality and an institution absurd in itself, since it supposes the inheritance of qualities appropriate for the fulfillment of public office. Every exception to the general law in favor of an individual is a violation of the rights of all. No ultimate power can be entrusted to an individual, either for his lifetime or for a long period, without conferring upon him an influence attached to his person and not to his office, without presenting his ambition with the means of subverting public liberty, or at least of attempting to do so.

Respect for an individual, the intoxication with which the pomp surrounding him afflicts feeble imaginations, and the sentiment of blind devotion that results; a man put in the place of the law and regarded as its living image; words devoid of sense, by which one seeks to lead men as if they were unworthy to follow reason alone: all these means of governing by error and corruption no longer suit an enlightened age, or a people whom enlightenment has led to liberty.

Unity, vigor, the strength to govern, are not attributes exclusively attached to such dangerous institutions. It is in the firm resolution of the people to obey the law that the strength of legitimate authority must reside. Unity and vigor can be the result of an organization of powers simply and wisely contrived. It would be vain to hope to secure this advantage by uniting them in a single individual, whom the pride of power would almost necessarily corrupt, and who would be more concerned with extending his prerogative than fulfilling his duties.

Without the kind of miracle upon which one must not count, any man endowed with hereditary or enduring authority is condemned to oscillate between weakness and ambition, apathy and perfidy. When the experience of monarchies has proved that they have been constantly governed by a council, it is difficult to find any utility in the existence of a monarch.

Monarchy, for these reasons, had to be abolished.

There is a great distance between the complete unity of the English constitution, which is broken only by territorial divisions necessary for the regular exercise of power, and the Swiss confederation, in which independent republics are united only by treaties formed for their mutual defense. Between these extremes, a multitude of different constitutions, approaching more closely to absolute unity on the one hand, or a simple confederation on the other, can be imagined.

The disposition of the French territory, the parts of which are not separated by any natural obstacle;[1] the complex relations and mutual obligations which have long been established between the inhabitants of its various regions; the long habit of being governed by a single power; the distribution of property in each province among men who inhabit them all; the association in each between individuals originating from all the others: all these factors seem to destine France for the most complete unity.

The necessity of being able actively to employ the force of the whole territory for the defense of each frontier; the difficulty of inducing federated regions, when they are situated in the interior with no enemies to fear or have nothing but the coast to defend, to contribute with equal zeal to such defense; the danger of destroying existing ties (at a time when all Europe is exerting its whole force and its whole cunning to break them) to create others more feeble; the necessity for the most intimate union among a people that alone professes the purest principles of reason and justice: these are new reasons for repudiating whatever might in the least injure political unity.

But it is useless here even to discuss all the importance of these reasons. To divide a single state into a republic of confederated states, or to unite confederated states into a single republic, there ought to be powerful motives of public interest—as, indeed, there ought to be for introducing any change not strictly required for the preservation of freedom and equality. But none of these motives exists among us. We could only want such a change in obedience to systematic views of perfection, to sacrifice the whole in favor of some parts, or to sacrifice the present generation to the uncertain good of generations to come. To effect a new revolution within, to establish a system which would necessarily weaken the means of defense of the nation adopting it, would be to expose the safety of the state to the threats of a league of powerful enemies.

Let us rather follow the example of a people worthy of imitation. Were the United States of America ignorant of the extent to which the weakness of their federal bond threatened the success of their war against the enemy of their independence? Every enlightened man, every patriot bewailed the lack of force in the general congress and the lack of unified action among the various republics. Yet during the war no one endeavored to correct this evil, even though it threatened its successful conduct. So thoroughly did they fear the effects of a great change executed under such dangerous circumstances. When our own circumstances oppose such a change most forcibly, should we attempt what the prudence of the Americans dared not undertake in circumstances which seemed to require it?

For these reasons, it has of necessity been declared that France should form a republic, one and indivisible.

The extent of the republic permits only a representative constitution. A constitution according to which the delegates formed a general will in conformity with the particular wills expressed in their mandates would be still more impracticable than one in which deputies, reduced to the simple function of drawing up the laws without even being accorded a provisional obedience, were obliged to present every law to the direct approval of the citizens.

But ought not the provisional obedience required for the laws passed by the representatives to have some other remedy against their errors or enthusiasms than the limits imposed on their power by constitutional laws which they cannot change, or their prompt replacement at regular intervals? Will the rights of citizens have been sufficiently respected if these constitutional laws, made by the representatives of the people, require a provisional obedience for a certain period irrespective of any national sanction? Will it be enough for them to be submitted as a whole to the approval of another assembly of popular representatives selected for that sole purpose?

Or should the people not rather have some legal means of protesting against all laws in a procedure that would necessarily subject any law to reexamination? Should it possess some legal means, continually open, of obtaining the reform of a constitution which appears to have violated its rights? Should a constitution be presented for its direct approval?

We live in a time when no law has the sanction of experience and the authority of custom, when the legislative body cannot confine itself to a few reforms, or to petty improvement in a code of laws already respected by the people. We live in a time when that vague suspicion, that active restlessness, which is the necessary consequence of a revolution, has not yet been able to calm itself. We have concluded that an affirmative answer to these last questions is the only one proper for the French nation at such a time, and the only one it could wish to hear. It is also the means of preserving and extending the enjoyment of the right of sovereignty, the direct exercise of which is useful (even under a representative constitution) to remind citizens of its reality and existence.

Two objections arise. It has been said that a common will formed by combining the wills of scattered assemblies does not really express the general will of the mass of citizens divided among them. It has been said that the citizens meeting in primary assemblies might occasion disturbances.

In examining the proceedings of a deliberative assembly, it is easily seen that its discussions have two quite distinct phases. First, principles are discussed which are to serve as a basis for decision on some general question: that question is examined under its various aspects and in terms of the consequences that would result from various ways of deciding it. So far, opinions are personal. Each is different from the rest, and none entirely commands the majority of votes. But this stage is succeeded by a new discussion. As the issues become clear, opinions approach and combine one with another. A small number of more general opinions is formed, and the question under discussion is soon reduced to a greater or lesser number of simpler questions, clearly posed, for a decision upon which it is possible to consult the will of the assembly. The point of perfection in such matters is obtained if these questions are such that each individual, answering yes or no to each of them, has truly expressed his opinion.

The first kind of discussion does not necessarily suppose men gathered together in an assembly; it can be achieved as well, and perhaps better, by the printed as by the spoken word. The second kind of discussion, on the contrary, could not be carried on by men isolated one from another without endless delays. The one suffices for men who seek only to enlighten themselves and form an opinion; the other can only be useful to those who are obliged to pronounce, or prepare for, a common decision.

Finally, when these two kinds of discussion have been concluded, there comes the moment of reaching a decision. If the object of the questions to be decided (by standing or sitting, by marking ballots "adopted" or "rejected," or by affirmative or negative voice vote) is fixed, it is evident that the decision is equally the expression of the opinion of all, whether the people vote together or separately, by voice vote or private ballot.

Thus the first kind of discussion does not more properly belong to a deliberative assembly than to men isolated one from another, nor to an assembly of public officials rather than to a private assembly. The second can only apply to a deliberative assembly, and is suitable only to a single body. It would be almost impossible, without a prior discussion held in an assembly instituted for that purpose, to prepare questions and to present them under a form admitting of immediate decision, whether by that assembly or by any other.

In short, the decision can be entrusted to separate assemblies, provided that the questions are definitively and unalterably posed in such a way that they can be decided by a simple vote of affirmation or negation. In that case, any discussion in these assemblies becomes superfluous. It is enough that those deciding have had time to examine the questions in silence or to discuss them freely in private meetings. The objection that citizens have not then been able to take part in the whole of the discussion, that all have not been able to be heard by all, can have no force.

It is not necessary, in order to decide any question responsibly, to have read or heard all that the men charged with formulating this decision have been able to think. It is not necessary to have heard them in preference to others who may have treated the subject better. It is enough not to have been deprived of any means of instruction, and to have been able to use them freely. Each individual must choose the method of enlightening himself that suits him best, matching to his enlightenment and powers of intelligence the study he is obliged to make of a question. Experience has proved, beyond a doubt, that men who wish to read all that has been written on any subject, and hear all that has been said, finish by rendering themselves incapable of deciding.

But to form a general will from the particular wills of a number of separate assemblies, it is necessary that the question to be decided be definitively posed. No one is ignorant of the extent to which the manner of posing a question can influence the resulting decision.

The right of separate assemblies to decide must therefore be regarded as illusory whenever the form under which that decision is demanded can influence their opinions, or even in some way determine it. Thus this method of deciding ought not to be used for every kind of question. On the contrary, it should be reserved for those decisions in which, whatever the manner of stating the proposition, the true purpose of seeking the express will of these assemblies is achieved by a simple affirmative or negative vote. One should only resort to it in the case of simple propositions, or of a series of propositions refusal to accept the whole of which, on the basis of objections to a single part, would nevertheless express the opinion that it was intended to make known.

Now what reasons occasion the proposal to submit a constitutional plan to the direct approval of the citizens? This is in order that the people, obeying only provisionally powers established by its consent, may preserve its sovereignty entirely; that no power contrary to its rights can be established, even for a moment; that its consent confer upon these laws the authority of the express will of the majority.

Acceptance of an entire constitution by the majority of citizens in separate assemblies, whose members have been able to subject it to examination, gives definitive expression to their belief that the establishment of such a constitution is neither dangerous to their liberty nor contrary to their rights; that it seems to guarantee these rights in all their integrity, opposing private ambitions with obstacles difficult to evade or destroy. Refusal to accept a constitution, on the contrary, expresses the citizens' conviction that it does not contain this certain guarantee, or that the plan submitted even violates their rights rather than preserving them. Now one or another of these decisions, formed even after examination of the plan by members of each assembly separately, expresses a fully informed opinion, a choice determined according to appropriate criteria.

It is not enough for acceptance that a part of this plan merit general approval: it is necessary that all its parts be acceptable. It is enough for the rejection of the plan, on the contrary, that in the eyes of the majority some of its parts present real dangers and approval cannot be given to it as a whole. This decision can then be stated with adequate justification; the form in which the question is posed leaves the people entirely free to do so. For, in truth, the people have only delegated the function of drawing up a constitution, which it cannot itself exercise. Refusal or acceptance of the constitutional plan then expresses its true will.

In the other circumstances in which we propose to consult the people in the same form, we have been careful to follow the same principles. These limit such consultation to simple questions—responses to which are entirely free and uninfluenced by the manner in which they have been posed—since this form is exclusively applied to cases in which refusal or acceptance expresses the will one is seeking to determine with equal lack of ambiguity.

But if the people wishes to exercise in its separate assemblies its right of sovereignty, or even its power to elect, reason requires that it subject itself rigorously to previously established forms. Each assembly is not sovereign: sovereignty can belong only to the people in its entirety; and this right would be violated if some fraction of the people did not act, in the exercise of a common responsibility, according to a form absolutely the same as that followed by others. In matters of general responsibility, the individual citizen belongs not to the particular assembly of which he is a member, but to the people of which he forms part. The majority of the assembly in which he votes has over him no other power than that explicitly conferred on it by law.

If a constitution already accepted by the people regulates the procedures to which these assemblies are subject, each portion of the people then obeys only the will of the direct majority of that same people: an authority which must be as supreme over every separate portion as it is over each single individual.

If, on the contrary, no constitution yet exists, then each portion of the people must submit to the rules drawn up by its representatives. It cannot be said, in any system, that this would result in the least violation of the rights of sovereignty. Indeed, uniformity in the mode of action being necessary here, it is equally important, in order to preserve such uniformity until the direct will of the sovereign can be expressed, to submit to the authority closest to that direct will.

Bringing citizens together in primary assemblies must be considered as a means of conciliating peace and liberty, rather than as a danger to public tranquillity. These assemblies, formed of men occupied in peaceful tasks and useful work, cannot experience disorders unless a session that goes on too long reduces the assembly to a rump of idle (and therefore dangerous) men; or unless, in abandoning such assemblies to their own devices, one exposes them to the temptations of error. We have therefore neglected no means to preserve all the natural usefulness of these assemblies, while insulating them from the influence of party or intrigue.

First of all, these primary assemblies in which citizens exercise their rights as members of the sovereign body—by accepting or rejecting a constitution; by responding to questions posed to them by the representatives of the nation; by directing at particular laws formal objections which oblige the legislative body to examine them—these assemblies in which the citizen votes not for himself but for the whole nation, are absolutely different, in form and in the territory to which they correspond, from those to which the same citizens could be called to deliberate as members of a particular territorial division. Hence, these assemblies can concern themselves only with matters for which the law prescribes their convocation.

Since the primary assemblies do not act each for itself as a portion of the whole, and since they will never be convoked except to decide questions already reduced to appropriate form, no discussion must be authorized within them. In the interval between the proposal of a question and a formal discussion of it, the citizens composing these assemblies can indeed discuss freely the questions submitted to their judgment; and they can do so in the regular meeting-place of the assembly. But the officers of the assembly do not then exercise any formal function. This discussion preserves the private character it ought to possess, and it can neither interfere with the decision nor delay it, since the voluntary meeting in which it takes place is absolutely distinct from the formal assembly in which the decision must be taken.

Partial and spontaneous protests, voluntary and private meetings assuming at will a public character they do not possess by law, municipal assemblies or meetings of a section: all these tend to transform themselves into primary assemblies. This we have wished to replace by regular and legal remonstrances, made by assemblies convoked in the name of the law and exercising precise and determined functions according to legally established forms.

By the very nature of things, when particular protests make themselves heard, when the people—agitated by disturbances that are inevitable, especially at the birth of a constitution and in times still close to a revolution—gather together, or concern themselves with these disturbances, in assemblies convoked for other purposes, the representatives of the nation find themselves falling between two stools. Acquiescence, which may be taken for weakness, encourages intrigue and faction, debases the law, and corrupts the national spirit. Resistance, on the other hand, can lead to insurrection. Such insurrections, which can be dangerous to freedom, are always dangerous to peace and are almost inevitably productive of particular evils. If such a state of unrest continues among the people, frequent disturbances present endless impediments to that tranquillity which is so necessary to the public good. If, on the other hand, the people itself becomes weary of these disturbances, the established powers soon learn to ignore its formal and timid remonstrances; and its petitions, peacefully presented, serve only to prove its apathy and encourage the desire to abuse it. These irregular protests have the further inconvenience of maintaining dangerous errors among the citizens concerning the nature of their rights, of the sovereignty of the people, and of the various powers established by the law.

In short, a real inequality between the various parts of the republic results. Indeed, irregular protests, and the insurrections or disturbances that can be their consequence, have a greater force if they occur in the capital, if they approach more closely to the seat of national power, or if the center of the agitation happens to be a rich town that is important in terms of its location and of the numerous establishments existing there.

In that case, certain portions of the country—because they include such towns, or because other local circumstances make it necessary to treat them with circumspection for fear of alienating them—exercise over a whole republic an influence contrary to that equality between the parts of a whole, the most scrupulous preservation of which is commanded by the law of nature, justice, the common good, and the general prosperity.

The form of remonstrance proposed by the committee appears to prevent all these inconveniences.

A single citizen may propose to his primary assembly that it demand the reexamination of a law, or that it express the desire for a new law to remedy a disorder which he regards as a matter of importance. It is only required that fifty other citizens join their signatures with his, to affirm not that his proposition is just but that it merits the consideration of a primary assembly.

If the primary assembly accepts such a proposition, it has the right to convoke all the assemblies of one of the territorial divisions to consider it. Should the will of the majority in these assemblies agree with the decision of the assembly proposing the reexamination, then all the assemblies of a more extensive territorial division are convoked. And if, in turn, the will of that majority is also affirmative, the national assembly is obliged to examine, not the proposal itself, but only whether it ought to be taken into consideration. If the national assembly decides negatively, all the primary assemblies of the republic are convoked to consider this same question: namely, whether the matter should be considered. In that case, either the will of the majority in the primary assemblies will declare in favor of the opinion of the national assembly, and the proposition will be rejected; or this majority will declare the contrary, and the national assembly, which will then appear to have lost the confidence of the nation, must be replaced with a new one. The new law enacted in consequence of the demand of the primary assemblies is subject to the same remonstrance and the same censure. In this way, neither the will of the representatives of the people, nor that of a group of citizens, can ever escape the sovereignty of the general will.

The same rules are to be observed if it is a question of deciding whether to call a convention charged with the responsibility of presenting to the people a new constitution. Such a constitution might simply be a corrected version of the old one; but the convention, which will necessarily be guided by the national spirit, must in all cases have the power to draw up a new constitutional plan. It would be absurd if it could only reform or correct a certain number of articles; for the very manner of changing them might necessitate changes in a great number of others. And in a work which must be a systematic whole, every alteration must involve a general reexamination, in order to make all the parts agree with the new element introduced into the system.

Should the majority desire a convention, the national assembly will be obliged to initiate its calling. The refusal of the national assembly to convoke the primary assemblies is the only case in which the right of insurrection can be legitimately exercised; and then the grounds for it would be so clear and universally felt, and the resulting upheaval would be so general and irresistible, that such a refusal, contrary to a positive law dictated by the nation itself, is wholly improbable.

These procedures, which can be made very expeditious in an emergency, nevertheless assure a necessary maturity and impose regular deliberations.

The remonstrances of the various territorial divisions would have equal authority, since they would lead with equal force, that is with the whole force of the law, to a consultation of the whole people. There would be no pretext for disturbances, since these disturbances could only be the work of a part against the whole, inspired by an evident intention to prevent the decision or render it useless. No system of intrigue which did not embrace the whole republic could hope for success.

The representative body, subject to legal renewal, could not—should it refuse to examine any question—become the object of resentment. For either the will of the nation would declare in its favor, or, in ceasing to exist, it would cease to excite unrest.

Finally, the provisional execution of the laws generates public tranquillity. And if precise knowledge of the will of a strong majority annihilates all factions, that of a weak majority, by showing the danger of not yielding to it, is sufficient to rally all good citizens and all true patriots in its support, and to convince them to unite in its favor even at the cost of sacrificing the success of their own personal opinions.

It must be added that a declaration of rights adopted by the people—that statement of the conditions to which each citizen submits on entering into the national association and of the rights he acknowledges as belonging to all other citizens; that boundary prescribed by the general will to the activities of social authorities; that compact to which all these authorities are committed relative to the rights of individuals—is yet another powerful shield for the defense of liberty and the maintenance of equality, and a sure guide for citizens in their protests. It is there that they can discover whether a particular law is contrary to the obligations which the whole society has contracted with respect to each individual; whether a particular law is one of the duties of the delegates of the common will; and whether the existing constitution offers a real and sufficient guarantee of the rights established by such a declaration. For just as it would be dangerous for the people not to delegate government in its interests, so would it be equally dangerous for it to place in other hands the preservation of its rights.

Having thus shown the guarantees that must secure the rights of the people, having determined those rights whose direct exercise it should retain, and the form under which they may be exercised, we turn to the question of the organization of the powers which it should delegate.

Two opinions have hitherto divided theorists. Some of them insist that a single force, limited and regulated by law, should motivate the social system; that a supreme authority should direct all others and be itself governed only by the law. In their view, the execution of the law against this supreme authority, should it attempt to arrogate to itself powers not entrusted to it or menace the freedom or the rights of citizens, would be guaranteed by the general will of the people.

Others, on the contrary, insist that certain independent forces should form a kind of balance, mutually serving to regulate one another; that each should become the defender of the general freedom against the other, so that each would oppose the usurpation of the others in order to defend its own authority. But what would become of the public liberty if these powers, instead of opposing each other, combined against it? What would become of the general tranquillity if opinions were divided, and the whole body of citizens was split in favor of this or that power and took action for or against them?

Has not the experience of all countries proved that either such complicated machines are destroyed by their own action, or, besides the system established by law, another is formed based on intrigue, corruption, or public apathy. In this latter case, two constitutions appear: one legal and public, but existing only in the text of the law; the other secret but real, the fruit of a tacit convention among the established powers.

One sole motive would have been sufficient to decide our opinion relative to these two systems. Those constitutions founded on a balance of powers suppose, or lead to, the existence of two parties; and one of the most pressing needs of the French republic is to be wholly free of party.

Thus the power to make laws, and that of deciding on measures of general administration which cannot without danger be confided to any but the representatives of the people, will be entrusted to a national assembly; and the other powers will be charged only to execute the laws and resolutions emanating from it.

The representatives of the people will meet in a single assembly. If this assembly were divided into two chambers, each composed of members equally elected by and from among all the citizens, such an institution would certainly not be contrary to natural equality.

But it is clear that if, for example, two separate assemblies were required to act in concert, the will of a very feeble minority would be enough, because of this division, to reject a motion that a great majority had really accepted. It is clear that such an institution would have the same effect as one in which a relative plurality, more or less strong, was required to adopt a proposition; but it would lead to this same end only in an uncertain and bizarre manner. This combination is not, therefore, the work of a political theory born in an enlightened age. For, not to mention some constitutions based on the prejudice that men may unite in the same society to exercise unequal rights, and that particular classes can pretend to preserve a will independent of the general will, this institution generally owes its origin to peoples whose ancient customs were their only laws; whose public expenses were paid either by territorial revenues or perpetual rents; who regarded every change with that dread which is always the concomitant of ignorance; whose virtually nonexistent administration had no need to take new measures. In a state like this, a power that could act was less to be sought than a power that could prevent change. This fear of innovation, one of the most fatal scourges of the human race, is still the strongest support of the constitutions described above. It is the justification on which their partisans insist with the greatest confidence. The inertia natural to such a system can only be overcome, in administrative measures, by the sheer necessity for action.

A constitution of this kind cannot, therefore, be appropriate for the French republic, where the reform of existing laws and the establishment of a new system of legislation are among the principal duties of representatives of the people; where so many losses to repair, and so many institutions to create, will long sustain recognition of the need for an incessantly active authority.

The very frequent renewal of the legislative body, the remonstrances that the people will be able to make against laws it regards as contrary to its liberty, and the immediate dissolution of the assemblies that refuse to listen to its voice are sufficient guarantees against the schemes for the usurpation of power and the systems destructive of liberty that might otherwise be feared from a single assembly instituted as the only source of every social power.

The use of this last means makes it necessary to distinguish between those acts of the legislative body which are truly laws, and those which can only be regarded as acts of general administration.

The laws are the object of a provisional obedience, just as they are subject to abrogation. By their nature, they continue in force until they are revoked by a legitimate authority; and they do not need to be renewed at definite intervals. Acts of administration, on the contrary, enjoy only a temporary execution or a definite duration. To fix the nature of a tax, to establish the manner in which it will be assessed, to determine how it will be collected, are truly legislative acts; but to declare the amount of the tax, to apply the principles of the assessment so as to produce such an amount, are acts of general administration. Against acts of this nature, remonstrance would either be useless, because too late, or dangerous, because it would suspend their necessary execution.

Thus, for example, determination of the public expenditure, and of the amount of each tax necessary to defray it, must be carried out annually. But this cannot be subject to remonstrance without incurring the risk of dislocating the whole social economy. Similarly, if decisions taken to undertake construction or form a particular establishment were to be subject to remonstrance, necessarily implying a reexamination, success would be rendered almost impossible by the continual uncertainty which would result. In such cases, remonstrances would be concerned not with the defense of rights that had been infringed, or of eternal principles that had been violated, but with matters of temporary or local concern, with considerations of public interest which the whole body of citizens cannot reasonably be supposed able to judge and upon which they do not even have the time to be able to instruct themselves.

Thus frequent renewal of the body to which public confidence has been granted, and the right to demand the reform of a bad constitution, are here the only guarantee that the common interest can require. This guarantee is sufficient.

Short duration of public offices, frequent elections, and the various modes of remonstrance regulated by law are therefore effective means of guaranteeing liberty. Nor should it be feared that they will be any less effective in protecting the public prosperity, or the rights of individuals, against the errors to which a numerous assembly could be carried by precipitation, prejudice, or even excess of zeal.

To remedy this obvious danger, it has more than once been proposed to divide a single assembly into two permanent sections deliberating separately. When their opinions differed, these sections would unite to come to a final determination, or the will of the majority would be obtained by counting the votes, for or against, in each section. It has also been proposed to give a separate body the right to examine the decisions of the assembly of representatives. This body would declare its grounds for disagreement with the assembly within a limited time; after which the assembly would engage in a new discussion before reaching a definitive decision.

There is nothing in these proposals contrary to liberty, or even to an entire unity of power. Each has its advantages and disadvantages. But neither has seemed appropriate to the French nation. Such permanent sections, such a body examining the laws, would necessarily excite division of opinion and become rallying points exciting alarm in some and enthusiasm in others. The rapid passage from despotism to liberty, and the no less rapid passage from a so-called constitutional monarchy to a republic; the agitation occasioned by these successive revolutions and the spirit of distrust that necessarily results from the errors and mistakes into which so many men have been carried: these all render such arrangements impracticable for us. For disagreements and conflicts of opinion between bodies invested with public authority cannot be reconciled with public tranquillity unless one supposes the people sufficiently calm and confident willingly to remain peaceful spectators judging these differences only by reason.

It was therefore necessary to seek procedures that would safeguard against the dangers of precipitate action, yet without rendering impossible that vigor, that promptness of decision-making, which is sometimes necessary (even though the law cannot determine in advance the cases in which that necessity is real).

It was also necessary that, even in the most imperious circumstances, these forms should still guard against the dangerous consequences of over-hasty decisions; that deliberations rapidly undertaken should not however be made without reflection; that even then the members of the national assembly should not be deprived of the means of forming an opinion; and that they should be able to enlighten themselves as to the grounds and consequences of the decision proposed to them.

Three legislative procedures have occupied our attention. All three have appeared adequate to the conditions required. In all three, the unity of the legislative body is entirely preserved. No external action, intruding itself into the legislative process, affords the least pretext for division or for the creation of parties, either in the legislative body or in the nation.

In the first of these procedures, acts of the legislative assembly not relating purely to its internal organization and rules of deliberation, are subject to two discussions. The purpose of the first discussion is to decide whether a proposal should be accepted for further consideration, rejected, or tabled. The proposal, once accepted for further consideration, must be sent to a committee charged to examine and report upon it; and it is only after this report that the second, definitive discussion begins.

Every proposal accepted for further discussion must be printed and distributed before the committee issues its report. The periods of delay for each of these operations are fixed. The assembly can shorten them, however, but only under the condition that the prescribed interval between the acceptance of a project for consideration and the final deliberation cannot be shortened without a decision by ballot. Acts will include in their title the date of their acceptance for consideration; the date of the committee report on them; and, finally, the date of the vote reducing the delay determined by law.

The assembly will thus have the power to give its deliberations all the promptness required, even in the most extraordinary circumstances. The printing of a proposed decree, deliberation by ballot, and the committee report—the only necessary formalities—will in these circumstances require but a short space of time. Yet, despite this promptness, each member will have read the proposal, and the committee will have examined whether it contradicts the general laws or preceding resolutions, before any resolution has been taken.

In ordinary circumstances, the examination and report of this committee will still have the advantage of adding more unity to the system of laws and measures of administration, more clarity and method to the drawing up of laws. It will prevent the too-frequent repeal of hasty resolutions. It will preclude that multiplicity of misinterpretations and uncertainties in the proceedings of the legislative body which is so injurious to its dignity, and so sure to deprive it of the confidence of the people.

The composition of this committee presented difficulties. It was decided to make it small, with a new committee formed monthly. Each committee would remain charged with the reports for which it had initially been given responsibility. And in the course of a single assembly, while no member would be twice elected to a committee, their numbers would always be complete.

In the second legislative procedure, the assembly can in like manner accelerate its deliberations. But it cannot undertake a definitive discussion without first dividing itself into two great committees and completing a preliminary discussion in each of them. This obligatory discussion counteracts the haste that stems from enthusiasm—especially the haste that can be produced by a faction formed by some members. For since creation of these committees will take place instantaneously, it will be impossible in advance to contrive means of swaying their deliberations.

In cases when the assembly follows its usual procedure, this does not present the advantage of submitting the law to the mature examination of a small committee. But this advantage is replaced by that of a more peaceful discussion. For in the separate committees, which would not come to any decision, or even deliberate, the discussion could not be disturbed by incidental motions, by points of order, or by those interruptions to which the necessity of attending to pressing affairs so frequently leads an assembly charged with important interests and numerous details.

It might perhaps be said that, in cases where the temper of the assembly threatened to produce a rash decision, discussion in the committees would be dispensed with. But this supposes that a majority in each committee strongly desires a prompt decision; and there is reason then to believe that such a decision would be demanded by the public interest.

In the third legislative procedure, two-thirds majority in a vote by name is required to decree urgency and to dispense with the delays established by law. This is the simplest of the three procedures, though there will be objections that it substitutes a two-thirds majority for a simple majority. But the objections against graduated pluralities have force only against those who would propose to apply them in cases where it is necessary to act, where action cannot take place without a new decision, and where there exist no grounds for preferring one or another of the proposed decisions. The laws of all civilized peoples require more than a mere majority for the condemnation of an accused person, because the evil resulting from the error of punishing the innocent is greater than that of mistakenly absolving the guilty. This greater majority can justly be required in important matters that it would be dangerous to decide badly, when a decision concerning them can be postponed without disadvantages so great as to balance this danger. It can likewise be required in cases in which the grounds for a decision must, if they are real, be evident to all; for then a feeble majority is a reason for doubting the existence of these grounds. It can be required, finally, when it is a question of an exception to a general law, the goodness of which is generally recognized.

Now these four conditions are united in this instance, since if the urgency is rejected and additional reasons for it occur, there is nothing to prevent a new deliberation. A mere day's delay is the only disadvantage to be balanced against the danger of multiplying over-hasty decisions. It should be observed, moreover, that it is not a question here of subjecting the majority to the will of the minority, but of obeying the will of the majority of the nation, which in this case has reserved the legitimacy of an exception to the general law, passed by itself. Does this majority not have the right to fix the conditions of the provisional obedience to which its will alone can subject the entire body of citizens?

By thus placing the sole principle of social action in an assembly of popular representatives, all other social authorities being only the executors of its laws and the agents of its administrative decisions, we believe we have seized the surest means of preserving unity and combining freedom and peace.

We are not ignorant of the fact that enlightened friends of liberty have envisaged with a kind of terror the creation of a single power whose authority, limited only by written laws, would have no other real limits but popular resistance. But this is because they have only envisaged such resistance as spontaneous and guided by the opinion of the moment; whereas in our plan this resistance is exercised according to forms that the law itself has prescribed. Furthermore, in every system—in the system of a balance of power as in that of unity of action—one is constantly led to a question that is equally difficult in politics and ethics: the question of the right of resistance to a law that is evidently unjust, even though it has been regularly instituted by a legitimate power. For if, on the one hand, continued obedience must then be regarded as a veritable abrogation of the rights of nature, it can be asked, on the other hand, who is to judge the reality of this injustice? According to the present plan, the judge—whose action is regulated by the law itself—is the direct majority of the people: the first of political powers, and that beyond which one cannot go without destroying the integrity of the social compact and returning man to a state of nature in which there exists no other authority but those immutable (but too often misunderstood) laws of reason and universal justice.

The maintenance of unity of action and of principle requires that the constitution place a council of national agents between the legislative body and the citizens who must obey the law, and between the legislative body and the public functionaries who must be responsible for the immediate execution of the laws or direct the detailed implementation of measures of general administration. This council will be charged to supervise the execution of the laws, to organize the details of measures of general administration so that they can be immediately realized, to act as the will of the nation has instructed, and to inform the representatives of the people of the facts that may require new determinations.

This necessary link in the social order must not be considered as a true power. This council must not will, but it must watch. It must act in such a way that the national will, once expressed, is executed with precision, order, and certainty.

There are only two means of preserving in this council the unity which all political action must possess. The first is to place at its head a chief to whom all must be referred, and whose signature would be necessary for every operation. The other members, among whom the labor would be divided, would act only in concurrence with him: if they agreed, their action would be independent of that of their colleagues; but if they differed in their opinions, the preponderance would either be given to this chief, or the council would decide between them. The second means consists of entrusting all general operations only to the whole body of the council, of granting it alone the power to decide, and of requiring that its members act separately only by virtue of a decision of the whole.

Whatever care is taken to avoid alarming even the most restless or most scrupulous concern for liberty, the first of these means will necessarily retain some semblance of royal forms. It will continually present to the imagination the idea of a man, when it is important that it see only the idea of the law. Furthermore, the necessity of taking precautions against excessive authority would inevitably render this means almost useless for the very purpose for which it would be instituted.

We have therefore preferred a council formed of equal members, each charged with the details of one branch of administration. All general resolutions, all determinations, would be taken on the report of that agent to whom the execution of these resolutions must then be entrusted.

It would be wrong to fear delays from a small council composed of men accustomed to public affairs. Its deliberations would be prompt; and they would almost always be limited to adopting, with certain modifications, the proposals of the member charged to prepare the reports for that department and to bring together the considerations that must determine decision.

Moreover, delays are to be feared not in general resolutions, but in the preparation of these decisions and their execution. Now both of these would be the responsibility of one man.

Half of this council will be renewed annually. As a result, since it will never be composed of men entirely new to their position, the chain of affairs cannot be broken. At the same time, there will be no fear of seeing the formation of that perpetuity of opinions and systems which opposes useful reforms and subjects everything to the empire of routine.

It is an error to believe that unity of policy and vigor of action depend entirely on employing a single agent; reason and experience alike prove that these advantages are characteristic of a small number of such agents. The difficulty of finding in a single individual both the powers of mind necessary to act only in accordance with constant principles and a vigor that applies itself equally to large and small matters, is perhaps much greater than that of finding several men in whom these qualities are combined to a lesser degree, but in a degree sufficient for the exercise of more limited functions.

These agents must be essentially subordinate to those who hold the legislative power, or the principle of unity of action would be violated. This council must be the hand by which the legislators act, the eye with which they can observe the details of the execution of their decrees and of the effects which those decrees have produced.

But the institutions of a free people cannot present the image of a servile dependence. If the members of the council are the agents of the legislative body, they must not be its creatures. This body must have the power to force their obedience and the authority to repress their deviations: but the law, protecting the rights of all, must be able to place itself between them. Thus the members of the council will not be elected by the legislative body, since they are the officers of the people and not of its representatives.

An arbitrary power of dismissal would have implied too great a dependence. The representatives of the people and the members of the council would be incessantly fatigued by the intrigues of men avid to obtain such posts, who would seek in their own interests to multiply changes of personnel. Yet it would be dangerous not to subject these officials to any threat of dismissal, leaving clear breaches of responsibility free of the rigors of the law.

Negligence (that incapacity which no precaution in the mode of choice can prevent) or loss of public confidence (which may be the result of involuntary errors) can render fatal to the nation the administration of a man whom it might nevertheless be unjust to accuse of guilt. In such a case, it would be necessary either to expose the public business to dangers, or to protect it by injustices or—what almost always comes to the same thing—by extreme rigor. We think we have found a means of avoiding both these difficulties, by giving the legislative body the right to arraign the members of the council for matters concerning which a national jury would pronounce simply whether the person arraigned ought or ought not to be dismissed from his office. By this means, involuntary mistakes would not be confounded with crimes; but at the same time the defects leading to them would cease to endanger public prosperity and safety.

This kind of censure will be exercised in the name of the people by men popularly elected, men free of any other function and hence of any political interest. These will be chosen by lot to decide particular cases and given adequate time to come to a decision. Such a censure seems to possess the impartiality that the interest and dignity of the nation demand. With such an arrangement, the legislative body exercises no improper functions, none but those of supervision. It will be freed even from the suspicion of the abuse of power, and from everything that can detract from that total public confidence which is the first need of the representatives of the people and the first foundation of order and tranquillity. . . .

Having thus explained the organization and form of the powers comprising the constitutional system, we must now consider their nature and origins.

In whom will the constitution acknowledge the capacity to exercise the political rights that men have received from nature; rights which, like all others, derive essentially from their existence as sensitive beings, susceptible to moral ideas and capable of reasoning? On this question, theorists have been divided between two antithetical opinions. Some have regarded the exercise of political rights as a kind of public function, eligibility for which can be made to depend on conditions determined by the public utility. They have argued that the exercise of the rights of all could be exclusively entrusted to some of the citizens, provided they had no interest in, and could have no motive for, abusing this power; and especially in situations that gave grounds for believing that the general interest of society would be better served if they alone exercised such rights. These theorists have concluded that there would be no real injustice involved in such a distinction, if the men so privileged were not allowed to make laws for themselves alone, and particularly if the exclusion established by the law could be regarded as in some sense voluntary as a result of the ease with which it might be avoided.

Others have thought, on the contrary, that political rights must belong to all individuals with absolute equality. They have insisted that the only conditions which can legitimately be required for their exercise are those necessary to prove that a particular individual is a citizen of a particular nation, and not of another; or, in cases where the citizens cannot vote in the same place, those determining to what assembly each citizen must belong.

Hitherto all free nations have followed the first opinion, as did the French constitution of 1791. But the second has appeared to us more in conformity with reason, justice, and even enlightened policy. We have not thought it legitimate to sacrifice a natural right, acknowledged by the most simple reason, to considerations the reality of which is at least uncertain. We have felt it necessary either to limit ourselves to distinctions that are insignificant and without any real object, or to give such exclusions an extent which a generous and just nation favoring equality would never debase itself to accept.

We have not thought it possible, in a nation enlightened as to its rights, to propose that half of the citizens abdicate some of these rights. Nor did we consider it conducive to public tranquillity to divide a people actively occupied with political interests into two parts: one of which, in the eye of the law, would be all, and the other nothing— despite the fact that nature, in making them men, wished them to remain equal.

In former times nations were composed of families supposed to have a common origin, or that at least went back to a first association. Political rights were hereditary, and it was by legal adoption that these families joined themselves with new ones. Now our nations are distinguished by territory; and it is the inhabitants of this territory who are essentially the members of each association.

It has been pretended that political rights should belong only to landholders. But if we observe the present order of societies, this opinion can be based only on one ground: that they alone exist on the territory in an independent manner, and cannot be excluded from it by the arbitrary will of anyone. Now, if we admit this argument, it is evident that it is equally conclusive in favor of those who, by agreement, have acquired the right of existing likewise upon the territory for a certain period in an independent manner. And if this inference is admitted, the force of the argument gradually diminishes, and the limits of the time required to establish residence can be fixed only in an uncertain and purely arbitrary manner. It would soon be seen that the limits of this kind of independence are not sufficiently clear to serve as a basis for a distinction as important as that between enjoyment and deprivation of political rights.

Dependence precluding the assumption that an individual acts from his own will could doubtless be legitimate grounds for exclusion. But we have not thought it possible to suppose the existence of such dependence under a truly free constitution, and in a people among whom the love of equality is a distinctive characteristic of the public spirit. Social relations implying such a humiliation cannot subsist among us, and they must soon assume another form. Finally, since our whole code of laws is consecrated to civil equality, is it not better that political equality should also reign in that code entirely, destroying every vestige of dependence rather than serving to consecrate it in our new laws?

Other considerations also determined us in this conclusion. Among them were the difficulty of fixing the point, in the chain of interdependence necessarily existing in society, at which an individual of the human species becomes incapable of exercising his rights. They also included the fear of rendering more dangerous the dependence of certain classes of men who would escape exclusion, and of providing a pretext for new exclusions in the future; the danger of separating a great number of individuals from the social interest, of rendering them indifferent to the common good or hostile to a liberty they are not allowed to share. We therefore concluded that justice and the public interest did not permit us to sully the system of our laws by any mark of inequality; that, for the first time on earth, it was possible to preserve in the institutions of a great people the entire quality of nature. . . .

For these reasons every man of the age of twenty-one, being a native of France or declaring his intention to reside there permanently, is admitted, after a year's residence, to enjoy all the rights of a French citizen. Three months' residence will entitle him to exercise these rights in the place where he has taken up his abode. An absence of six years, except in the public service, will require an individual to renew his residence for six months before he can again exercise the rights of the citizen.

We have thought it good to limit the austerity of the law to the simple precautions necessary to prevent arbitrariness in admission to the rights of citizens, to avoid disputes, and to subject them to uniform principles throughout the whole republic. Each citizen will be eligible for every office which the election of his fellow citizens can bestow. The only condition required is twenty-five years of age. This interval between being admitted to the exercise of political rights and being eligible for public functions allows the time necessary to judge the new citizens, to observe their conduct, and to learn their principles.

The youth whose individual and theoretical education is ended enjoys the personal rights he derives from nature. A kind of political education then begins for him, and the very exercise of these first rights forms part of this second education.

Whether one considers the rights of the electors, which must be exercised freely, or the rights of those who may be elected, and who must be able to aspire equally to the same advantages, no condition of eligibility can be established without violating political equality, unless the utility of such a condition is self-evident. When elections are made only by a portion of the people, the majority of the nation (and consequently the law, which expresses its will) can say to this portion "You do not elect for yourselves alone, but for all; and the public good requires that your choice be subject to certain conditions." The majority can likewise say to the minority: "We all possess the right to choose freely among all the citizens. But we wish to choose only among those who fulfill certain conditions; and we have the right to limit the forms of election to those that will permit us to fulfill this purpose. Consequently we have the right to make a law which, by requiring these conditions, saves us from establishing that form which would become embarrassing to you."

But the right of the majority, considered according to the principles of justice, is not the right to be arbitrary; it cannot constrain the minority to satisfy a mere caprice, and any restriction pronounced by the majority can be legitimated only by an evident utility. Now what conditions of eligibility could be required according to this principle? Would they be relative to age? Whether the majority followed the torrent of established opinions or obeyed reason, youth would not be preferred. It can be the age of genius, the age of enthusiasm for virtue; but it is not the time of true enlightenment or of virtue purified by reason. A man whose youth gives promise of talent will sometimes be preferred to one whose maturity reveals only mediocre ability, but not to the citizens whose superior merit has received the seal of experience and earned the authority of renown.

Would these conditions be based on wealth? Since we can have neither the stupidity nor the baseness to believe that rich men are more inaccessible to vice and corruption than poor men, the only grounds for such a law would be the utility of limiting the choice to men in whom a more extended early education must imply enlightenment. But then it would be necessary to require a considerable fortune. Thus all the conditions of this kind are either illusory or conducive to a real oligarchy.

Will one demand, for certain positions, proof of a certain course of study or success in particular examinations? Conditions like these, which are almost always eluded, have the disadvantage of creating powers foreign to the general order of society. They give some men, or some classes of citizens, an influence contrary to equality.

It could, further, be required that more important positions be conferred only on persons who had already fulfilled lesser functions: requiring, for example, that a member of the national assembly have prior experience as a member of a departmental administration; or that members of departmental administrations have exercised municipal offices. But such conditions have one grave disadvantage. Men would then be distinguished in the political order not only by the offices they occupy—a distinction which is in the nature of things—but by those they had previously filled, which would become a real personal distinction. Citizens eligible for different kinds of office would form different classes; they would soon join together as an exclusive elite, suffering no man to enter their class who did not suit their pride or their plans. It is even easy to foresee that in time a kind of heredity would be created. The sons of persons eligible for a particular office would find it easy to become eligible themselves, while a thousand little tricks would be employed to exclude new men.

The tendency toward hereditary politics is as real in nature as the establishment of such heredity is a violation of its rights. And this observation, which the history of all nations confirms, does not allow us to regard as a matter of indifference to freedom institutions which favor this fatal propensity, even indirectly.

We have therefore determined to establish no conditions of eligibility. We propose that the citizens preserve in its entirety their freedom of choice; and we believe them worthy to place this confidence in themselves without danger.

The mode and form of elections form an essential part of the constitutional laws, for a legislative body that could change them at will would equally have the power to violate the constitution itself, or to render it unworkable as a means of overthrowing it. Such a body could perpetuate its own existence despite the constitution, if it wished to exercise a tyranny.

The first question to be resolved concerns the possibility of direct elections, and of the utility of substituting them for those carried out, since the year 1790, by electoral bodies. Under the old constitution the departmental bodies necessarily became a support for royal power, serving to defend it against the representatives of the people. The nature of their functions must give them a tendency (even involuntary) in favor of everything that can strengthen the force of government, or appear to maintain tranquillity and preserve the status quo.

On the other hand, electors chosen by the citizens had to regard themselves as the most direct representatives of the people, seeing the deputies they chose as their creatures, and endeavoring to become something more in the political order than mere electors. But at the same time they necessarily united with the popular parts of the national assemblies, and aided them in opposing the usurpations of the other powers. From this point of view, they could appear a counterweight useful to freedom, but dangerous to peace, the general tranquillity, and even the unity of the empire.

But since the republic has replaced the incoherent and servile system of limited royalty; since everything points to the desirability of a single body as the principle of all social actions, preserving unity in its full force, the electoral bodies could exert their influence in the future only against the representatives of the whole nation. Hence they would become the support of particular administrations against the assembly and the national agents. Their continuation would incessantly menace the indivisibility of the republic and give a dangerous force to any party that wished to transform France into a league of confederated republics, since each department would then offer a kind of particularistic representation, which it would be enough simply to assemble, and render active, to create a separate and independent center of power.

Thus it was sufficient for the committee to be assured of the possibility of dispensing with these electoral bodies to hasten to restore to the citizens the right of direct elections which had been taken from them.

In examining the various forms of election which might be established, it will be found that they cannot make known the persons whom the majority regards as most worthy of office, unless the number of candidates is first limited by a declaration of the majority that the choice must be made among a group of candidates alone considered capable of exercising such functions. But to fulfill this first condition even imperfectly, it would be necessary for each elector to designate an indefinite number of persons whom he regards as worthy of the office; and for all the electors to vote on the capacity of every person nominated, even by a single elector. This initial judgment could not be dispensed with, without making it obligatory to consider as candidates all those nominated, even by a single elector. Each elector must then express his complete opinion by a comparative judgment among all the candidates, taken in pairs; and from the result of the will of the majority in each of these comparisons, the result of its general will can be derived. It must be observed, further, that this result would frequently differ from what is demanded as the preference of the majority; for it can happen that this apparent preference does not really exist.

If one considers the length and inconvenience of this first declaration concerning the capabilities of the candidates, the difficulty for the electors in listing according to merit a great number of candidates, the time necessary for each to vote on this list of candidates taken in pairs, and the labor necessary to arrive at the general result, it will be seen that this method—which can only designate those whom a relative plurality, and not the majority, regards as most worthy—is impracticable even for an electoral assembly composed almost entirely of enlightened and unimpassioned men. Since the only method which leads to the choice of those whom the majority has declared most worthy cannot be employed, and since the other methods can only make known those whom a greater majority judges very worthy of an office, we have thought it our duty to choose the most practicable and most simple of these methods; that which is least liable to be influenced by party and intrigue; that, in short, which can most certainly produce the only end to which it is possible to aspire.

In the method we have preferred, the will of each primary assembly is carried to the capital of the department, there to form the general will of the citizens of the department; and the will of the citizens of each department, carried to the national capital, can there form the common will of the citizens of the whole republic.

Whatever the number of places to be filled for one and the same function, each citizen will only have two occasions to vote: once to form a list of candidates, the number of which will be fixed; a second time to complete the election. In the first vote, he will write down a fixed number of names. For example, in an election of deputies from a department to the national assembly, each citizen will write a number of names equal to the number of deputies to be chosen. The list of candidates, which will be triple the number of representatives, will be formed from the names of those who have obtained the most votes; and it is from this list alone that candidates must be elected. Thus, if the number of deputies to be chosen is ten, only the thirty citizens with the most votes on the first list will form the second list of candidates.

In the second vote, each citizen will first choose the candidates whom he judges most worthy, in number equal to the number of deputies to be chosen. He will then choose the same number of those whom he regards as next most worthy. Thus, for example, should the number of deputies required be ten, each citizen will first name the ten most worthy of the thirty candidates, and then the ten most worthy of the remaining twenty. The result of these first votes will first be determined, and those candidates who have obtained an absolute majority—or, if their number surpasses the number of deputies to be chosen, those who have obtained a greater majority—will be elected.

If all the places are not filled by the result of the first votes, the second will then be reverted to. And according to the general results of these votes, the persons obtaining a greater majority will be elected. . . .

This method of election requires of the citizens only very short and simple operations, which can be facilitated still further by removing everything that could embarrass the most simple man.

All the details of these operations fall on the persons charged to formulate the results, whether of individual votes, or of the votes of separate assemblies. And there are also means of abridging and facilitating this labor.

If we examine this method in itself, it will be found that requiring a list of candidates which is triple the number of places reduces the real limits of the election very little. Few of those in favor of whom citizens would be inclined to vote will be excluded.

It is possible for the list of candidates to contain an insufficient number of names, because the votes of the citizens will agree only on a small number of individuals. In such a case, which will never occur even though it is physically possible, there will be a simple means of ending the election in conformity with the spirit of the method.

In the first votes for the definitive election, the opinion of each citizen will be expressed in the most natural, simple, and complete manner. Indeed, the idea of naming by successive votes men who are destined to fill absolutely equal places is absurd in itself, because—under the appearance of leading first to a choice of the man whom the majority prefers to all others, which in this case is of no utility—it gives a false result instead of a correct one, since it does not make the choice fall on men who, in the opinion of the majority, should be called to fulfill these places. Not only does this method fail to prevent cabals, but it renders them almost inevitable, and abandons to chance elections that it does not subject to the influence of party.

In the method we propose, those who are elected by the first votes are necessarily regarded by the majority as more worthy to occupy a position than the other candidates.

In circumstances that make it necessary to turn to the subsidiary list, the vote of the greatest majority will again indicate their preference. Its vote in their favor will not be as pronounced; it will only be more favorable to them than to others. But it will be a true expression of the preferences involved; and what would be gained by requiring the appearance of a larger majority, by appearing to have obtained a vote that did not really exist? . . .

Elections thus carried out in separate assemblies will be much less exposed to intrigue. It would be almost impossible to prevent a man of real merit from being put on the list of candidates, if the wishes of his fellow citizens naturally place him there. It would be equally difficult for any faction to prevent the majority from uniting in the favor of a superior man, or to seduce it into voting for someone really worthless.

Let us now examine this form of election on the hypothesis that two parties divide the people. Any method of election which would become vicious in such a circumstance is inadmissible in a constitution; for, if it is possible to dispense with political parties, it is not possible to prevent parties of opinion from forming and perpetuating themselves.

Now, on this hypothesis, the method we propose presents very real advantages. First, the most numerous party must inevitably place on the list a number of candidates large enough to satisfy it, and at least equal to that their opponents could introduce; but it will be difficult for them to fill the list entirely. Thus this list will not present the always dismal spectacle of the power of a party. Then, in the election itself, it will be enough to secure the preponderance of the most numerous party that it obtain a number of names on the list equal to the number of places. This party will then necessarily have the advantage without needing to have recourse to any of those corrupt means so contrary to public peace, the practice of which, if long continued in a country, ultimately perverts public spirit and imperils freedom.

The most that can happen is that some of the places will be given to men of each party who, by their character or their wisdom, have earned the esteem or the indulgence of the opposite party: i.e., to those who can hold a useful balance between the two parties, thereby preventing party quarrels from degenerating into fatal feuds. In a word, since this form of election will deprive the less numerous party of the hope of succeeding by seduction or threats, and give the opposite party an assurance of success which will make recourse to its force unnecessary, elections will necessarily be peaceful, even when the electors are divided. They will serve to indicate the power of the parties, but they will not be their work.

The deputies forming the legislative body are elected in each department and their number is fixed according to population alone. This is yet another tribute to equality. A provision that allocated three deputies to each department, while a third of the total was distributed in proportion to taxation, would doubtless correct the advantage that distribution according to taxation alone would confer upon the richest departments. But we have preferred introducing no inequality to having one for which to compensate.

The idea of having the national council chosen by all citizens is made very practicable by following this method of election, modified only by the necessity for a proportionally more numerous list of candidates for a single place, and by the need to be able to name several substitutes for each place at the same time. It has appeared very important to us that these high agents of the national power be chosen by the citizens themselves; that reputation alone direct this choice; that intrigue be avoided; that these places no longer appear to be reserved almost solely to the inhabitants of a single city, as they would be if the assembly of representatives or a single body was charged with this election. One of the first duties of this position is to promote the entire union of every part of a republic. It is therefore right that such men belong equally to all parts. It is right that men responsible for the interests of their country in a negotiation with foreign nations be invested with the direct confidence of the majority of the citizens.

Voting aloud cannot be admitted in the primary assemblies without introducing disorder and confusion. It has the further inconvenience of giving those who vote first a kind of influence over the voters who follow, which is a sufficient reason to reject this method of election. It also supposes a permanent assembly during the whole time of voting, which would impose upon the citizens a useless inconvenience. But a written ballot is not necessarily a secret ballot. The name of each citizen can be attached to his vote, and these names can be read when the votes are counted.

We propose that in the vote forming the list of candidates, each ballot be accompanied by the name of the voter. There seem to us to be no disadvantages in each person's being responsible for his choice to public opinion. But we have at the same time concluded that in the ballot for election the name of the voter ought not to be revealed. In the first vote, which is only a simple nomination, there can be no danger to the public good if voters sometimes list names for personal reasons. The names not being read until after the election is over, it will not be influenced by murmurs or signs of disapprobation that certain names might excite. And the publication of this first vote can be useful to national manners, without harming the tranquillity of individuals or giving too much power to intrigue.

Moreover, since the vote forming the list of candidates represents the citizens' opinion as to the best choices to be made, it can be a good thing that those men who have merited this confidence not remain unknown; and it can be useful for persons not acquainted sufficiently themselves with men worthy of the places to be able to direct their judgment according to the public and avowed judgment of citizens whose probity and enlightenment they respect. This is an additional reason for preferring written and signed votes to voting aloud, in which each citizen knows only the opinion of the members of his own assembly.

The second vote, on the contrary, is a vote of preference. For this reason alone, it is good to preserve it from every kind of influence, to render it independent both of public opinion and of the engagements which men may have made from weakness. Such a vote must be made the fullest expression of the will of those voting.

The simplicity of the forms of election makes it possible to hold them frequently.

The utility of preserving the same principles of administration and of consistently following measures once adopted must yield to the danger of imposing upon the confidence of citizens. In a truly free nation, the basis of such consistency must be sought in the very principles of the people. And what are the principles of the French people? A love of freedom, common to all nations not degraded by slavery; the love of equality, which in some way constitutes its particular character; and respect for the rights of men, rendered sacred in a declaration from which each citizen learns what he has a right to expect from all, and what all have a right to expect from him. These principles, well known and well developed, are sufficient to give to every law and every act of administration that consistency which would be expected in vain from the mere duration of particular offices.

In establishing these frequent elections of public officials, we thought it our duty to set no limits upon re-eligibility. Such limits might have been useful when elections were entrusted to electoral bodies; but once they are entrusted to the citizens themselves, unlimited liberty, if it is not a consequence of the national sovereignty, is at least a tribute the law must pay to the majesty of the people, a mark of confidence which its courage in the defense of liberty has deserved. Jealous precautions would be an outrage to its zeal for the maintenance of its rights.

This re-eligibility is, moreover, useful to counterbalance the disadvantages of the frequent change of offices. These two institutions appear to be intimately connected, never to be separated. . . .

But to have established the forms of a constitution on the principles of equality; to have organized powers in such a manner as to secure freedom and peace; to have prevented the plots of ambition and the spirit of party by frequent renewal of offices and direct elections, the form of which preserves them from intrigue; to have offered the people peaceful means of protest against laws injurious to its rights or its opinions; to have regulated the means by which it can give itself a new constitution should the first appear to threaten its liberty: to have done all this was still not all. It was also necessary that the national assembly, in a better position than individual citizens to recognize the vices of the constitution and anticipate the abuses to which it might lead, have the right to inform the citizens of these defects or dangers, and to ask whether the people would wish for a national convention to consider the means of correcting the one and preventing the other. It also remained to guard the people against the dangers of that profound indifference which often follows revolutions; against the effects of those slow and secret abuses which in the long run corrupt human institutions; and against the vices which must corrupt the best contrived constitution, should it remain the same while the men for whom it was written have changed with the very progress of knowledge and civilization.

For these reasons, we have thought it our duty to establish a constitutional mode of subjecting the constitution itself to reform at fixed intervals, independent of the people's demand.

The period of such a reform would doubtless be a period of internal commotion, if all of a sudden one saw the formation of a body of representatives invested with the dual power of making laws and presenting a constitutional plan; for this accumulation of authority would give it the idea of placing itself, in advance, above the constitution it was about to change.

But this difficulty will be avoided by allowing all the former powers to exist until the new constitution has been accepted; and by entrusting the responsibility for drafting and presenting it to the people to a less numerous assembly, required to hold its sessions separately from the legislature, elected for this purpose alone and unable to exercise any other function. Limits thus set cannot be transgressed. The purely theoretical function of examining a constitution and reforming it, in order to present it for acceptance (before which this constitution is nothing more than philosophical speculation), has nothing in common (nor can it be confused) with the active function of making detailed laws that are provisionally binding, and of taking measures of general administration that are immediately executed. If the constitution of a people is based on the principle of the balance of the vicious powers combatting or combining one with another; if it gives different classes of citizens prerogatives that must balance one another; if it creates permanent bodies and establishes powers long entrusted to the same individuals, no doubt the moment of examining such a constitution will be a moment of alarm because these diverse interests it has created will raise vigorous and implacable war upon each other.

But it is not the same when a constitution is based on unity of action, frequent renewal of public officials by direct elections, and the most perfect equality between men. Then, making a new constitution can only be a matter of modifying procedures, and of improving the organization of assemblies or councils charged with public functions, the method of electing their members, and the manner in which these authorities must act. What great unrest could then excite troubles? Would not those who might desire or attempt public disturbances be restrained by that sacred principle of entire equality which is the only basis of enduring freedom: a principle engraved on the hearts of all men; a principle that, leading of itself to clear consequences within the grasp of all minds, can never be violated with impunity once it has been acknowledged and put into practice.

In this report we have confined ourselves to an exposition of the general principles which have guided us, and the grounds for our most important decisions.

In the natural sense of the word, a constitution ought to contain all the laws that relate to the establishment, formation, organization, function, mode of action, and limits of all the social powers. But from the moment we attach to the laws contained in the constitution an irrevocability proper to them; from the moment they cannot be changed, like other laws, by a power always subsisting in society, it becomes necessary to include there only those laws relating to the social system, the irrevocability of which will not injure the workings of that system, nor make necessary a too-frequent convocation of an extraordinary power.

It is at the same time necessary that the changes which depend on the will of a single legislative assembly should allow it neither to invade the authority nor to corrupt the spirit of the constitution under the appearance of changing different forms. Such a defect, in a constitution which gave the people legal means of obtaining its reform, would lead equally to the too-frequent calling of national conventions.

All that pertains to the legislative body, to the limits of powers, to elections, and to arrangements necessary to guarantee the rights of citizens, must therefore be developed in the greatest detail, and determined in such a manner as to leave no fear that the social action would be subject to delay, difficulty, or upheaval.

A constitution expressly adopted by the citizens, and including regular means of correcting and changing it, is the only means of attaining a regular and enduring order in a society whose members, enlightened as to their rights and jealous to preserve them, have just recovered these rights and still fear that they may again be lost.

Enthusiasm and exaggerated suspicion, the fury of party and the dread of faction, pusillanimity (which regards every agitation as dissolving the state) and restlessness (which suspects tyranny the moment it perceives peace and order): all these must vanish in the presence of these salutary arrangements.

In every great society that has undergone a revolution, men are divided into two classes. Some, actively occupied in public affairs, either from motives of interest or of patriotism, become involved in every dispute, divide themselves among all factions and parties. One would think them the whole nation, though they are often only a small part. Others, given over to their own work and restricted to their personal occupations either by necessity or the love of ease, love their country without seeking to govern it, and serve the nation without wishing to make their opinions or their party prevail. Forced either to divide into factions and to place their confidence in the leaders of opinion, or to be reduced to inactivity and silence, they need a constitution to show them their interest and their duty in an unequivocal manner, so that they can learn without difficulty the goal to which they should direct their efforts. Once this imposing mass is directed toward this common goal, the active portion of the citizens ceases to appear to be the entire people. Then individuals are nothing, and the nation alone exists.

It must therefore be expected that all those whose vanity, ambition, or avarice need to feed on troubles; all those who fear that the establishment of a peaceful order would cast them from the limelight of public esteem back into the obscurity of the crowd; all those who can be something in a party but nothing in a nation, will unite their efforts to delay, disturb, or perhaps prevent, the establishment of a new constitution. They will be seconded by those who regret some part of what the revolution has destroyed, who deny that the formation of a republic founded on equality is possible, because they fear to see it established; and by those, still more guilty, who have calculated that the long duration of our internal divisions could alone give to our foreign foes the success that would be fatal to freedom.

Thus intriguers of every party, aristocrats of every class, and conspirators of every order, will share a single will, employ the same means, and speak the same language, against the establishment of a new constitution. If they cannot attack what may be too evidently useful or wise, they will seek to discover secret intentions in those who have proposed or defended it. For it is easier to give birth to a suspicion than to destroy a rational argument; and even less talent is necessary to invent a slander than to contrive a sophistical argument.

But the Convention will destroy these shameful hopes. It will hasten to present to the people a constitution worthy of itself, and worthy of the nation. It will not fail to discover the snares intriguers will scatter along the route.

The citizens, all of whom feel the necessity for laws at last fixed, will join the Convention. They are not ignorant that its glory, and the future fate of its members, are attached to the success of this great act of the national will. It is by this act that the French nation, Europe, and posterity will judge our intentions and our conduct; this idea will sustain the popular confidence; and the people will judge the plan that your wisdom must submit to its sovereign authority according to reason alone.

As for your committee, we present our labors with the confidence of men who have sought what is useful and just, without passion, without prejudice, without the spirit of party, without motives of personal interest or vanity, but with the humility inspired in us by the difficulty of such a work in itself, and by all those other difficulties with which, in the present circumstances, it is surrounded.

The sovereignty of the people, equality among men, and the unity of the republic, have been the principles ever present to our thoughts, guiding us in the choice of the means we have adopted. We have been persuaded that the constitution that is best in itself and most in conformity with the present spirit of the nation, would be that in which these principles will be most respected.

Frenchmen, to you we owe the truth in its entirety. Vainly would a simple and well-formed constitution, accepted by you, assure your rights. You will neither know peace, nor happiness, nor even freedom, if submission to the laws that the people has enacted for itself is not the first duty of every citizen; if that scrupulous respect for the law, which characterizes free nations, does not extend itself even to those laws the reform of which is demanded by the public interest; if, charged to choose all those entrusted with authority, you listen rather to the murmurs of calumny than to the voice of fame; if an unjust suspicion condemns virtue and talent to silence and retreat; if you put faith in accusers instead of judging accusations; if you prefer the mediocrity that envy spares to the merit that it delights to persecute; if you judge men according to their opinions, which are easy to feign, and not according to their conduct, which is difficult to sustain; if, in short, from culpable indifference, you do not exercise peacefully, yet with dignity and zeal, the important functions that the law has reserved to you as citizens. Where would there be liberty and equality, if the law which regulates rights common to all were not equally respected? And what peace, what happiness, could be hoped for by a people whose imprudence and carelessness abandoned its interests to incapable or corrupt men? Yet, whatever defects a constitution may contain, if it offers the means of reforming itself to a people who love the laws, who are occupied with their interests, and who obey the voice of reason, these defects will soon be repaired even before they have been able to do harm. Thus nature, which has willed that each people preside over its own laws, has decreed equally that each people be the arbiter of its own prosperity and happiness.

NOTE TO ''ON THE PRINCIPLES OF THE CONSTITUTIONAL PLAN''

1. "Supposing a surface equal to that of France represented as a circular figure (the figure in which the greatest distance between two points of the contour is the smallest possible), this distance would still be more than 180 leagues. And in France it is scarcely more than 200 leagues" [Condorcet's note].

A General View of the Science of Social Mathematics (1793)

This article, never completed by Condorcet, was published in the *Journal d'instruction sociale* [Journal of Social Instruction], 29 June and 6 July 1793. It was left unfinished when the philosophe, denounced in the Convention on 8 July, fled into hiding. Appropriately, this last article of Condorcet's free political life represents a comprehensive attempt to set forth the principles and methods of the science he now came to call "social mathematics," and to demonstrate the indispensability of that science as a guide to rational social action.

While the sciences are in their infancy an individual can cultivate them all at once. Nevertheless they remain isolated, for the imaginary systheses produced in such circumstances by a few enthusiastic minds can only be placed in the category of scientific dreams. Once scholars are forced by scientific progress to divide up the various branches of the sciences, however, lines of communication develop between them and the application of one science to another often becomes its most useful or brilliant aspect.

Such an application not only requires that each of the two sciences has attained a certain development. It also demands knowledge of them widespread enough that there are men expert in both disciplines who are able to pursue the problems of each with an equally sure step.

Thus the application of mathematical calculation to the moral and political sciences could only have come about in an age when mathematics was being studied successfully, and among peoples whose liberty was enhanced by tranquillity and buttressed by enlightenment. In Holland the celebrated Johan de Witt, disciple of Descartes, and in England the knight [Sir William] Petty, took the first steps in this science during the last century,[1] at about the same time that Fermat and Pascal were creating the calculus of probabilities that is now one of its principal foundations.[2] However, Fermat and Pascal only dared to apply the calculus of probabilities to games of chance, or did not even conceive of the possibility of putting it to more useful and important applications.

The extent to which these applications have now been developed makes it possible to regard them as constituting a separate science. I shall attempt in what follows to sketch its general outline.

Since all these applications are immediately related to social interests or to the analysis of the operations of the human mind, and since in the latter case their object is still only man perfected by society, I conclude that the term "social mathematics" is most appropriate for this science.

I prefer the term "mathematics"[3] . . . to "arithmetic," "geometry," or "analysis," on the grounds that the latter terms refer only to certain aspects of mathematics, or to one of its methods. The application of algebra or geometry is as relevant here as that of arithmetic; and we are concerned with applications in which all mathematical methods may be used. Furthermore, the expression "analysis" is ambiguous, since it sometimes means algebra and sometimes the analytic method, and we will sometimes even be obliged to use this same word in the general sense given to it in other sciences.

I prefer the term "social" to the terms "moral" or "political," because the sense of these latter words is less comprehensive and less precise.

The following account will demonstrate the wide utility of this science. It will be seen that none of our interests—individual or public—is foreign to it; nor is there an interest which it fails to elucidate by giving us more precise ideas and more certain knowledge. It will also be seen how much this science would contribute, if it were more widespread and better cultivated, both to the happiness and to the perfection of the human race.

Two observations will serve to make this clear. In the first place, almost all the opinions, almost all the judgments that direct our conduct, rest on a greater or lesser probability, always evaluated according to a vague and almost mechanical sentiment, or on the basis of crude and uncertain guesses.

It would doubtless prove impossible to subject all these opinions and judgments to calculation, just as it would be equally impossible to calculate all the eventualities in a game of dice or cards. Nevertheless, one could still acquire the same advantage that the player who today knows how to calculate his game enjoys over one who plays only by instinct and routine.

In the second place, absolute truths—truths which exist independently of all measure and of all calculation—are often inapplicable and vague. In matters open to quantitative treatment, or admitting of numerous alternative possibilities, they do not go beyond the statement of first principles and therefore become inadequate from the very outset. Thus if we restrict ourselves to reasoning without calculation, we are open to the danger of falling into error and even of acquiring prejudices, either by ascribing to certain maxims a generality they do not possess, or by deriving conclusions from them that do not result if they are taken in the sense and to the extent that they are true. In short, the point would soon be reached where all progress becomes impossible without the application of rigorous methods of calculation and of the science of combinatorial analysis; and the advances of the moral and political sciences—as of the physical sciences—would soon come to a halt.

When a revolution draws to a close, this method of teaching the political sciences acquires a new kind and a new degree of utility. Indeed, to recover promptly from the disorders inseparable from any great social movement, to restore public prosperity (the return of which can alone consolidate a social order menaced by so many diverse interests and prejudices), there is a need for more exact policies and methods calculated with more precision. These can only be made to carry on the basis of proofs which, like the results of calculation, impose silence on prejudices and bad faith. It therefore becomes necessary to destroy the empire that talk has usurped over reasoning, the passions over truth, active ignorance over enlightenment. Since all the principles of public economy have been overthrown, since all the truths recognized by enlightened men have been confounded in the mass of uncertain and changing opinions, men must be bound to reason by the precision of ideas and the rigor of proof. The truths presented to them must be set beyond reach of the eloquence of words or the sophisms of interest. It is necessary to accustom minds to the slow and peaceable march of discussion, to preserve them from that perfidious art which lays hold of their passions to drag them down into error and crime, and which acquires so fatal a perfection in times of trouble.

But how much force would this rigor, this precision which accompanies all the operations to which calculation is applied, not add to that of reason! How much would it not contribute to ensure the advance of reason over this debris-covered terrain, long shaken by violent tremors and still suffering from internal commotions.

Social mathematics can be concerned with men, things, or men and things together.

It is concerned with men when it teaches us how to determine the mortality rate in a given region, or when it calculates the advantages or disadvantages of a method of election. It deals with things when it evaluates the advantages of a lottery, and when it seeks the principles that must determine the rates of maritime insurance. Lastly, it is concerned with both men and things together when it deals with life annuities and life insurance.

Social mathematics can consider man as an individual, the duration and relations of whose existence is subject to the order of natural events. Or it can be applied to the nature of the operation of the human mind.

It considers man as an individual when it reveals, precisely and on the basis of facts, the influence that climate, customs, and occupations have on the duration of life. It considers the operations of the mind when it weighs the grounds for belief and calculates the probable truth of testimony or decisions.

Calculation could only be applied directly to one thing at a time, and its uses would be very limited, if men had not been led by necessity to establish a common measure of the values of things. But the existence of this common measure makes it possible to compare all things one with another, and to submit them to calculation in spite of their natural differences (which are therefore abstracted).

Yet the determination of this common measure, such as it results from human needs and social laws, is very far from the precision and invariability that a true science requires; and the theory of the reduction of values to a common measure becomes a necessary part of social mathematics.

The value of a thing cannot be the same, if one considers it as freely and indefinitely available, as available only for a limited period (after which it ceases to be available for the same individual), or as only becoming available again at a certain time.

These various considerations apply to all commodities that can be utilized without being altered, or the alterations of which can be evaluated.

From this, there derives the theory of what is called interest on money.

Whatever object this science considers, it comprises three principal parts: the determination of facts, their evaluation (which includes the theory of mean values), and their results.

But in each of these parts, the facts, the mean values, or the results, having been considered, it remains to determine their probability. Thus the general theory of probability is at one and the same time a part of the science of which we are speaking, and one of the foundations for all the other parts.

Facts may be divided into two classes: real facts, given by observation; and hypothetical facts, resulting from combinations made at will. Of a given number of individuals born the same day, so many die the first year, so many the second, and so many the third: these are real facts. Supposing two six-sided dice, I can derive all the numbers from 2 to 12: these are hypothetical facts. The table of real facts is formed by observation; whereas that of hypothetical facts comprises the list of possible combinations.

Among these hypothetical facts there are some that are similar, either absolutely, or in terms only of certain characteristics. The method of classifying them, that of knowing the number of different combinations considered from one point of view or another, or the number of times that each combination is repeated, depends on the general theory of combinations, the first foundation of the science that we are dealing with.

Likewise, in considering a succession of observed facts differing among themselves, it often becomes necessary to abstract some of these differences, classifying together all those facts showing similarities in terms of the remaining characteristics, in order to discover the numerical ratio between those differing on a given point, or to learn what other circumstances more or less constantly accompany the facts placed in one or another separate class.

Thus in tables of births and deaths, for example, men and women are separated so that we can know their respective numbers or examine the mortality rate peculiar to each sex. It is by this means alone that one can advance from particular facts to the discovery of those general facts that result from observation. The general means of classifying observed facts according to the order that one needs to give them, which makes it possible to elicit with ease the relations they present, is for observed facts what the theory of combinations is for hypothetical facts. This art of deriving general facts from observed facts is yet another of the foundations of social mathematics. It has two parts: first, the search for general facts; second, the search for the general laws that may result from them. This is properly the art of making discoveries by observation.

A table expressing how many of a given number of men born the same day survive after the first year, how many after the second, etc., presents a series of general facts, such as the following: in a given country, half of the men die before reaching age 10. But if I can represent this same table by a formula, then I have a general law, such as the following: of a given number of men of a certain age, an equal number dies each year; or (what comes to the same thing) the ratio of the number of dead to that of survivors, for each year, increases in an arithmetic progression.[4]

Among the facts given by observation, it will often be found that no two are exactly alike. When the difference is very small, however, one is obliged to regard them as absolutely the same if one wants to arrive at general results and avoid being lost in the immensity of detail. In such a case, it is necessary to substitute for these observed facts a single fact that can accurately represent them.

The same individual fact, if observed several times, can also present deviations resulting from observational error. Since in most cases there exist no grounds for preferring one of these observations to the exclusion of all the others, it is then necessary, using these same observations, to seek the one that seems most appropriate to represent the real fact.

Finally, it is possible to consider a large number of facts of the same kind, but which give rise to different effects. If these are facts that have already occurred, the result of such consideration is a common value for these effects. If they are facts equally possible in the future, the result—for the man who, having to experience one of these effects, can expect any of them equally—is a situation that one must seek to evaluate, in order to be able to compare this common effect or this expectation to other effects or other situations of the same kind.

The determination of this single fact representing a great many others, which can be substituted for them in reasoning or calculation, is a kind of estimate of observed facts, or facts regarded as equally possible. This is what is called a mean value.

The theory of mean values must be considered as a preliminary to social mathematics, for it is not limited to this particular mathematical application.

In all the physico-mathematical sciences it is equally useful to have mean values of observations or experimental results.

Thus the science that we are discussing here must naturally be preceded by five mathematical theories, which can be developed independently of any application:

1. The theory of quantities susceptible of increase in proportion to time, which includes that of interest on money;
2. The theory of combinations;
3. That of the method of deriving from observed facts either general facts or even more general laws;
4. The theory of the calculus of probabilities;
5. Lastly, that of mean values.

In this science, as in all other applications of mathematics, if profound mathematical knowledge is necessary to resolve certain questions, even to establish certain theories and to make new steps forward, elementary knowledge is sufficient to understand the solution of at least the majority of these questions, to comprehend these theories, and to deduce their most immediate practical applications.

The science can make progress only to the extent that it is cultivated by mathematicians who have thoroughly studied the social sciences. But in terms of its practical utility, it can become an object of almost general knowledge among all those who wish to enlighten themselves regarding the important subjects with which it is concerned.

It is possible to treat it in a simple and elementary manner, to put it within reach of all those who have some acquaintance with elementary mathematical theories and some practice in calculation.

All the sagacity, all the genius of several great mathematicians were necessary to yield a theory of the moon according to which reliable lunar tables could be developed. But the development of these tables and their application to the determination of longitudes require only elementary knowledge.

Thus it is a common, everyday science that is being presented here, not an occult science, the secret of which is reserved to a few adepts. It is a question, at one and the same time, of accelerating the progress of a theory upon which depends the advance of the sciences most important for public happiness, and of illuminating several aspects of these same sciences with knowledge of a general and practical utility.

I shall now sketch the various objects of social economy to which calculation can be applied [See Chart].

[I. MAN]

1. Man considered as an individual

We know how much man is affected by climatic conditions, the nature of the soil, his food, the general habits of life, medical practices, social institutions. And we can investigate the ways in which these various causes affect the duration of life, the numerical proportion of individuals of each sex (either at birth or at different ages), the ratio of births, marriages, and deaths to the number of individuals in the population, as well as that of married, unmarried, and widowed, of either sex or of both.

We shall then see in what manner these causes influence the mortality produced by different classes of disease.

Finally, we shall see to what point one can discover their influence on the force, size, and build of individuals, or even on their moral qualities.

OBJECTS OF SOCIAL MATHEMATICS

1. MAN

    1. Individual man.
    2. The operations of the human mind.

2. THINGS

    Reduction of things to a common measure. Calculation of values (1).

3. MAN AND THINGS

METHODS OF THE SCIENCE

1. DETERMINATION OF FACTS:
    A. 1. Observed facts.
       2. Hypothetical facts.

    B. 1. Enumeration of facts.
       2. Classification of facts. Combinations (2). Probability of facts (5).

2. ESTIMATION OF FACTS (3). FORMATION AND USES OF MEAN VALUES (4). THEIR PROBABILITY (5).

3. RESULTS OF FACTS. PROBABILITY OF RESULTS (5).

PRELIMINARY THEORIES
THAT MUST PRECEDE THESE APPLICATIONS

1. Theory of quantities susceptible of proportional increase.
2. Theory of combinations.
3. Method of deriving from particular observed facts (a) the facts resulting from them; (b) the general laws observed in them.
4. General theory of mean values.
5. General theory of probabilities.

NOTE: Numbers in parentheses refer to "preliminary theories" 1–5 listed in the chart under that heading.—ed.

Either the separate action of each of these causes can be considered, or that of several of them combined. In this latter case, it is necessary at one and the same time to examine whether these two or three combined causes act in a manner isolated one from another, or whether they are really combined in the sense that they correct or aggravate the effects that each of them would have produced individually.

Here observation can only reveal the coexistence between the fact regarded as cause and that regarded as effect. It remains to determine, by means of the calculus of probabilities, whether or not this coexistence must be regarded as the result of a constant law, and whether the effect must be attributed to the supposed cause or to chance, i.e., to an unknown cause.

I throw two dice fifty times in succession, getting an uneven number 27 times and an even number 23 times. Although I know that of the 36 possible combinations yielding numbers from 2 to 12, eighteen produce an even number and eighteen an uneven number, I do not immediately conclude that I must attribute the superiority of uneven numbers in this case to an inequality in the dice. But if I repeat this experiment with fifty throws of the dice a hundred times, getting an uneven number about 2,700 times and an even number about 2,300 times; if of these hundred experiments 98 against 2 have presented the same advantage in favor of the uneven numbers, would I not then have grounds for believing that the dice are made in such a way that, the one more easily yielding an even number and the other an uneven number, it is consequently easier to get an uneven number when throwing them both together?

It will be seen that this same observation applies equally to natural facts, and that it would expose one to quite ridiculous errors to infer their mutual dependence from a small number of coincidences: if, for example, having found that at a certain time there were six blind men in a certain place with 3,000 inhabitants while there were only four in another place with the same population, one went on to conclude that the climate of the first was more unfavorable to the preservation of sight.

It is clear that in such cases the relevant facts can only be collected with the assistance of the public authority. Indeed, if the number of facts is small, they do not lead to any conclusion probable enough to yield useful consequences. Nor can the researches of one or several individuals provide what could easily be obtained from examination either of the registers of births, marriages, and deaths, or of the lists of citizens or of the national guard.

But then, if one wishes these registers to be truly useful for the knowledge of man, it is necessary to give them the form and the extent required by this too long neglected goal. It is also necessary to find ways of organizing the data gathered from these numerous registers, in such a way that the resulting tables can offer the observer all the general facts deriving from this mass of data, and not only those that it was intended to seek when the tables were being drawn up.

2. [THE OPERATIONS OF THE HUMAN MIND]

The applications of calculation to the intellectual operations of a single individual, or of several, presents a scope no less vast.

Considering them in themselves, one can apply the theory of combinations.

The theory of the syllogism, the invention of Aristotle, is the first and almost the only example.

All the rigorous proofs of intellectual truths can be reduced to this form. But since it is not the only path that can be followed, and since it would be a long or difficult task to reduce to syllogistic form a sequence of reasoning that was at all extensive, it would be useful to apply the theory of combinations either to other methods or to the means of facilitating or simplifying this reduction.

The calculus of probabilities teaches us to know and to measure the true weight of our grounds for belief, from the adherence we give to truths demonstrated by calculation or rigorous reasoning to the opinion we form on the basis of testimony. It teaches us how to evaluate, from the natural relationship of facts among themselves, the ground for believing the truth of a fact which it has not been possible to observe immediately; and from their order, the ground for belief in the existence of an intention to produce them.

The same calculus will teach us equally to evaluate the grounds for belief, whether of similar or different kinds, that can combine or conflict in relation to the same proposition: as, for example, when a fact improbable in itself is nevertheless supported by evidence of imposing testimony.

The application of calculation to these last questions will have the advantage of bringing the light of reason to questions too long abandoned to the seductive influences of the imagination, of interest, or of the passions.

Instead of yielding mechanically to the force of certain impressions, one will know how to calculate it and evaluate it. It is by this means alone that the final blows can be dealt both to superstition and pyrrhonism, to the exaggeration of credulity as to that of doubt.

In this way one will see how and why the force of the sentiment which leads us to belief is weakened, as the ground for belief is assessed with more exactness; and, consequently, why a sort of suspension of belief so constantly accompanies the greatest enlightenment, while total conviction is the lot of ignorance.

Finally, it is in this way that one will recognize the true difference between the instinctual judgments that imperiously direct our customary actions, and those judgments resulting from reason, which determine our conduct in important actions or fix our opinions in speculative matters.

It is then necessary to fix the limits of the probability according to which one can direct one's conduct, depending on the nature of the question; and to see how, according to the difference in the effects resulting from one or another contrary actions, one course of action must be decided upon only on the basis of proofs, and another on the basis of the slightest degree of probability.

Among these applications of social mathematics to the operations of the human mind, there should also be included the technical or even mechanical means of executing intellectual operations: such as the art of arranging historical, chronological, or scientific materials in tables or registers, or that of forming or deciphering codes; such as arithmetical machines, or those that might be used to discover more easily the result of a large vote. Turning then to intellectual operations carried out by several men at the same time and analyzing the way in which they take place, the theory of combinations can be applied to the form, the calculation, and the probability of decisions arrived at by majority vote, to examination of the advantages and disadvantages of various modes of election, and to the probability that their result is a good decision.

Here there is a distinction to be made between decisions in which a simple majority is adequate and those in which a larger majority must be required. If in the latter case this larger majority is not attained, it is necessary either to appeal for another decision, or to postpone decision, or finally to act on the basis of the will of the minority, because the opinion of the majority is among those that should not be followed so long as they remain below a certain degree of probability.

In the same way, in elections, one distinguishes between those that express the preference of the majority; those that only express a judgment regarding the absolute capacity of the candidates preferred; those in which one gives both a relative statement of preference in some respects, and a statement concerning absolute capacity in others.

The extent to which the inequality of the minds involved in these operations, the necessary differences in the probability of different decisions made by a single individual in different circumstances, the bad faith that can sometimes be suspected, can introduce into questions simple in themselves considerations that are essential but difficult to subject to calculation: this will be readily apparent. So will be the necessity to find empirical means of discovering the probability of an individual's judgment, or at least the more or less narrow limits within which that probability can be comprised.

Such is the very imperfect outline of the first two parts of social mathematics.

[II. THINGS]

The theory of values, and of the prices that express the relationship of values by reducing them to a common measure, must serve as the foundation for that part of social mathematics which is concerned with things.

Without this, since calculation can only be applied to things homogeneous among themselves, it would have only very limited applications and a very feeble utility.

Everything that serves an individual's needs, everything that has some utility in his eyes, everything that affords him some pleasure or saves him from pain, has a value for him. The natural measure of this value is the importance of the need served, the degree of the utility, the intensity of the pleasure afforded or of the pain avoided.

Since all men who inhabit the same country have more or less the same needs, since in general they also have the same tastes and the same ideas of utility, what has a *value* for one of them generally has a value for all.

If a man who needs grain and can dispose of a certain quantity of wine meets another who needs wine and can dispose of a certain quantity of grain, an exchange occurs between them, the one giving the other two measures of grain, for example, for one measure of wine.

It can first be said that these two values are equal, in the sense that the two measures of grain have, for one of these men, the same value as a measure of wine for the other.

Moreover, if a similar exchange occurs between a certain number of individuals in the same place, following such a proportion, these values are still equal, in the sense that each can if he wishes have two measures of grain for a measure of wine, or vice versa.

Thus a relationship of *value* is established between determinate quantities of grain and of wine; and it can be said that 25 measures of wine are worth 50 of grain, concluding from this that a man who has 50 measures of wine, one who has 25 measures of wine and 50 of grain, and one who has 100 measures of grain, possess equal values.

If, in these exchanges, a certain thing is generally exchanged against all the others—as, for example, in the case where savage peoples might exchange animal skins for the produce they need—then this thing serves as a common measure of values and is called the price. Thus, for these peoples, the price of a knife or a hatchet would be so many animal skins. And consequently, when the price of two things is known, so is the ratio of their values. The values of all things can therefore be included in a single calculation, deriving results common for all these values simply by calculating in terms of the units of the thing that has become their common measure.

But for this it is necessary to choose as a measure either similar things that can be counted, or a single thing that can constantly be obtained in determinate quantities. It is also necessary to be able to suppose that these similar things are equal among themselves, or that this single thing is always of the same quality.

Indeed, it would soon have been realized that if a knife were worth two skins and a hatchet twenty, it could not be concluded that a hatchet was worth 10 knives unless the skins serving as a common measure were supposed equal among themselves.

It can happen, as in this example, that the thing taken as a common measure might not be susceptible to this constancy. In this case the idea develops of taking as a unit one of these things in the size and condition in which it is most often presented in real exchanges. Thus, for example, the common measure will be a beaver skin of roughly a given length and breadth, or a sheep of roughly a given age and size. This is a kind of mean value which develops naturally, because the need for it is felt. From this the next step has been to a kind of abstract unit, the original name of which is retained even after it has been agreed to attach it to something of an entirely different nature.

Other peoples have had the idea of taking as a common measure shells that cannot be put to any other use, but which also acquire a real value because they therefore become useful in facilitating exchanges.

Finally, in a more advanced state of society, metals have been taken that are exactly divisible, homogeneous, found everywhere the same and remaining so at all times: having a real value because they serve other uses, and acquiring a greater one on account of the new utility that they assume when they are employed as a common measure of exchange.

But if this common measure is of the same nature in different countries and at different times, what real conclusions can be drawn from the relationships of values that knowledge of prices can reveal?

If, for example, I know that in China a quintal (or 1,600 ounces) of rice is exchanged for an ounce of silver, and that in Europe the same quantity of rice would be exchanged for 2 ounces of silver, then I can conclude that a given weight of rice is worth 1,600 times less in China, and only 800 times less in France, than an equal weight of silver.

From this then I draw the practical conclusion that it is profitable to send silver to China in order to bring back rice.

In the same way, if in Athens a certain measure of flour cost an ounce of silver, and the same measure costs 2 ounces of silver in France today, one could conclude that the relationship of value of equal weights of flour and of silver had doubled since that time.

But this is as far as these consequences go, and these relationships tell us nothing about the mass of needs that are satisfied by this quantity of rice or of flour, or about the price that in different countries and periods has been attached to the enjoyment that can result from the possession of such and such a thing.

These observations must be extended further if one wishes to penetrate to more advanced conclusions.

Before advancing so far, it is also necessary to know the influence on prices of various monetary systems, either metallic or representative, and to calculate the extent to which commerce existing between countries that have adopted different systems has been affected by these differences; i.e., to know the theory of money, exchange, and banking.

It is also necessary to learn to recognize or form the distinction between the individual price of a thing just being bought, the common price of this same thing in the same place and at the same time, its ordinary price, and its average price, either for different countries or for a certain number of years. It is then necessary to see how the cost of producing such a thing affects the price that it must have at each period, and in each country: either in the case that its production can be regarded as restricted within certain limits (as with the fruits of the earth, animals, or natural products, the mass of which remains smaller than our needs), or in the case that this production can be regarded as of indefinite extent (as with certain manufactured products, lace or prints for example).

Having learned not to confuse these different kinds of prices of the same thing, having guarded oneself against the confusion of ideas that derives from the inexactness of language, one will see that beyond this measure recognized in everyday life—in which is included the unit of measure for all values that makes it possible to subject them to calculation—there can be set a natural measure less susceptible to frequent variation, indicating more constant and more important relationships for the general order of societies.

Such, for example, would be the most general and most common quantity of food sufficient for one day, for a grown man of ordinary size and physical constitution. Such would be the common daily wage of a man without particular skill, or even the value of the annual expenditure of a healthy man as limited to the most simple necessities.

This preliminary information once established, one is naturally led to the means of evaluating exactly the wealth of a nation, the increase or decrease of its wealth.

The annual reproduction is the unique source of this wealth in each isolated nation: if consumption exceeds this reproduction, wealth diminishes and with it the size and well-being of the population. If, on the contrary, reproduction exceeds consumption, wealth increases and there exists a superfluity that produces more well-being for those who exist, and consequently more means of preserving children, which leads to an increase in population.

A portion of the annual reproduction is necessarily used to ensure an equal reproduction for the following year, the rest constitutes what is called the net product.

This net product is also called the disposable product, because it can be used at will, without altering the reproduction. A part of it is consumed; the rest can constitute an increase in wealth.

Thus three classes of men come into being: those working at the cultivation of the soil, who produce more than they consume; those using these first productions to make manufactured products of one kind or another, who only change their form and confer upon them a value equal to that which they have consumed; and finally the simple consumers, who destroy while producing nothing.

One can even identify a fourth and a fifth class: first, that of the merchants charged with preserving and transporting the productions of the soil or the products of manufacture, who sell them with an increase in value equal to that of the work employed or the values consumed in securing this preservation and effecting this transportation; and then the class of men who, even without any labor on their part, can exercise the choice to preserve or even augment the value of a portion of their disposable wealth that they could have consumed. For example, a rich man consumes 10,000 *livres* a year, dressing himself luxuriously and nourishing himself with delicate or exotic foods: this sum of values can be regarded as uselessly destroyed, even though it has served to provide a living for the men employed by him and to support industry. Another individual spends this same amount of money acquiring pictures, prints, books. In this case the value has been preserved: he has equally provided for the living of some men, but in employing them in a more useful manner. Finally, a third individual spends the same amount of money draining a marsh or clearing a piece of land: from this there results an increase in value, a new reproduction.

Now it is easy to see what different results, both for the national wealth and the public prosperity, can stem from these different uses of equally disposable values; and how, depending upon the way in which prevailing opinion shapes the conduct and behavior of the men to whom the disposition of this wealth is entrusted, the state of society can improve, be maintained, or deteriorate.

From this formation, distribution, and utilization of wealth, social relations develop among men necessitating a mass of different operations, the function of which is the circulation of values. In these operations, mathematical calculation is necessarily employed. Thus it is here that one should place the application of calculation to commercial and banking operations.

All the calculations applied to the theories affecting the questions we have just indicated, and to the general facts that we have just outlined, naturally become complicated by the necessity of introducing a further element of consideration: that of the interest on the capital which furnishes the advances indispensable to operations relating to the production of values, to their transformation and transmission.

This brings us to the whole theory of commerce, in which it is necessary, when considering profit, to distinguish carefully between the real interest on the capital advanced, the merchant's reward for his work, and the price of the risk to which he exposes himself. This risk ranges from the loss that can result from the fact that a commodity kept too long will have lost its value, to that which can stem from shipwreck on a distant expedition; from the minor insurance calculation that each merchant could make for himself, to that of maritime insurance taken in its greatest extent. The general theory of insurance of values of any kind, under whatever form these operations present themselves, here takes its place in the overall system of the science which we are presenting.

Thus, knowing all the causes that affect the formation of prices, all the elements that must enter into it, it will become possible to analyze the phenomena presented by their variations, to distinguish their laws, and to derive from these observations truly useful consequences.

One must then turn to the calculation both of the results of commerce between different nations, and of the formation of its true balance, which must not be confused with the balance in which only the metals used as currency are considered. Then one will see what this latter balance, the only one on which facts have been collected, can really express; and what errors have been committed by the majority of those who have been concerned with this question.

Here the principal utility of the application of calculation will be to show that several principles too often adopted as absolute and precise truths are susceptible of exceptions and even of modifications. They are consequently true only in general, and will not even lead to sufficiently approximate results. For in almost all cases men have reasoned about these objects in much the same way as if, in calculating the operations of a great hydraulic machine, one had restricted oneself to the simple application of the general principles of mechanics. The second utility of the application of calculation will be to show how one has often forgotten to pay attention, in the course of reasoning, to data that it is not permissible to neglect. And, finally, it will show that in this mass of operations exercised in an independent manner by a great number of men—and directed by the interest, by the opinion, one might even say by the instinct of each of them—an order, a regularity has been supposed, of which they are not susceptible.

Until now we have considered nations only as aggregates of individual men occupied with their interests or with their labors.

It remains for us to consider them as a body which the social pact has made, in a certain way, into a moral individual.

From this point of view, the common defense, maintenance of security and of property, the public works and establishments useful to all, demand expenses that can only be met by taxation.

These taxes are either approximately the same each year for a long period of time, or they are levied only for one or several years at irregular periods determined by the conjuncture of events.

On what part of the annual reproduction are these constant taxes necessarily to be paid? How, depending on their nature and their mode, are they to be distributed among the diverse portions of this part of the annual product?

Going on to consider the greater or lesser extent of the sum to which they amount each year, the objects that they affect directly, the mode according to which they are levied or distributed, the amount spent on raising them, the severe laws necessary to ensure their collection, one will ask what effects these various causes must have on the national wealth, on its distribution, on its increase or preservation, and in what ways these same causes influence the cultivation of the soil, industry or commerce, or interest rates.

Simple reasoning is sufficient to reply to all these questions. But calculation must give more precision to the responses since it teaches how to balance off those effects that can contradict one another.

The effects of taxes that are only temporary in duration must be examined separately. It is clear that the total system of the national wealth must be affected by any establishment of a mass of contributions more or less constant in its value and in its forms; and that under the influence of this cause, if continued for a long time, it must take on a sort of equilibrium or regular movement. Thus it is necessary to investigate what this constant state will be, and by what intermediary states it can be arrived at.

But if it is a question of a temporary tax, producing a kind of transitory disturbance from which the social economy will soon regain its equilibrium, it is necessary to know the effects of this disturbance.

If this disturbance is complete enough, however, or if it is repeated frequently enough to produce long-term alterations, then it is necessary to examine both the temporary effects and the final result of these irregular movements.

It will be seen that these disturbances are almost always harmful, precisely because they necessarily change the distribution of wealth, thereby also changing the distribution of the means of subsistence. For in this kind of thing all change must be made in such a way that the movement occurs peaceably and without causing disruptions in the general chain of its effects.

Public loans are a means of avoiding these disruptions, and it is clear that calculation alone can teach us how to choose the operations of this kind that must meet with the most success and yield consequences that are least onerous.

Here we come to the calculation of lotteries, which can be relevant both to taxes or loans, according to the manner in which they are formed.

Without doubt, one must speak of them only to demonstrate their ruinous and deadly effects, adding the authority of a calculated truth to the force of morality, which has until now been all too powerless.

The effects that the existence of a public debt or a national bank can have on the distribution of wealth, on agriculture, industry, and commerce, are another of the objects to which the application of calculation will not be useless.

One can also add to this list an examination of the influence that different monetary systems can have.

Several public expenditures also have effects on the national wealth that are more or less direct, more or less important. Such are those concerned with public assistance, public works, and public establishments.

For example, assistance badly distributed can transform into useless consumers men whose work would have increased the mass of the productions of the soil or of the products of the different manufactures; and this assistance thereby becomes a source of impoverishment.

The expense of a public work can exceed its utility, and the loss occasioned by this expense can be such that the good produced can never make up for it.

If an educational establishment diminishes the expense necessary to acquire a certain trade, then its effect will be to lower the price of the products. The entire mass of institutions and laws affect wealth, and this influence can consequently be submitted to calculation. For example, from this point of view one can examine the effect of the destruction of the privileged orders and of feudal rights, of the equality of succession, of the suppression of the right to testament; and one can examine especially with what rapidity these two last acts of justice would affect a more equal distribution of properties.

Finally, several questions of jurisprudence cannot be resolved without invoking the aid of calculation.

The first of these is fixing a legal rate of interest, that is to say one which must be set, but which has not however been determined by a particular agreement.

Another is fixing the value of a thing that an individual must furnish in kind, when the execution of the condition is found to be impossible and it must be replaced by an equivalent.

Another would be the distribution of an obligation to be fulfilled in common, or of a thing to which several individuals have rights, every time that these rights are mixed up in the consideration of various contingencies which necessitate recourse to the calculus of probabilities, or necessitate evaluations for which this calculus or the theory of mean values are indispensable.

Another is the manner in which an agreement between several individuals should be terminated, when it is found to be annulled by a cause not foreseen in the original agreement, and when uncertain events or complicated evaluations affecting the rights of the parties also make it necessary to have recourse to these same means.

This second part of the table of objects to which calculation can be applied seems to embrace almost the whole of political economy. This must necessarily be the case since political economy only considers things relative to their value. However these two sciences must not be confused.

In all the questions of political economy, in all the practical operations it treats theoretically, and which suppose or require only very simple calculations, social mathematics must be limited to a general exposition of the methods while concentrating only on questions where the difficulties of solution depend on calculation itself.

It must be concerned with the analysis of ideas or of facts only to the extent that this is necessary to ensure that the calculation is based on solid foundations.

It is the feebleness of the human mind and the necessity of husbanding our time and energies that oblige us to divide the sciences, to circumscribe them, to classify them sometimes according to the objects with which they deal, sometimes according to the methods they employ. In this latter division, the lines of separation must be more uncertain; and it is with a division of this kind that we are dealing here.

Mineralogy and the application of chemical analysis to the study of minerals are not the same science, but they are concerned with the same subject while employing different methods. They each throw light upon the other; and the one cannot be handled well without the help of the other.

In mineralogy, observation of minerals—their description and their history—forms the basis of the science; but it often invokes chemistry when faced with difficulties that observation alone cannot resolve. In the application of chemistry to metallic substances, their chemical analysis is the basis of the science; but chemistry often needs to be illuminated by observation.

In the same way, although political economy employs observation and reasoning, one is constantly reminded of its need for calculation. Conversely, social mathematics teaches us only to calculate abstractions if it does not borrow from political economy the data that it must utilize, and if this latter subject does not indicate the questions that it is important to resolve.

There is perhaps no portion of the political sciences concerning which there remain more prejudices to be destroyed, and where these prejudices can have more fatal consequences. Until now they have resisted the force of reason. Defeated more than once, they have been seen to rise up again with yet more force. Where they have disappeared from one country, we have seen them reappear in another.

Let us dare to hope that once they are attacked by reason and calculation, we will no longer have to fear these unexpected resurrections, these oscillations between truth and error.

NOTES TO ''A GENERAL VIEW OF THE SCIENCE OF SOCIAL MATHEMATICS''

1. On De Witt, see above, p. 70, note 7. His concern as Grand Pensionary to strengthen the public finances of his state prompted him to seek to calculate more precisely the actuarial problems involved in annuities on lives, a common method of raising funds among seventeenth-century governments. Sir William Petty (1623–1687), one of the founders of the Royal Society, was the principal English protagonist of the science he called "political arithmetic," meaning the application of mathematics and empirical reasoning to questions of national wealth and power.

2. The foundations of the calculus of probabilities were first developed in a celebrated

exchange of letters between the French mathematician, Pierre Fermat (1601–1665), and the philosopher, scientist, and mathematician, Blaise Pascal (1623–1662). While Pascal's discussion was limited to questions of probability as raised in games of chance, the theory of probability was soon recognized by his successors as potentially applicable to the probabilities of the social world more generally.

3. In the French original, Condorcet argued here for the term *mathématique,* "although no longer commonly used in the singular," to emphasize the fact that the new science would draw on all available mathematical techniques.

4. "This law was proposed by Moivre. It agrees well enough with observation for the ages between 10 and 80, and it can be used in several circumstances to shorten calculations. Lambert and citizen Duvillard [de Durand] have both presented other laws of mortality that are more exact but also more complicated" [Condorcet's note]. Abraham de Moivre (1667–1754), whose work, *The Doctrine of Chances,* is one of the classics in the development of probability theory, was a French Protestant who left his native land for England after the revocation of the Edict of Nantes. His *Annuities on Lives* became a standard eighteenth-century work on the applications of probability theory to actuarial problems.

III Condorcet in Hiding

Sketch for a Historical Picture of the Progress of the Human Mind (1793)

Driven into hiding in July 1793, Condorcet devoted his remaining months of life to the *Historical Picture of the Progress of the Human Mind* he had long contemplated. The introduction intended for that work, generally known as the *Sketch for a Historical Picture of the Progress of the Human Mind*, forms part of a much larger body of material related to his project that Condorcet prepared during this period. The *Sketch*, uniting all the strands of Condorcet's thinking in a passionate vision of human progress, was published posthumously in 1795. It has often been regarded as the authentic testament of the Enlightenment, written in the shadow of death by the last of the philosophes.

Condorcet divided the historical progress of mankind into nine stages, adding a tenth epoch in which he sketched his hopes for the future. The following selection includes the introduction to the *Sketch*, in which he explained the philosophical basis for his belief in progress and the manner in which his work was written; the chapter on the Ninth Stage, which describes the advance of reason in Europe in the seventeenth and eighteenth centuries; and the chapter sketching the future Tenth Stage inaugurated by the French Revolution. The selection presented here is taken from the modern translation by June Barraclough, which was first published in 1955. Passages printed within square brackets represent additions to the *Sketch*, as printed in 1795, which do not appear in the original manuscript among Condorcet's papers (dated 13 October 1793). The origin of these passages is obscure. They were probably added by

Condorcet, between October 1793 and March 1794, on another copy of the manuscript now lost.

INTRODUCTION

Man is born with the ability to receive sensations; to perceive them and to distinguish between the various simple sensations of which they are composed; to remember, recognize and combine them; to compare these combinations; to apprehend what they have in common and the ways in which they differ; to attach signs to them all in order to recognize them more easily and to allow for the ready production of new combinations.

This faculty is developed in him through the action of external objects, that is to say, by the occurrence of certain composite sensations whose constancy or coherence in change are independent of him; through communication with other beings like himself; and finally through various artificial methods which these first developments have led him to invent.

Sensations are attended by pleasure or pain; and man for his part has the capacity to transform such momentary impressions into permanent feelings of an agreeable or disagreeable character, and then to experience these feelings when he either observes or recollects the pleasures and pains of other sentient beings.

Finally, as a consequence of this capacity and of his ability to form and combine ideas, there arise between him and his fellow-creatures ties of interest and duty, to which nature herself has wished to attach the most precious portion of our happiness and the most painful of our ills.

If one confines oneself to the study and observation of the general facts and laws about the development of these faculties, considering only what is common to all human beings, this science is called metaphysics. But if one studies this development as it manifests itself in the inhabitants of a certain area at a certain period of time and then traces it on from generation to generation, one has the picture of the progress of the human mind. This progress is subject to the same general laws that can be observed in the development of the faculties of the individual, and it is indeed no more than the sum of that development realized in a large number of individuals joined together in society. What happens at any particular moment is the result of what has happened at all previous moments, and itself has an influence on what will happen in the future.

So such a picture is historical, since it is a record of change and is based on the observation of human societies throughout the different stages of their development. It ought to reveal the order of this change and the influence that each moment exerts upon the subsequent moment, and so ought also to show, in the modifications that the human species has undergone, ceaselessly renewing itself through the immensity of the centuries, the path that it has followed, the steps that it has made toward truth or happiness.

Such observations upon what man has been and what he is today, will instruct us about the means we should employ to make certain and rapid the further progress that his nature allows him still to hope for.

Such is the aim of the work that I have undertaken, and its result will be to show by appeal to reason and fact that nature has set no term to the perfection of human faculties; that the perfectibility of man is truly indefinite; and that the progress of this perfectibility, from now onwards independent of any power that might wish to halt it, has no other limit than the duration of the globe upon which nature has cast us. This progress will doubtless vary in speed, but it will never be reversed as long as the earth occupies its present place in the system of the universe, and as long as the general laws of this system produce neither a general cataclysm nor such changes as will deprive the human race of its present faculties and its present resources.

The first stage of civilization observed among human beings is that of a small society whose members live by hunting and fishing, and know only how to make rather crude weapons and household utensils and to build or dig for themselves a place in which to live, but are already in possession of a language with which to communicate their needs, and a small number of moral ideas which serve as common laws of conduct; living in families, conforming to general customs which take the place of laws, and even possessing a crude system of government.

The uncertainty of life, the difficulty man experiences in providing for his needs, and the necessary cycle of extreme activity and total idleness do not allow him the leisure in which he can indulge in thought and enrich his understanding with new combinations of ideas. The means of satisfying his needs are too dependent on chance and the seasons to encourage any occupation whose progress might be handed down to later generations, and so each man confines himself to perfecting his own individual skill and talent.

Thus the progress of the human species was necessarily very slow; it could move forward only from time to time when it was favored by exceptional circumstances. However, we see hunting, fishing, and the natural fruits of the earth replaced as a source of subsistence by food obtained from animals that man domesticates and that he learns to keep and to breed. Later, a primitive form of agriculture developed; man was no longer satisfied with the fruits or plants that he came across by chance, but learned to store them, to collect them around his dwelling, to sow or plant them, and to provide them with favorable conditions under which they could spread.

Property, which at first was limited to the animals that a man killed, his weapons, his nets, and his cooking utensils, later came to include his cattle and eventually was extended to the earth that he won from its virgin state and cultivated. On the death of the owner this property naturally passed into the hands of his family, and in consequence some people came to possess a surplus that they could keep. If this surplus was absolute, it gave rise to new needs; but if it existed only in one commodity and at the same time there was a scarcity of another, this state of affairs naturally suggested the idea of exchange, and from then onwards, moral relations grew in number and increased in complexity. A life that was less hazardous and more leisured gave opportunities for meditation or, at least, for sustained observation. Some people adopted the practice of exchanging part of their surplus for labor from which they would then be absolved. In consequence there arose a class of men whose time was not wholly taken up in manual labor and whose desires extended beyond their elementary needs. Industry was born; the arts that were already known, were spread and perfected; as men became more experienced and attentive, quite casual information suggested to them new arts; the population grew as the means of subsistence became less dangerous and precarious; agriculture, which could support a greater number of people on the same amount of land, replaced the other means of subsistence; it encouraged the growth of the population and this, in its turn, favored progress; acquired ideas were communicated more quickly and were perpetuated more surely in a society that had become more sedentary, more accessible, and more intimate. Already, the dawn of science had begun to break; man revealed himself to be distinct from the other species of animals and seemed no longer confined like them to a purely individual perfection.

As human relations increased in number, scope, and complexity, it became necessary to have a method of communicating with those who were absent, of perpetuating the memory of an event with greater precision than that afforded by oral tradition, of fixing the terms of an agreement with greater certainty than that assured by the testimony of witnesses, and of registering in a more enduring manner those respected customs according to which the members of a single society had agreed to regulate their conduct. So the need for writing was felt, and writing was invented. It seems to have been at first a genuine system of representation, but this gave way to a more conventional representation which preserved merely the characteristic features of objects. Finally by a sort of metaphor analogous to that which had already been introduced into language, the image of a physical object came to express moral ideas. The origin of these signs, like that of words, was ultimately forgotten, and writing became the art of attaching a conventional sign to every idea, to every word, and so by extension, to every modification of ideas and words.

And so mankind had both a written and spoken language, both of which had to be learned and between which an equivalence had to be established.

Certain men of genius, humanity's eternal benefactors, whose names and country are forever buried in oblivion, observed that all the words of a language were nothing but the combinations of a very limited number of primary sounds, but that their number, though very limited, was enough to form an almost limitless number of different combinations. They devised the notion of using visible signs to designate not the ideas or the words that corresponded to ideas, but the simple elements of which words are composed. And here we have the origin of the alphabet; a small number of signs sufficed to write everything, just as a small number of sounds sufficed to say everything. The written language was the same as the spoken language; all that was necessary was to know how to recognize and reproduce these few signs, and this final step assured the progress of the human race forever.

[Perhaps it would be useful today to invent a written language that, reserved exclusively for the sciences, expressing only the combinations of those simple ideas which are the same for every mind, and used only for the reasoning of strict logic, for the precise and calculated operations of the understanding, would be understood by the people of every country and could be translated into every vernacular and would not have to be altered, as happens now, when it passed into general use.

[So by a strange revolution this type of writing, whose survival would only have helped to prolong ignorance, would now become, in the hands of philosophy, a useful tool for the swift propagation of enlightenment and for the perfection of scientific method.]

All peoples whose history is recorded fall somewhere between our present degree of civilization and that which we still see among savage tribes; if we survey in a single sweep the universal history of peoples we see them sometimes making fresh progress, sometimes plunging back into ignorance, sometimes surviving somewhere between these extremes or halted at a certain point, sometimes disappearing from the earth under the conqueror's heel, mixing with the victors or living on in slavery, or sometimes receiving knowledge from some more enlightened people in order to transmit it in their turn to other nations, and so welding an uninterrupted chain between the beginning of historical time and the century in which we live, between the first peoples known to us and the present nations of Europe.

So the picture that I have undertaken to sketch falls into three distinct parts.

In the first our information is based on the tales that travellers bring back to us about the state of the human race among the less civilized peoples, and we have to conjecture the stages by which man living in isolation or restricted to the kind of association necessary for survival, was able to make the first steps on a path whose destination is the use of a developed language. This is the most important distinction and indeed, apart from a few more extensive ideas of morality and the feeble beginnings of social order, the only one separating man from the animals who like him live in a regular and continuous society. We are therefore in this matter forced to rely upon theoretical observations about the development of our intellectual and moral faculties.

In order to carry the history of man up to the point where he practices certain arts, where knowledge of the sciences has already begun to enlighten him, where trade unites the nations and where, finally, alphabetical writing is invented, we can add to this first guide the history of the different societies which have been observed in all their intermediary stages, although none can be traced back far enough to enable us to bridge the gulf which separates these two great eras of the human race.

Here the picture begins to depend in large part on a succession of facts transmitted to us in history, but it is necessary to select them from the history of different peoples, to compare them and combine them in order to extract the hypothetical history of a single people and to compose the picture of its progress.

The history of man from the time when alphabetical writing was known in Greece to the condition of the human race at the present day in the most enlightened countries of Europe is linked by an uninterrupted chain of facts and observations; and so at this point the picture of the march and progress of the human mind becomes truly historical. Philosophy has nothing more to guess, no more hypothetical surmises to make; it is enough to assemble and order the facts and to show the useful truths that can be derived from their connections and from their totality.

When we have shown all this, there will remain one last picture for us to sketch: that of our hopes, and of the progress reserved for future generations, which the constancy of the laws of nature seems to assure them. It will be necessary to indicate by what stages what must appear to us today a fantastic hope ought in time to become possible, and even likely; to show why, in spite of the transitory successes of prejudice and the support that it receives from the corruption of governments or peoples, truth alone will obtain a lasting victory; we shall demonstrate how nature has joined together indissolubly the progress of knowledge and that of liberty, virtue and respect for the natural rights of man; and how these, the only real goods that we possess, though so often separated that they have even been held to be incompatible, must on the contrary become inseparable from the moment when enlightenment has attained a certain level in a number of nations, and has penetrated throughout the whole mass of a great people whose language is universally known and whose commercial relations embrace the whole area of the globe. Once such a close accord has been established between all enlightened men, from then onwards all will be the friends of humanity, all will work together for its perfection and its happiness.

We shall reveal the origin and trace the history of those widespread errors which have somewhat retarded or suspended the progress of reason and which have, as often as forces of a political character, even caused man to fall back into ignorance.

The operations of the understanding that lead us into error or hold us there, from the subtle paralogism which can deceive even the most enlightened of men, to the dreams of a madman, belong no less than the methods of right reasoning or of discourse to the theory of the development of our individual faculties; on the same principle, the way in which general errors are insinuated among peoples and are propagated, transmitted, and perpetuated is all part of the historical picture of the progress of the human mind. Like the truths that perfect and illuminate it, they are the necessary consequences of its activity and of the disproportion that forever holds between what it knows, what it wishes to know, and what it believes it needs to know.

It can even be observed that, according to the general laws of the development of our faculties, certain prejudices have necessarily come into being at each stage of our progress, but they have extended their seductions or their empire long beyond their due season, because men retain the prejudices of their childhood, their country, and their age, long after they have discovered all the truths necessary to destroy them.

Finally, in all countries at all times there are different prejudices varying with the standard of education of the different classes of men and their professions. The prejudices of philosophers harm the progress of truth; those of the less enlightened classes retard the propagation of truths already known; those of certain eminent or powerful professions place obstacles in truth's way: here we see three enemies whom reason is obliged to combat without respite, and whom she vanquishes often only after a long and painful struggle. The history of these struggles, of the birth, triumph, and fall of prejudices, will occupy a great part of this work and will be neither the least important nor the least useful section of it.

[If there is to be a science for predicting the progress of the human race, for directing and hastening it, the history of the progress already achieved must be its foundation.

[Philosophy has had to proscribe in no uncertain terms that superstition which believes that rules of conduct can be found only in the history of past centuries, and truth only in the study of ancient opinions. But ought it not to condemn with equal vigor the prejudice that arrogantly rejects the lessons of experience? Without doubt it is only by meditation, which furnishes us with fruitful combinations of ideas, that we can arrive at any general truths in the science of man. But if the study of inividual human beings is useful to the metaphysician and the moralist, why should the study of societies be any less useful to them and to the political philosopher. If it is useful to observe the various societies that exist side by side, and to study the relations between them, why should it not also be useful to observe them across the passage of time? Even if we suppose that these observations can be neglected in the search for speculative truths, ought they to be ignored when it is a question of applying these truths in practice and of deducing from science the art which should be its useful result? Do not our prejudices and the evils that proceed from them have their origins in the prejudices of our ancestors? Is not one of the most certain ways of undeceiving ourselves from the one and of guarding ourselves against the other, to study their origins and their effects?

[Are we now at the stage when we have nothing further to fear, neither new errors nor the return of old ones; when no corrupting institution can any longer be devised by hypocrisy, and adopted by ignorance or enthusiasm; when no evil combination can any longer ruin a great nation? Would it then be useless to know how in the past nations have been deceived, corrupted or plunged into misery?

[Everything tells us that we are now close upon one of the great revolutions of the human race. If we wish to learn what to expect from it and to procure a certain guide to lead us in the midst of its vicissitudes, what could be more suitable than to have some picture of the revolutions that have gone before it and prepared its way? The present state of enlightenment assures us that this revolution will have a favorable result, but is not this only on condition that we know how to employ our knowledge and resources to their fullest extent? And in order that the happiness that it promises may be less dearly bought, that it may be diffused more rapidly over a greater area, that it may be more complete in its effects, do we not need to study the history of the human spirit to discover what obstacles we still have to fear and what means are open to us of surmounting them?]

I shall divide the area that I propose to cover into nine great stages [and in a tenth I shall venture to offer some observations on the future destiny of the human race.

[I shall confine myself here to presenting the main features that characterize each of these stages; I shall deal only with the outlines, and not stop to mention exceptions or details.

[I shall point out the subjects and the conclusions; the work itself will offer the development and the proof.] . . .

THE NINTH STAGE: FROM DESCARTES TO THE FOUNDATION OF THE FRENCH REPUBLIC

We have watched man's reason being slowly formed by the natural progress of civilization; we have watched superstition seize upon it and corrupt it, and tyranny degrade and deaden the minds of men under the burden of misery and fear.

One nation alone escapes the two-fold influence of tyranny and superstition. From that happy land where freedom had only recently kindled the torch of genius,[1] the mind of man, released from the leading-strings of its infancy, advances with firm steps toward the truth. But this triumph soon encourages tyranny to return, followed by its faithful companion superstition, and the whole of mankind is plunged once more into darkness, which seems as if it must last forever. Yet, little by little, day breaks again; eyes long condemned to darkness catch a glimpse of the light and close again, then slowly become accustomed to it, and at last gaze on it without flinching; once again genius dares to walk abroad on the earth, from which fanaticism and barbarism had exiled it.

We have already seen reason lift her chains, shake herself free from some of them, and, all the time regaining strength, prepare for and advance the moment of her liberation. It remains for us to study the stage in which she finally succeeds in breaking these chains, and when, still compelled to drag their vestiges behind her, she frees herself from them one by one; when at last she can go forward unhindered, and the only obstacles in her path are those that are inevitably renewed at every fresh advance because they are the necessary consequence of the very constitution of our understanding—of the connection, that is, between our means of discovering the truth and the resistance that it offers to our efforts.

Religious intolerance had forced seven of the Belgian provinces to throw off the yoke of Spain and form a federal republic. Religious intolerance alone had aroused the spirit of English liberty, which, exhausted by a protracted and bloody civil war, was finally embodied in a constitution that was for long the admiration of philosophers, but owes its preservation merely to the superstition of the English nation and the hypocrisy of their politicians. And, finally, it was also through priestly persecution that the Swedish nation found courage to reclaim a portion of their rights.

However, in the midst of all these advances, which owed their origin to theological disputes, France, Spain, Hungary, and Bohemia saw their feeble liberties extinguished, or so at least it seemed.

It would be vain to look, in those countries which we call free, for that liberty which infringes none of the natural rights of man; a liberty which not only allows man to possess these rights but allows him to exercise them. For the liberty we find there is based on a system of positive rights, unequally distributed among men, and grants them different privileges according to the town in which they live, the class into which they have been born, the means of which they can dispose, and the profession that they follow. A comparative sketch of the curious inequalities to be found in different countries is the best retort that we can make to those who still uphold their virtue or necessity.

But in these same countries the law guarantees individual and civil liberty, so that if man has not there reached a state of perfection, his natural dignity is not degraded; at least some of his rights are recognized; he can no longer be said to be a slave though he can be said to be not truly free.

In those nations where at this time there was, to a greater or lesser extent, a genuine loss of liberty, the political rights enjoyed by the great mass of the people had been confined within such narrow limits that the destruction of the virtually arbitrary power of the aristocracy under which man had groaned, seems to have more than compensated for their loss. Man lost the title of citizen, which inequality had rendered little more than a name, but the quality of man was accorded greater respect; royal despotism saved him from feudal oppression, and relieved him from a state of humiliation all the more painful because the awareness of his condition was constantly kept alive in him by the number and actual presence of his tyrants. The system of laws tended to improve, both in those states whose constitution was partly free, and in those ruled by despots: in the former because the interests of those who exercised the real power did not invariably conflict with the interests of the people; in the latter because the interests of the despot were often indistinguishable from those of public prosperity, or because the despot's endeavors to destroy the vestiges of feudal or clerical power had imparted to the law a spirit of equality, whose inspiration may have been the desire to establish equality in slavery, but whose effects were often salutary.

We shall give a detailed exposition of the causes that have produced in Europe a kind of despotism for which there is no precedent in earlier ages or in other parts of the world, a despotism in which an all but arbitrary authority, restrained by public opinion, controlled by enlightenment, tempered by self-interest, has often contributed to the progress of wealth, industry, and education, and sometimes even to that of liberty.

Manners have become less violent through the weakening of the prejudices that had maintained their savagery, through the influence of the spirit of industry and commerce which is inimical to unrest and violence as the natural enemies of wealth, through the sense of horror inspired by the none too distant picture of the barbarism of the preceding stage, through a wider diffusion of the philosophical ideas of equality and humanity, and, finally, through the influence, slow but sure, of the general progress of enlightenment.

Religious intolerance remains, but more as an instrument of human prudence, as a tribute to popular prejudice, or as a precaution against popular unrest. Its fury abates; the fires at the stake are seldom lit, and have been replaced by a form of oppression that, if it is often more arbitrary, is less barbarous; and of recent years the persecutions have become much rarer, and the result rather of complacency or habit. Everywhere, and in every respect, governmental practice has slowly and regretfully followed the progress of public opinion and even of philosophy.

Indeed, if in the moral and political sciences there is always a large interval between the point to which philosophers have carried the progress of enlightenment and the degree of enlightenment attained by the average man of education (and it is the body of beliefs held in common by such men that constitutes the generally accepted creed known as public opinion), those who direct public affairs and who immediately influence the fate of the common people, under whatever constitution they may hold their powers, are very far from rising to the level of public opinion; they follow its advance, without ever overtaking it and are always many years behind it and therefore always ignorant of many of the truths that it has learned.

This sketch of the progress of philosophy and of the dissemination of enlightenment, whose more general and more evident effects we have already examined, brings us up to the stage when the influence of progress upon public opinion, of public opinion upon nations or their leaders, suddenly ceases to be a slow imperceptible affair, and produces a revolution in the whole order of several nations, a certain earnest of the revolution that must one day include in its scope the whole of the human race.

After long periods of error, after being led astray by vague or incomplete theories, publicists have at last discovered the true rights of man and how they can all be deduced from the single truth, that *man is a sentient being, capable of reasoning and of acquiring moral ideas.*

They have seen that the maintenance of these rights was the sole object of men's coming together in political societies, and that the social art is the art of guaranteeing the preservation of these rights and their distribution in the most equal fashion over the largest area. It was felt that in every society the means of assuring the rights of the individual should be submitted to certain common rules, but that the authority to choose these means and to determine these rules could belong only to the majority of the members of the society itself; for in making this choice the individual cannot follow his own reason without subjecting others to it, and the will of the majority is the only mark of truth that can be accepted by all without loss of equality.

Each man can in fact genuinely bind himself in advance to the will of the majority which then becomes unanimous; but he can bind only himself; and he cannot engage even himself toward this majority when it fails to respect the rights of the individual, after having once recognized them.

Here we see at once the rights of the majority over society or its members, and the limits of these rights. Here we see the origin of that unanimity which allows the decisions taken by the majority alone to impose an obligation upon all: an obligation which ceases to be legitimate when, with a change in the individuals constituting the majority, the sanction of unanimity no longer exists. Doubtless there are issues on which the decision of the majority is likely to be in favor of error and against the interests of all: but it is still this majority that must decide which issues are not to be subjected to its own direct decision; it is the majority that must appoint those persons whose judgment it considers to be more reliable than its own; it is the majority that must lay down the procedure that it considers most likely to conduct them to the truth; and it may not abdicate its authority to decide whether the decisions they take on its behalf do or do not infringe the rights that are common to all.

So, in the face of such simple principles, we see the disappearance of the belief in the existence of a contract between the people and their lawgivers, which can be annulled only by mutual consent or by the defection of one of the parties; and along with it there disappeared the less servile but no less absurd opinion according to which a nation was forever chained to its constitution once this constitution had been established—as though the right to change it were not the guarantee of every other right, and as though human institutions, which are necessarily defective and capable of perfection as men become more enlightened, could be condemned to remain forever in their infancy. Man was thus compelled to abandon that astute and false policy, which, forgetful of the truth that all men possess equal rights by nature, would seek to apportion those rights unequally between countries, according to the character or prosperity of a country, and the conditions of its industry and commerce, and unequally between men, according to a man's birth, fortune, or profession, and which then calls into being conflicting interests and opposing forces to restore the balance, measures which would have been unnecessary without this policy and which are in any event impotent to control its more dangerous tendencies.

Nor did men any longer dare to divide humanity into two races, the one fated to rule, the other to obey, the one to deceive, the other to be deceived. They had to recognize that all men have an equal right to be informed on all that concerns them, and that none of the authorities established by men over themselves has the right to hide from them one single truth.

These principles, which the noble Sydney paid for with his blood and on which Locke set the authority of his name, were later developed by Rousseau with greater precision, breadth, and energy, and he deserves renown for having established them among the truths that it is no longer permissible to forget or to combat. Man has certain needs and also certain faculties with which to satisfy them; from these faculties and from their products, modified and distributed in different ways, there results an accumulation of wealth out of which must be met the common needs of mankind. But what are the laws according to which this wealth is produced or distributed, accumulated or consumed, increased or dissipated? What, too, are the laws governing that general tendency toward an equilibrium between supply and demand from which it follows that, with any increase in wealth, life becomes easier and men are happier, until a point is reached when no further increase is possible; or that, again, with any decrease in wealth, life becomes harder, suffering increases, until the consequent fall in population restores the balance? How, with all the astonishing multifariousness of labor and production, supply and demand, with all the frightening complexity of conflicting interests that link the survival and well-being of one individual to the general organization of societies, that make his well-being dependent on every accident of nature and every political event, his pain and pleasure on what is happening in the remotest corner of the globe, how, with all this seeming chaos, is it that, by a universal moral law, the efforts made by each individual on his own behalf minister to the welfare of all, and that the interests of society demand that everyone should understand where his own interests lie, and should be able to follow them without hindrance?

Men, therefore, should be able to use their faculties, dispose of their wealth and provide for their needs in complete freedom. The common interest of any society, far from demanding that they should restrain such activity, on the contrary, forbids any interference with it; and as far as this aspect of public order is concerned, the guaranteeing to each man his natural rights is at once the whole of social utility, the sole duty of the social power, the only right that the general will can legitimately exercise over the individual.

But it is not enough merely that this principle should be acknowledged by society; the public authority has specific duties to fulfill. It must establish by law recognized measures for the determination of the weight, volume, size, and length of all articles of trade; it must create a coinage to serve as a common measure of value and so to facilitate comparison between the value of one article of trade and that of another, so that having a value itself, it can be exchanged against anything else that can be given one; for without this common measure trade must remain confined to barter, and can acquire very little activity or scope.

The wealth produced each year provides a portion for disposal which is not required to pay for either the labor that has produced it or the labor required to ensure its replacement by an equal or greater production of wealth. The owner of this disposable portion does not owe it directly to his work; he possesses it independently of the use to which he puts his faculties in order to provide for his needs. Hence it is out of this available portion of the annual wealth that the public authority, without violating anyone's rights, can establish the funds required for the security of the State, the preservation of peace within its borders, the protection of individual rights, the exercise of those powers established for the formation or execution of the law, and, finally, the maintenance of public prosperity.

There are certain undertakings and institutions which are beneficial to society in general, and which it therefore ought to initiate, control, and supervise; these provide services which the wishes and interests of individuals cannot provide by themselves, and which advance the progress of agriculture, industry, or trade or the prevention or alleviation of inevitable natural hardships or unforeseen accidents.

Up to the stage of which we speak and even for a long time afterwards, these various undertakings were left to chance, to the greed of governments, to the skill of charlatans or to the prejudices or self-interest of powerful sections of the community. A disciple of Descartes, however, the famous and ill-starred Johan de Witt, felt that political economy ought like every other science to submit itself to the principles of philosophy and the rigor of calculation.

Political economy made little progress until the Peace of Utrecht gave Europe the promise of lasting peace. From then onwards one notices an increasing intellectual interest taken in this hitherto neglected subject; and the new science was advanced by Stewart, Smith, and more particularly the French economists, at least as far as precision and the purity of its principles are involved, to a point that one could hardly have hoped to reach so soon after such a long period of indifference.

But this progress in politics and political economy was caused primarily by the progress in general philosophy and metaphysics, if we take the latter word in its broadest sense.

Descartes had brought philosophy back to reason; for he had understood that it must be derived entirely from those primary and evident truths which we can discover by observing the operations of the human mind. Soon, however, his impatient imagination snatched it from the path that he had traced for it, and for a time it seemed that philosophy had regained her independence only to be led astray by new errors.

At last, Locke grasped the thread by which philosophy should be guided; he showed that an exact and precise analysis of ideas, which reduces them step by step to other ideas of more immediate origin or of simpler composition, is the only way to avoid being lost in that chaos of incomplete, incoherent, and indeterminate notions which chance presents to us at hazard and we unthinkingly accept.

By this same analysis he proved that all ideas are the result of the operations of our minds upon sensations we have received, or, to put it more exactly, that they are the combinations of these sensations presented to us simultaneously by the faculty of memory in such a way that our attention is arrested and our perception is thereby limited to no more than a part of such compound sensations.

He showed that if we attach a word to each idea after analyzing it and circumscribing it, we shall succeed in remembering the idea ever afterwards in a uniform fashion; that is to say, the idea will always be formed of the same simple ideas, it will always be enclosed within the same limits, and it can in consequence be used in a chain of reasoning without any risk of confusion. On the other hand, if a word is used in such a way that it does not correspond to a determinate idea, it can at different times arouse different ideas in the same person's mind, and this is the most fecund source of error in reasoning.

Locke, finally, was the first man who dared to set a limit to the human understanding, or rather to determine the nature of the truths that it can come to know and of the objects it can comprehend.

This method was soon adopted by all philosophers and, by applying it to moral science, to politics and to social economy, they were able to make almost as sure progress in these sciences as they had in the natural sciences. They were able to admit only proven truths, to separate these truths from whatever as yet remained doubtful and uncertain, and to ignore whatever is and always will be impossible to know.

[Similarly, the analysis of our feelings leads to our finding, in the development of our capacity to feel pleasure and pain, the origin of our moral ideas, the foundation of those general truths which, resulting from these ideas, determine the necessary and immutable laws of justice and injustice, and, finally, the motives that we have for conforming to them, motives which spring from the very nature of our sensibility, from what might be called our moral constitution.]

This metaphysical method became virtually a universal instrument. Men learned to use it in order to perfect the methods of the physical sciences, to throw light on their principles and to examine the validity of their proofs; and it was extended to the examination of facts and to the rules of taste.

Thus it was applied to all the various undertakings of the human understanding, and by means of it the operations of the mind in every branch of knowledge were subjected to analysis, and the nature of the truths and the kind of certainty we can expect to find from each of these branches of knowledge was thereby revealed. It is this new step in philosophy that has forever imposed a barrier between mankind and the errors of its infancy, a barrier that should save it from relapsing into its former errors under the influence of new prejudices, just as it should assure the eventual eradication of those that still survive unrecognized, and should make it certain that any that may take their place will exercise only a faint influence and enjoy only an ephemeral existence.

In Germany, however, a man of vast and profound genius laid the foundations of a new doctrine. His ardent and passionate imagination could not rest satisfied with a modest philosophy and leave unsolved those great questions about the spirituality or the survival of the human soul, about man's freedom or the freedom of God, about the existence of pain and evil in a universe governed by an all-powerful intelligence whose wisdom, justice, and loving-kindness ought, it would seem, to exclude the possibility of their existence. He cut the knot which the most skillful analysis would never have been able to untie and constructed the universe from simple, indestructible entities equal by their very nature. The relations of each of these entities with all the others, which with it form part of the system of the universe, determine those qualities of it whereby it differs from every other. The human soul and the least atom of a block of stone are, each of them, one of these monads, and they differ only in the different place assigned to them in the universal order. Out of all the possible combinations of these beings an infinite intelligence has preferred one, and could have preferred one only, the most perfect of all. If that which exists offends us by the misery and crime that we see in it, it is still true that any other combination would have had more painful results.

We shall explain this system which, being adopted, or at least upheld, by Leibniz's compatriots, has retarded the progress of philosophy among them. One entire school of English philosophers enthusiastically embraced and eloquently defended the doctrine of optimism, but they were less subtle and less profound than Leibniz, for whereas he based his doctrine on the belief that an all-powerful intelligence, by the very necessity of its nature, could choose only the best of all possible worlds, the English philosophers sought to prove their doctrine by appealing to observation of the particular world in which we live and thereby sacrificing all the advantages possessed by this system so long as it remains abstract and general; they lost themselves in details, which were too often either revolting or ridiculous.

In Scotland, however, other philosophers finding that the analysis of the development of our actual faculties led to no principle that could provide a sufficiently pure or solid basis for the morality of our actions, thought to attribute a new faculty to the human soul, distinct from but associated with those of feeling or thinking, a faculty whose existence they proved only by showing that they could not do without it. We shall recount the history of these opinions and shall show how, if they have retarded the progress of philosophy, they have advanced the dissemination of philosophical ideas.

Up till now we have shown the progress of philosophy only in the men who have cultivated, deepened, and perfected it. It remains for us to show what have been its effects on public opinion; how reason, while it learned to safeguard itself against the errors into which the imagination and respect for authority had so often led it, at last found a sure method of discovering and recognizing truth; and how at the same time it destroyed the prejudices of the masses which had for so long afflicted and corrupted the human race.

At last man could proclaim aloud his right, which for so long had been ignored, to submit all opinions to his own reason and to use in the search for truth the only instrument for its recognition that he has been given. Every man learned with a sort of pride that nature had not forever condemned him to base his beliefs on the opinions of others; the superstitions of antiquity and the abasement of reason before the transports of supernatural religion disappeared from society as from philosophy.

Soon there was formed in Europe a class of men who were concerned less with the discovery or development of the truth than with its propagation, men who while devoting themselves to the tracking down of prejudices in the hiding places where the priests, the schools, the governments, and all long-established institutions had gathered and protected them, made it their life-work to destroy popular errors rather than to drive back the frontiers of human knowledge—an indirect way of aiding its progress which was not less fraught with peril, nor less useful.

In England Collins and Bolingbroke, in France Bayle, Fontenelle, Voltaire, Montesquieu, and the schools founded by these famous men, fought on the side of truth, using in turn all the weapons with which learning, philosophy, wit, and literary talent can furnish reason; using every mood from humor to pathos, every literary form from the vast erudite encyclopædia to the novel or the broadsheet of the day; covering truth with a veil that spared weaker eyes and excited one to guess what lay beyond it; skillfully flattering prejudices so as to attack them the better; seldom threatening them, and then always either only one in its entirety or several partially; sometimes conciliating the enemies of reason by seeming to wish only for a half-tolerance in religious matters, only for a half-freedom in politics; sparing despotism when tilting against the absurdities of religion, and religion when abusing tyranny; yet always attacking the principles of these two scourges even when they seemed to be against only their more revolting or ridiculous abuses, and laying their axes to the very roots of these sinister trees when they appeared to be lopping off a few stray branches; sometimes teaching the friends of liberty that superstition is the invincible shield behind which despotism shelters and should therefore be the first victim to be sacrificed, the first chain to be broken, and sometimes denouncing it to the despots as the real enemy of their power, and frightening them with stories of its secret machinations and its bloody persecutions; never ceasing to demand the independence of reason and the freedom of the press as the right and the salvation of mankind; protesting with indefatigable energy against all the crimes of fanaticism and tyranny; pursuing, in all matters of religion, administration, morals, and law, anything that bore the marks of tyranny, harshness, or barbarism; invoking the name of nature to bid kings, captains, magistrates, and priests to show respect for human life; laying to their charge, with vehemence and severity, the blood their policy or their indifference still spilled on the battlefield or on the scaffold; and finally, taking for their battle cry—*reason, tolerance, humanity.*

Such was the new philosophy: an object of common hatred to all those many sections of society which owe their existence to prejudice, their survival to error, their power to credulity; welcomed nearly everywhere, but persecuted none the less; numbering kings, priests, great men and lawyers among its disciples and among its enemies. Its leaders were, in general, astute enough to escape vengeance, although exposing themselves to hatred; and to hide from persecution, though remaining sufficiently in evidence to lose none of the glory.

A government would often reward them with one hand, and pay their slanderers with the other; proscribe them, and feel honored that they had been born on their soil; punish their opinions, and yet feel humiliated if they were suspected of not sharing them.

These opinions were to become those of all enlightened men, professed by some, dissimulated by others, with a hypocrisy whose transparency varied with their strength or timidity of character, and which was dependent on whether they yielded to the interests of their profession or to those of their vanity. But already the interests of vanity were so strong, that, in place of the profound dissimulation of preceding ages, men were content with a prudent reserve for themselves and often even in others.

We shall trace the progress of this philosophy in different parts of Europe where it was soon rapidly diffused, despite governmental and priestly inquisitions, by the almost universal medium of the French language. We shall show how skillful policy and superstition recruited against it every motive for mistrusting reason that human ingenuity could suggest, every argument that demonstrated its weakness and its limitations, and how people contrived to employ even total skepticism in the service of credulity.

That simple system which regarded the enjoyment of an unlimited freedom as the surest encouragement to trade and industry; which delivered the masses from the destructive scourge and humiliating yoke of taxes unjustly imposed, and extravagantly and often cruelly raised, and substituted for them just, equal, and almost imperceptible contributions; which linked the state's true power and wealth to the well-being of the individual and a respect for his rights; which bound together in bonds of mutual happiness the different classes into which societies are naturally divided; which preached the comforting doctrine of the brotherhood of man, whose gentle harmony should no longer be upset by the self-interest of nations: all these principles, attractive on account of their nobility, simplicity, and breadth of vision, were propagated enthusiastically by the French economists. Their success was less prompt and less general than that of the philosophers, for the prejudices they had to fight were less crude, and the errors subtler. They had to enlighten before they could disabuse of error, and to teach common sense before they could employ it as an arbiter.

If, however, they were able to win only a small number of converts to their doctrine in its entirety, if people were frightened of the universality of their maxims and the inflexibility of their principles, and if they themselves harmed their cause by affecting an obscure and dogmatic manner of exposition, by appearing to favor free trade at the expense of political liberty and by presenting in too magisterial and dogmatic a fashion certain parts of their system that they had insufficiently investigated, at least they succeeded in showing how odious and dispicable were those cowardly, crafty and corrupt political doctrines which looked for the prosperity of a nation in the impoverishment of its neighbors, in the short-sighted policy of a protectionist regime and in the petty calculations of a tyrannical exchequer.

The salutary influence of the new truths with which genius had enriched philosophy, politics, and public economy, and which had been adopted more or less generally by enlightened men, was felt far afield.

The art of printing had spread so widely and had so greatly increased the number of books published; the books that were published catered so successfully for every degree of knowledge, or industry, or income; they were so proportioned to every taste, or cast of mind; they presented such easy and often such pleasant means of instruction; they opened so many doors to truth that it was no longer possible that they should all of them be closed again, that there was no class and no profession from which the truth could be withheld. And so, though there remained a great number of people condemned to ignorance either voluntary or enforced, the boundary between the cultivated and the uncultivated had been almost entirely effaced, leaving an insensible gradation between the two extremes of genius and stupidity.

Thus, an understanding of the natural rights of man, the belief that these rights are inalienable and indefeasible, a strongly expressed desire for liberty of thought and letters, of trade and industry, and for the alleviation of the people's suffering, for the proscription of all penal laws against religious dissenters and the abolition of torture and barbarous punishments, the desire for a milder system of criminal legislation and jurisprudence which should give complete security to the innocent, and for a simpler civil code, more in conformance with reason and nature, indifference in all matters of religion which now were relegated to the status of superstitions and political impostures, a hatred of hypocrisy and fanaticism, a contempt for prejudice, zeal for the propagation of enlightenment: all these principles, gradually filtering down from philosophical works to every class of society whose education went beyond the catechism and the alphabet, became the common faith, the badges of all those who were neither Machiavellians nor fools. In some countries these principles formed a public opinion sufficiently widespread for even the mass of the people to show a willingness to be guided by it and to obey it. For a feeling of humanity, a tender and active compassion for all the misfortunes that afflict the human race and a horror of anything that in the actions of public institutions, or governments, or individuals, adds new pains to those that are natural and inevitable, were the natural consequences of those principles; and this feeling exhaled from all the writings and all the speeches of the time, and already its happy influence had been felt in the laws and the public institutions, even of those nations still subject to despotism.

The philosophers of different nations who considered the interests of the whole of humanity without distinction of country, race, or creed, formed a solid phalanx banded together against all forms of error, against all manifestations of tyranny, despite their differences in matters of theory. Activated by feelings of universal philanthropy, they fought injustice even when it occurred in countries other than their own and could not harm them personally; they fought injustice even when it was their own country that was guilty of acts against others; they raised an outcry in Europe against the crimes of greed that sullied the shores of America, Africa, and Asia. English and French philosophers considered themselves honored to be called the *friends* of the black races whom their foolish tyrants disdained to consider as members of the human race. In France writers lavished encomiums on the new-won tolerance accorded in Russia and Sweden: while in Italy Beccaria denounced the barbarous tenets of French jurisprudence. In France writers sought to free England from her commercial prejudices and her superstitious respect for the vices of her constitution and her laws, while the worthy Howard denounced to the French the callous indifference which was causing the death of so many human victims in their prison-cells and hospitals.

Force or persuasion on the part of governments, priestly intolerance, and even national prejudices, had all lost their deadly power to smother the voice of truth, and nothing could now protect the enemies of reason or the oppressors of freedom from a sentence to which the whole of Europe would soon subscribe.

Finally, we see the rise of a new doctrine which was to deal the final blow to the already tottering structure of prejudice—the doctrine of the indefinite perfectibility of the human race of which Turgot, Price, and Priestley were the first and the most brilliant apostles. This doctrine belongs to the tenth stage of our history, and there we shall examine it in greater detail. But here we must describe the origin and the progress of a false philosophy against which the support of that doctrine is so necessary if reason is to triumph.

Born of pride in some and of self-interest in others, conniving at the perpetuation of ignorance and the continued reign of error, it has had its numerous adherents ready to corrupt men's reason with brilliant paradoxes or to lull it into the comfortable indolence of absolute pyrrhonism; so to despise the human race as to teach it that the progress of knowledge would be ·not only useless but dangerous both to its happiness and to its freedom; ready to infuse it with a false enthusiasm and grandiose illusions about a new species of wisdom that would absolve virtue from the need of enlightenment and common sense from the verdict of fact; ready, on the one hand, to speak of philosophy and the sciences as subjects too arduous for a mere human being with limited powers, at the mercy of his wants, weighed down with the pressing cares of daily life; and, on the other, to pour scorn on these sciences as a heap of uncertain and extravagant speculations, and to maintain that in all matters the skill, the practical experience of the statesman should be preferred to them. The adherents of this philosophy chose the moment when knowledge was progressing more rapidly than ever before, to complain incessantly of its decline; the moment when men were at last beginning to remember their rights and to employ their reason, to deplore the degeneration of mankind: they even went so far as to predict that by a swing of the pendulum mankind was about to plunge once more into barbarism, ignorance, and slavery, just when everything combined to show that men had left these evils behind them forever. Indeed, it seemed that they were either humiliated by the progress of mankind because they had made no contribution toward it, or terrified because it presaged their fall from power and importance. [Moreover, some charlatans, less foolish than those who were still clumsily trying to shore up the fabric of ancient superstitions whose foundations had been undermined by philosophy, endeavored to construct out of their ruins a religious system in which reason would be called upon to make only a partial submission and would remain free to believe what she wished, so long as she consented to believe something incomprehensible. Others tried through secret societies to revive the forgotten mysteries of ancient theurgy; abandoning the masses to their errors while chaining their disciples in new superstitions, they had the audacity to hope that they might bring back, for the benefit of a few initiates, the ancient tyranny of the pontiff kings of India and Egypt. But philosophy, resting on the unshakable foundations prepared for her by science, opposed to their attempts a wall against which they broke in vain.]

A comparison of the attitude of mind I have already described with the forms of government prevalent at that time would have made it easy to foresee that a great revolution was inevitable, and that there were only two ways in which it could come about; either the people themselves would establish the reasonable and natural principles that philosophy had taught them to admire, or governments would hasten to anticipate them and carry out what was required by public opinion. If the revolution should come about in the former way it would be swifter and more thorough, but more violent; if it should come about in the latter way, it would be less swift and less thorough, but also less violent: if in the former way, then freedom and happiness would be purchased at the price of transient evils; if in the latter, then these evils would be avoided but, it might be, at the price of long delaying the harvest of the fruits that the revolution must, nevertheless, inevitably bear. The ignorance and corruption of the governments of the time saw that it came about in the former way, and the human race was avenged by the swift triumph of liberty and reason.

Simple common sense taught the inhabitants of the British colonies that Englishmen born beyond the Atlantic Ocean had been endowed by nature with exactly the same rights as other Englishmen born under the meridian of Greenwich, and that a difference of 70 degrees of longitude was not enough to change these rights. They had, perhaps, a better idea than most Europeans of what were the rights common to every member of the human race and among them they included the right not to pay taxes without consent. But the British government affected to believe that God had created America, as he had created Asia, for the pleasure of the inhabitants of London; for it wanted to have in its power a vassal nation beyond the seas that, when the time came, could be used to crush revolt in England. It therefore ordered the compliant representatives of the English people to violate the rights of America, and to impose taxation on her without asking her consent. America proclaimed that this injustice released her from the obligations binding her to England, and she declared her independence.

We see then for the first time, a great people delivered from all its chains, giving itself in peace the laws and the constitution that it believed most likely to bring it happiness. Its geographical situation and its old political form obliging it to form a federal republic, there were at once set up thirteen republican constitutions, each based on a solemn recognition of the natural rights of man, and having for its chief end the preservation of these rights. We shall sketch the form of these constitutions, and show how much they owed to the progress of the political sciences; and we shall show how they were tainted with the prejudices that those who drafted them had imbibed in their youth: how, for example, their simplicity was impaired by the determination to preserve a balance of power within the state, and how they had as their principle the identity of interests rather than the equality of rights. We shall demonstrate not only that this principle of the identity of interests, once made the basis for political rights, is a violation of the rights of those who are thereby debarred from a complete exercise of them, but also that this identity ceases to exist once it gives rise to genuine inequality. We shall insist on this point because the fallacy involved in accepting this principle is the only one still likely to be dangerous, since it is the only one to which intelligent men are not yet wholly alive. We shall show how the American republics put into practice the idea, which was still new even in theory, of the necessity for establishing by law a regular and peaceful procedure for reforming the constitution itself, and of distinguishing the authority entrusted with such reforms from the ordinary legislative authority.

But in the war that arose between two enlightened peoples, of which one defended the natural rights of humanity while the other opposed to it the impious doctrine that these rights could be submitted to prescription, to political interests, to written conventions, the issue was pleaded at the bar of public opinion before the whole of Europe, and the rights of men were nobly upheld, and expounded without restriction or reserve, in writings that circulated freely from the shores of the Neva to those of the Guadalquivir. Reports of this great debate penetrated to the most oppressed countries and the most isolated settlements, and the men who lived there were astonished to hear that they had rights. They learned what they were, and they learned that other men had had the courage to defend them or to win them back.

The American revolution, then, was about to spread to Europe; and if there existed a country where sympathy with the American cause had diffused more widely than elsewhere its writings and its principles, a country that was at once the most enlightened and the most enslaved of lands, a country that possessed at the same time the most enlightened philosophers and the most crassly and insolently ignorant government, a country whose laws were so far below the level of public intelligence that not even patriotism or prejudice could attach the people to its ancient institutions, was not this country destined by the very nature of things to start that revolution which the friends of humanity awaited with such impatience and such high hopes? It was inevitable, then, that the revolution should begin in France.

The maladroitness of her government precipitated it, her philosophers guided its principles and the power of her people destroyed the obstacles which might have stood in its way.

The revolution in France was more far-reaching than that in America and therefore more violent: for the Americans, who were content with the civil and criminal code that they had received from England; who had no vicious system of taxation to reform; and no feudal tyrannies, no hereditary distinctions, no rich, powerful, and privileged corporations, no system of religious intolerance to destroy, limited themselves to establishing a new authority in place of that which had been exercised up till then by the British. None of these innovations affected the ordinary people or changed the relations between individuals. In France, on the contrary, the revolution was to embrace the entire economy of society, change every social relation and find its way down to the furthest links of the political chain, even down to those individuals who, living in peace on their private fortune or on the fruits of their labor, had no reason to participate in public affairs—neither opinion nor occupation nor the pursuit of wealth, power, or fame.

The Americans, who gave the impression that they were fighting only against the tyrannical prejudices of the mother country, had the rivals of England as their allies; and, at the same time, other powers, jealous of her wealth and her pride, lent the support of their good-will to the triumph of justice so that the whole of Europe was united against the oppressor. The French, on the contrary, attacked at once the despotism of kings, the political inequality of any constitution only partly free, the pride of the nobility, the domination, intolerance, and wealth of the priesthood, and the abuses of the feudal system, all of which are still rampant in most of Europe, so that the European powers inevitably united on the side of tyranny. Consequently, all that France found raised in her favor were the voices of a few wise men, and the timid prayers of the down-trodden masses, and even this support calumny endeavored to wrest from her.

We shall show in what ways the principles from which the constitution and laws of France were derived were purer, more precise, and more profound than those that guided the Americans; how they more successfully escaped every kind of prejudice; how the equality of rights was nowhere replaced by the identity of interest, which is only a feeble and hypocritical substitute; how the theory of the limitation of powers took the place of that futile balance of powers which had so long been admired; and how for the first time in a great nation necessarily divided into a large number of isolated factions, men had the courage to allow the people to exercise their sovereign right—the right to obey only those laws the procedure for whose enactment is sanctioned by their direct assent, even if the actual enactment is delegated to their representatives, laws which, if the people should find them injurious to their interests or rights, they can revoke by the legitimate assertion of their sovereign will.

From the moment when the genius of Descartes gave men's minds that general impetus which is the first principle of a revolution in the destinies of the human race, to the happy time of complete and pure social liberty when man was able to regain his natural independence only after having lived through a long series of centuries of slavery and misery, the picture of the progress of the mathematical and physical sciences reveals an immense horizon whose different parts must be distributed and ordered if we wish to grasp the significance of the whole and properly observe its relations.

Not only did the application of algebra to geometry become a fruitful source of discoveries in these two sciences, but in proving by this great example how in general the methods of calculating magnitudes could be extended to all questions that were concerned with the measuring of extension. Descartes announced in advance that they would be applied with equal success to all the objects whose relations are capable of precision; and this great discovery, showing for the first time this final objective of the sciences, which is to subject all truths to the rigor of calculation, gave hope of reaching it and afforded a glimpse of the means toward that end.

Soon this discovery was followed by the discovery of a new calculus, showing how to find the rate of increase or decrease of a variable quantity, or to rediscover the quantity itself from the knowledge of this rate, regardless of whether one imputes a finite magnitude to this increase, or whether the rate is to be determined for a given instant—that is, when the increase is nil; a method which, as it applies to all combinations of variable magnitudes and to all hypotheses concerning their variations, also allows us to determine, for all objects whose changes are capable of precise measurement, either the relations between the elements when only those between the objects are known, or the relations between the objects when only those between the elements are known.

We owe to Newton and to Leibniz the invention of these calculi for which the work of the geometers of the previous generation had prepared the way. Their continuous progress for more than a century has been the work of several men of genius whose glory they made. They present to the eyes of the philosopher who can observe them even without being able to follow them, an imposing monument to the power of the human intelligence.

When we come to describe the formation and the principles of the language of algebra, the only really exact and analytical language yet in existence, the nature of the technical methods of this science and how they compare with the natural workings of the human understanding, we shall show that even though this method is by itself only an instrument pertaining to the science of quantities, it contains within it the principles of a universal instrument, applicable to all combinations of ideas.

Rational mechanics soon became an extensive and profound science. The true laws of the collision of bodies about which Descartes had been mistaken finally became known.

Huyghens discovered the laws of circular motion. At the same time he furnished the method of determining to what circle each element of any curve ought to belong. By combining these two theories Newton discovered the theory of curvilinear motion and applied it to those laws which Kepler had found to be followed by the planets in their elliptical orbits.

It was discovered that a planet, imagined to be projected into space at a certain moment with a certain speed and in a predetermined direction, described an ellipse round the sun by reason of a force acting upon it and inversely proportional to the square of the distance. The same force keeps the satellites in their orbits round the principal planet. And it extends to the entire system of heavenly bodies and acts reciprocally between all the elements composing them.

The regularity of planetary ellipses is disturbed by this force and the calculus explains in detail these perturbations. It acts upon the comets for which the same theory holds, and determines their orbits and predicts their return. The movements we notice in the axes of rotation of the earth and of the moon prove once again the existence of this universal force. It is finally the cause of the weight of bodies on the earth, in which it appears to be constant because we cannot observe them at sufficiently varied distances from the center of action.

Thus man at last discovered one of the physical laws of the universe, a law that has hitherto remained unique, like the glory of the man who revealed it.

A hundred years of labor have confirmed that law which appears to govern all celestial phenomena to a degree that is, so to say, miraculous. Every time that a phenomenon appears not to come under that law, this uncertainty soon becomes the occasion of a new triumph.

Philosophy is nearly always obliged to look into the writings of a man of genius in order to find the secret thread that guided him; but in this case, interest, inspired by admiration, has discovered and preserved some precious stories which enable us to follow Newton's progress step by step. These will be useful to us in showing how the happy conjunctions of chance combined with the efforts of genius to lead to a great discovery, and how less favorable conjunctions might have retarded them or reserved them for other hands.

But Newton perhaps did more for the progress of the human mind than discover this general law of nature; he taught men to admit in physics only precise and mathematical theories, which account not merely for the existence of a certain phenomenon but also for its quantity and extension. Nevertheless he was accused of reviving the occult qualities of the Ancients because he confined himself to locating the general cause of celestial phenomena in one simple fact, whose incontestable reality was proved by observation. And this accusation itself proves how much the methods of science still stood in need of enlightenment from philosophy.

A host of problems of statics and dynamics had been successively formulated and solved when d'Alembert discovered a general principle, which alone was enough to determine the movement of any number of particles urged by any number of forces, and related to each other by certain conditions. Soon he extended this same principle to finite bodies of a determinate figure, to those which, being elastic or flexible, could change their figure according to certain laws while still preserving certain relations between their parts. Finally he extended it to fluids themselves whether of a constant density or in a state of expansion. A new calculus was required for the solution of these latter questions. It could not escape his genius, and consequently mechanics was transformed into a pure calculus.

These discoveries belong to the mathematical sciences. But the nature of the law of universal gravitation and of the principles of mechanics and their consequences insofar as they reflect on the eternal order of the universe are within the province of philosophy. It was learned that all bodies are subject to necessary laws which tend by themselves to produce or maintain equilibrium and create or preserve regularity of motion.

The knowledge of the laws that govern celestial phenomena; the discoveries of mathematical analysis, leading to more exact methods of calculating those phenomena; the perfection beyond all expectation attained by optical instruments and instruments whose precise calibration determines the precision of the observations made with their help;

the precision of machines destined to measure time; the more general interest in the sciences and the concern of governments which made for an increase of astronomers and observatories—all these causes contributed to the progress of astronomy. The sky was enriched for man with new stars and he learned how to determine and predict with exactitude their position and their movements.

Physics, having gradually delivered itself from the vague explanations introduced by Descartes, just as it had shaken off the scholastic absurdities, is now merely the art of putting nature to the question by experiment so as then to be able by calculation to deduce more general facts.

The weight of the air has been measured and found out. It was discovered that the transmission of light is not instantaneous, and its speed was measured. From this a calculation was made of the effects that should result for the apparent position of the heavenly bodies. The sun's rays were divided up into simpler light rays having different degrees of refrangibility and diversely colored. The rainbow was explained and the means of producing its colors or making them disappear have been submitted to calculation. Electricity, which was known only as the property possessed by certain substances of attracting light bodies when rubbed, became one of the general phenomena of the universe. The cause of lightning is no longer a mystery, and Franklin has revealed to men the art of harnessing it and using it as they wish. New instruments were employed to measure variations in the weight of the atmosphere, in the humidity of the air, and in the temperature of a body. A new science under the name of meteorology taught us how to understand and sometimes to predict atmospheric phenomena whose laws we shall doubtless discover one day.

In presenting the picture of these discoveries we shall show how the methods which led the physicists in their researches were purified and perfected; how the art of making experiments and of constructing instruments progressively acquired greater precision, so that physics was not only enriched day by day with new truths but the truths which had already been proved acquired greater exactitude; not only has a mass of hitherto unknown facts been observed and analyzed, but all have been submitted in detail to the most rigorous methods.

Physics had had to fight only against the prejudices of scholasticism and the appeal, so seductive to idle minds, of general hypotheses. Other obstacles impeded the progress of chemistry. People had imagined that it would yield the secret of making gold and the secret of immortal life.

Great interests make for superstition. People thought that such promises, which flattered the two strongest passions of the vulgar and excited the desire for glory, could not be fulfilled by any ordinary methods, and all the extravagances that demented credulity had ever invented, seemed crammed together into the heads of chemists.

But these dreams gradually gave way to the mechanical philosophy of Descartes, which in turn was rejected and replaced by a truly experimental chemistry. Observation of the phenomena that accompany the composition and decomposition of bodies, the search for the laws governing these operations, the analysis of substances into ever simpler elements acquired an increasing precision and rigor.

But we must mention in addition to this progress in chemistry some of the improvements that, affecting, as they do, a given scientific system in its entirety by extending its methods rather than by increasing its truths, foretell and prepare a successful revolution. Such was the discovery of new methods of collecting and subjecting to experiment the expansible fluids that had hitherto eluded such examination. [This was a discovery that changed the entire system of chemistry; for it made possible control over a whole range of new entities as well as over those that were already known but had remained beyond the reach of research, and it added a new element to almost all compounds.] Another such improvement was the formation of a language in which the names designating the substances indicate either the relations or differences between those substances having a common element, or the class to which they belong. Other such improvements were the introduction of a scientific notation in which these substances are represented by analytically combined characters and that can express even the most common operations; the general laws of affinities; the use of all the methods and instruments that are employed in physics for calculating the results of experiments with rigorous precision; and finally the application of mathematics to the phenomena of crystallization and to the laws describing how the elements of certain bodies unite and take regular and constant form. Men who had for so long been satisfied with superstitions or philosophical dreams about the formation of the earth rather than proper inquiry, now at last felt the need to study, with scrupulous attention, the substances found on its surface or, where they had been led by necessity to penetrate it, in its interior, their disposition and their regular or fortuitous distribution. They learned to recognize the marks of the slow and prolonged action of sea-water, subterranean water, and fire upon it; and to distinguish those parts of the surface and external crust of the earth where the irregularities and disposition of substances, and often the substances themselves, are the work of fire, subterranean water, and sea-water from other parts of the earth which have been formed for the most part from heterogeneous substances and bear the impress of earlier revolutions whose causes are still unknown to us.

Minerals, vegetables, and animals are divided into several species whose members differ only in an imperceptible and irregular fashion, or for purely local causes. Several of these species resemble one another and possess a certain number of common qualities which serve to establish the successive and increasingly extensive divisions. Naturalists have learned to classify individuals methodically according to determined characteristics which are easy to grasp, the only method of distinction possible with this innumerable multitude of different beings. These methods are a kind of real language in which every object is designated by some of its more constant qualities and by means of which, knowing these qualities, we may find the name of the object in the conventional language. These same languages, when they are well constructed, also tell us what are, for each class of natural beings, the really essential qualities whose conjunction implies a more or less complete resemblance in the remaining properties.

If we have sometimes seen men, in their pride so very conscious of the toil that the invention of these methods cost them, attach an exaggerated importance to them and take for the science itself what is merely its dictionary and its grammar, a false philosophy has also led them into the opposite excess, of holding too low an opinion of these same methods and identifying them with an arbitrary system of nomenclature, barren, painstaking compilations.

The chemical analysis of substances in the three great kingdoms of nature; the description of their external form; the exposition of their physical qualities and their ordinary properties; the history of the development of organic bodies, whether animals or plants, and of their nutrition and reproduction; the details of their organic structures; the anatomy of their different parts and the functions of each of these parts; the history of the habits of animals and of their efforts to procure food and shelter, to seize their prey, or to hide from their enemies; the family or species societies which they form together; that body of truths which is attained by going through the enormous chain of natural entities; the successive links that lead from brute matter to the lowest degree of organic life, from organic matter to that which gives the first indications of spontaneous movement and sensitivity, and finally from that to man; the relations of all these entities to man, either relative to his needs or in the analogies which bring him nearer to them, or in the differences that separate him from them:—this is the picture which natural history gives us today.

Physical man has become himself the object of a separate science; *anatomy*, which in its ordinary meaning includes physiology, that science which had been retarded by a superstitious respect for the dead, profited from the general enfeeblement of prejudice and successfully undermined the support that it received from powerful men who were interested in its preservation. Its progress seems somehow to have come to a stop, and to await the discovery of improved instruments and new methods. And it now seems to be almost reduced to the study of the comparisons between the parts of animals and those of men, the organs common to different species, and the manner in which similar functions are exercised, in its search for those truths which are at the moment not open to human observation. Almost everything which the eye of the observer has been able to discover with the aid of a microscope is already unveiled. The future development of anatomy seems to depend on the possibility of experiment which has proved so useful to the progress of other sciences. But this necessary means of improvement has been denied to anatomy by the very nature of its subject.

The circulation of the blood was for long known; but the disposition of the vessels carrying the chyle which is destined to mix with it so as to make good its losses; the existence of a gastric juice which brings about the necessary decomposition of food in order to separate those parts fit to be assimilated to living fluids and organic matter; the changes that various parts and organs undergo, both in the period between conception and birth, and after birth in the different ages of life; the identification of the parts endowed with sensitivity or with that property of irritability discovered by Haller and found common to almost all organic beings—this is what physiology discovered and established by certain observation during that brilliant era; and so many important truths should secure general forgiveness for those earlier mechanical, chemical, and organic explanations which have successively overburdened physiology with hypotheses baneful to the progress of science and dangerous when their application was extended to medicine.

To this picture of the sciences we must append a picture of the arts. For the arts, now resting on the sciences, made sure progress and broke the chains in which routine had hitherto bound them.

We shall show the influence that the progress of mechanics, astronomy, optics, and the science of measuring time exercised over the art of building, moving, and guiding ships. We shall explain how the increase in the number of observers, the greater skill of the navigator, and a stricter precision in the astronomical determination of position and in topographical methods, at last laid bare the whole of the terrestrial globe which had been almost unknown at the end of the previous century; how the mechanical arts proper owed their perfection to that of the art of constructing instruments, machines, and looms, and how the perfection of the latter was due to the progress of rational mechanics and of physics; we shall also show what these arts owed to the science of using existing engines with less loss and expense, and to the invention of new engines.

We shall see how architecture borrowed, from the science of equilibrium and the theory of liquids, methods for making a roof that was at once less expensive and more convenient, but with no danger to the solidity of the construction; ways of resisting the impact of water in a more scientific fashion; and means of controlling its course and exploiting it by building canals with greater ingenuity and success.

We shall show how the chemical arts were enriched by new methods; and how the old methods were purified and simplified; how the useless or harmful substances, the ineffectual or imperfect practices introduced by routine were cast away; while at the same time means were discovered of preventing the terrible dangers to which workmen were often exposed, so that now they could enjoy themselves more and earn more, and no longer at a heavy price in painful sacrifice and regret.

Chemistry, botany, and natural history were of use in the economic arts, and in the cultivation of useful plants; in the feeding, breeding, and rearing of domestic animals; in perfecting their stocks and bettering their produce; in the preparation and conservation of the earth's supplies and animal produce.

Surgery and pharmacy have become almost new arts ever since anatomy and chemistry offered them their enlightened and certain guidance.

Medicine, which as far as its practice is concerned must be regarded as an art, was at least delivered from false theories, pedantic jargon, murderous routine, servile submission to the authority of men and the doctrine of faculties. It now teaches men to believe nothing but experience. It has increased its methods and learned better how to combine and employ them. If in certain aspects its progress has been somewhat negative, limited to the abandonment of dangerous practices and harmful prejudices, new methods of studying chemical medicine and combining observations foretell real and far-reaching progress.

We shall above all try to follow the progress of scientific genius, which sometimes descends from a profound abstract theory to skillful and delicate applications of this theory, and, by simplifying its methods and by adapting them to our needs, extends its benefits to the most ordinary occasions; and then, at other times, stimulated by these practical needs, seeks the realm of the most elevated speculation for the assistance that was denied it by ordinary knowledge.

We shall show that declamations about the inutility of theories even in the simplest arts have never proved anything save the ignorance of those who make them. We shall point out that it is not to the profundity of these theories but on the contrary to their imperfection that we must attribute the inutility or tragic consequences of so many unfortunate applications.

These observations will lead us to this general truth, that, in all the arts, truths of theory are necessarily modified in practice; that there exist certain genuinely inevitable inexactitudes whose effects we should attempt to render nugatory without entertaining any illusory hopes of avoiding them altogether; that a great number of conditions, relating to needs, methods, time, expense, which are necessarily neglected in theory, must enter into the problem when it is a question of a real and immediate practical application; and if we consider these conditions with the true skill of practical genius, we can at once go beyond the narrow limits within which prejudice against theory threatens to constrain the arts, and also avoid the mistakes into which a clumsy application of theory might lead us.

Sciences which had been divided could not develop without closer association, without making points of contact.

Exposition of the progress within each science suffices to show what has been the utility, in several of them, of the immediate application of calculation; and how in all of them it has been used to give a greater precision both to experiment and to observation; how much they owe to mechanics, which has provided them with more perfect and more exact instruments; the extent to which the discovery of microscopes and meteorological instruments has contributed to the perfection of natural history; what this latter science owes to chemistry, which alone has been able to lead it to a deeper knowledge of the objects it deals with, to unveil for it the most intimate secrets of nature and her most essential differences, by showing the mode of composition of chemical elements; while, on the other hand, natural history provides chemistry with so many products to separate and collect, so many different operations to conduct, so many natural combinations whose true elements must be separated and whose secrets may sometimes be discovered or even imitated; and finally, physics and chemistry afford assistance to each other, and anatomy receives it so plentifully from natural history and the other sciences.

Even so we have described only a very small portion of the benefits that we have received, and are still to receive from this application. Several geometers have supplied us with general methods for finding the empirical laws of phenomena on the basis of observation, methods that can be extended to all the sciences since they lead equally to knowledge of the law giving the successive values of a given quantity for a series of moments or of positions, or the law according to which different properties, or the different values of a similar quality, are distributed between a given number of objects.

Some applications have already proved that we can successfully use the science of combinations for arranging observations in such a way as to be able to grasp more easily the relations between them, the conclusions that follow from them, and their general scheme.

The existing applications of the calculus of probability foretell how they can aid the progress of the other sciences. In some cases they can determine the probability of unusual facts and inform us whether they should be rejected or whether they deserve to be verified. In other cases they can determine the probability of the constant recurrence of those facts which often present themselves in the practice of the arts and which are not by themselves linked to an order already regarded as a general law: as, for example, in medicine the salutary results of certain remedies and the success of certain preservatives. Other applications show us what is the probability of a class of phenomena being the result of the intention of an intelligent being or of their being dependent on other preceding or coexisting phenomena; the probability too that must be attributed to that necessary and unknown cause which we call chance, a word whose true meaning can be determined only by the study of this calculus.

These applications have also taught us to recognize the different degrees of certainty that we can hope to attain; the degree of likelihood an opinion must possess before we can adopt it and use it in argument, without infringing the rights of reason or the principles of conduct, without sacrificing prudence or offending justice. They show us the advantages and disadvantages of the different systems of voting and the different ways of deciding an issue by a majority vote; the different degrees of probability that these methods produce, and for any question the degree that the public interest may rightly demand. They tell us how to determine the degree of probability with virtual certainty in cases where a decision is not necessary or where the disadvantages of the two possible courses of action are discrepant and so one of them should not be adopted as long as its chances of success remain below this degree of probability; or alternatively how to determine the degree of probability in advance and with complete certainty in cases where a decision is necessary and where even the slightest likelihood of its being right justifies its adoption.

We may number among these applications the examination of the probability of facts for those who cannot base their beliefs on their own observations—a probability which arises either from the reliability of witnesses or from the relation of the facts in question to others that have been directly observed.

The knowledge of physical man, medicine, and public economy are bound to benefit from the researches about the duration of human life and the way this is influenced by differences in sex, temperature, climate, profession, government, and ordinary habits; about the dependence of the death-rate on various illnesses; about changes in population, and the extent to which they depend on the action of various causes; about the distribution of population in the various countries according to age, sex, and occupation.

And how useful to public economy has been the application of these same calculi in the organization of life annuities, tontines, private savings banks, benefit schemes and insurance policies of every kind! Ought not the application of the calculus of probability to be applied to that part of public economy which includes the theory of measures, money, banking, financial operations, as well as taxation, its legal distribution, its actual distribution which so often contradicts the law, and its consequences for all sections of the social system?

How many important questions in this same science have been resolved only by the aid of our knowledge of natural history, agriculture, the physical constitution of plants, and the mechanical or chemical arts!

Such, in a word, has been the general progress of the sciences that there is not really one of them whose principles and details can be fully developed without the help of all the others. In presenting our picture of the new truths with which each of the sciences has been enriched and of how much each owes to the application of theories or methods that seem to belong more particularly to other systems of knowledge, we shall investigate the nature and limits of the truths to which observation, experiment, and meditation can lead us in each science. We shall also inquire what precisely constitutes, for each one of them, the talent of invention, that primary faculty of the human intelligence which has been given the name *genius;* by which means the mind can make the discoveries that it seeks or sometimes be led to those which it did not seek and could not even have foreseen. We shall point out how the methods which lead us to discoveries can be exhausted so that science is somehow forced to stop, unless new methods appear to provide genius with a new instrument, or to facilitate the use of those which, it seemed, could no longer be employed without waste of time and energy.

If we were to confine ourselves to showing the benefits that we have derived from the sciences in their immediate uses or in their applications to the arts, either for the well-being of individuals or for the prosperity of nations, we should display only a very small portion of their blessings.

The most important of these, perhaps, is to have destroyed prejudices and to have redirected the human intelligence, which had been obliged to follow the false directions imposed on it by the absurd beliefs that were implanted in each generation in infancy with the terrors of superstition and the fear of tyranny.

All errors in politics and morals are based on philosophical errors and these in turn are connected with scientific errors. There is not a religious system nor a supernatural extravagance that is not founded on ignorance of the laws of nature. The inventors, the defenders of these absurdities could not foresee the successive perfection of the human mind. Convinced that men in their day knew everything that they could ever know and would always believe what they then believed, they confidently supported their idle dreams on the current opinions of their country and their age.

Advances in the physical sciences are all the more fatal to these errors in that they often destroy them without appearing to attack them [, and that they can shower on those who defend them so obstinately the humiliating taunt of ignorance].

At the same time the habit of correct reasoning about the objects of these sciences, the precise ideas gained by their methods, and the means of recognizing or proving the truth of a belief should naturally lead us to compare the sentiment that forces us to accept well-founded opinions credible for good reasons, with that which ties us to habitual prejudices or forces us to submit to authority. Such a comparison is enough to teach us to mistrust opinions of the latter kind, to convince us that we do not really believe them even when we boast of believing them, even when we profess them with the purest sincerity. This secret, once discovered, makes their destruction immediate and certain.

Finally this progress of the physical sciences which neither the passions nor self-interest can disturb, in which neither birth, nor profession, nor position are thought to confer on one the right to judge what one is not in a condition to understand, this inexorable progress cannot be contemplated by men of enlightenment without their wishing to make the other sciences follow the same path. It offers them at every step a model to emulate and one by which they may judge of their own efforts, recognize the false roads on which they may have set out and preserve themselves equally from pyrrhonism, from credulity, from extreme diffidence, and from a too great submission even to the authority of learning and fame.

Admittedly, metaphysical analysis led to the same results but it gave only abstract principles, while now these same abstract principles, put into practice, are illuminated by example and fortified by success.

Up to this stage, the sciences had been the birthright of very few; they were now becoming common property and the time was at hand when their elements, their principles, and their simpler methods would become truly popular. For it was then, at last, that their application to the arts and their influence on men's judgment would become of truly universal utility.

We shall follow the progress of European nations in the education both of children and of adults. This progress may appear to have been slow, if one considers only the philosophical foundations on which education has been based, for it is still in the grip of scholastic superstition: but it appears swift enough if one considers the nature and the extent of the subjects taught, for these are now confined almost completely to genuine inquiries, and include the elements of nearly all the sciences; while dictionaries, abstracts, and periodicals provide men of all ages with the information they require—even if this does not always appear in an unadulterated form. We shall examine the utility of combining oral instruction in the sciences with the immediate instruction to be acquired from books and private study, and we shall also examine whether any advantage has accrued from the development of compilation into an accredited profession in whose practice a man may hope to earn a livelihood; a development that has augmented the number of indifferent books in circulation, but has also increased the roads to knowledge open to men of little education. We shall give an account of the influence exercised by learned societies, for these will long remain a useful bulwark against charlatanry and false scholarship. Finally we shall unfold the story of the encouragement given by certain governments to the progress of knowledge, and also of the obstacles that were laid in its path often enough by these same governments, at the same time, in the same country. We shall expose, on the one hand, the prejudices and Machiavellian principles that have directed these governments in their opposition to men's progress toward the truth, and on the other, the political opinions originating either from self-interest or even from a genuine concern for the public good, that have guided them when they have seemed interested in accelerating and protecting it.

The spectacle presented by the fine arts has no less brilliant results to show. Music has become almost a new art, and, at the same time, its theory has been illuminated by the application of numerical calculation to the vibration of resonating bodies and the oscillation of the air. The graphic arts, which had already passed from Italy to Flanders, Spain and France, rose in the latter country to the heights they had attained in Italy during the preceding stage, and there shone with even greater brilliance than in Italy itself. The art of our painters is still the art of Raphael and the Carracci. Their methods, so far from dying out, have not only been kept alive in the schools, but have been more widely diffused. Nevertheless, too much time has elapsed without the appearance of a genius comparable to Raphael for us to attribute so long a period of sterility to chance alone. It is not that the methods of the art have been exhausted, although major achievements in it have become more difficult: it is not that nature has denied us faculties as perfect as those of the Italians of the sixteenth century; it is solely to changes in politics and in manners that we must attribute, not indeed the decadence of the art, but the feebleness of its products.

The art of letters, which, though in no way decadent in Italy, is cultivated there with less success, has made such progress in the French language that it has earned for it the honor of becoming the all but universal language of Europe. In the hands of Corneille, of Racine, of Voltaire, tragedy has risen step by step to a hitherto unknown perfection; and, in the hands of Molière, comedy has risen even more rapidly to heights as yet unattained in any other nation.

At the beginning of this period, the English language was brought to perfection, and so, more recently was the German. Both in England and in Germany, the arts of poetry and prose learned to accept, if with less docility than in France, the yoke of those universal rules of reason and of Nature which ought to be their guide. These rules are true for all languages and all peoples, although until now only very few have been capable of understanding them and of attaining that justice and certainty of taste which is merely a feeling for these rules, which presided over the works of Sophocles and Virgil as over those of Pope and Voltaire, which taught the Greeks and the Romans, as later the English and the French, to be delighted by the same beauties and to be shocked by the same faults.

We shall show what factors have favored or impeded the progress of the arts in each nation, the reasons for the so unequal degrees of excellence attained in each nation by the various kinds of poetry and prose, and the way in which the literary rules can be modified, with no infraction of the universal principles on which they are based, by the manners and the opinions of the nation in which a given *genre* is practiced, and by the use for which it is destined. So, for example, tragedy intended to be spoken in daily performance, before a small audience in a room of moderate size, cannot have the same practical rules as tragedy intended to be sung in an immense theatre, as part of solemn festivities to which a whole nation is convened. We shall endeavor to prove that the rules of taste have the same universality, the same constancy as the other laws of the physical or the moral universe, but are susceptible to the same kind of modification as they are when it is a question of their application in some practical art.

We shall show how the printing press multiplies and spreads abroad even those works primarily intended to be performed or read aloud in public, and so allows them to reach incomparably more people as readers than they ever could as mere listeners; we shall show how, as a consequence of the way that any important decision taken in a large assembly is now determined by what the members of that assembly have learned through the written word, a new art of persuasion has arisen among the moderns, different from that practiced by the ancients, a difference that is analogous to the differences in the effects produced, in the means employed between this modern art and that of the ancients; and, finally, we shall show how in those branches of literature where even the ancients confined themselves to the written word, such as history or philosophy, the invention of printing makes it so much easier for the author to expand and develop his ideas, that here again it has inevitably modified those rules.

The progress of philosophy and the sciences has favored and extended the progress of letters, and this in turn has served to make the study of the sciences easier, and that of philosophy more popular. The sciences and the arts have assisted one another despite the efforts of the ignorant and the foolish to separate them and make them enemies. Scholarship, which seemed doomed by its respect for the past and its deference toward authority always to lend its support to harmful superstitions, has nevertheless contributed to their eradication, for it was able to borrow the torch of a sounder criticism from philosophy and the sciences. It already knew how to weigh up authorities and compare them; it now learned how to bring every authority before the bar of Reason. It had already discounted prodigies, fantastic anecdotes, facts contrary to all probability; but after attacking the evidence on which such absurdities relied, it now learned that all extraordinary facts must always be rejected, however impressive the evidence in their favor, unless this can truly turn the scale against the weight of their physical or moral probability.

Thus all the intellectual activities of man, however different they may be in their aims, their methods, or the qualities of mind they exact, have combined to further the progress of human reason. Indeed, the whole system of human labor is like a well-made machine, whose several parts have been systematically distinguished but none the less, being intimately bound together, form a single whole, and work toward a single end.

Turning now our attention to the human race in general, we shall show how the discovery of the correct method of procedure in the sciences, the growth of scientific theories, their application to every part of the natural world, to the subject of every human need, the lines of communication established between one science and another, the great number of men who cultivate the sciences, and most important of all, the spread of printing, how together all these advances ensure that no science will ever fall below the point it has reached. We shall point out that the principles of philosophy, the slogans of liberty, the recognition of the true rights of man and his real interests, have spread through far too great a number of nations, and now direct in each of them the opinions of far too great a number of enlightened men, for us to fear that they will ever be allowed to relapse into oblivion. And indeed what reason could we have for fear, when we consider that the languages most widely spoken are the languages of the two peoples who enjoy liberty to the fullest extent and who best understand its principles, and that no league of tyrants, no political intrigues, could prevent the resolute defense, in these two languages, of the rights of reason and of liberty?

But although everything tells us that the human race will never relapse into its former state of barbarism, although everything combines to reassure us against that corrupt and cowardly political theory which would condemn it to oscillate forever between truth and error, liberty and servitude, nevertheless we still see the forces of enlightenment in possession of no more than a very small portion of the globe, and the truly enlightened vastly outnumbered by the great mass of men who are still given over to ignorance and prejudice. We still see vast areas in which men groan in slavery, vast areas offering the spectacle of nations either degraded by the vices of a civilization whose progress is impeded by corruption, or still vegetating in the infant condition of early times. We observe that the labors of recent ages have done much for the progress of the human mind, but little for the perfection of the human race; that they have done much for the honor of man, something for his liberty, but so far almost nothing for his happiness. At a few points our eyes are dazzled with a brilliant light; but thick darkness still covers an immense stretch of the horizon. There are a few circumstances from which the philosopher can take consolation; but he is still afflicted by the spectacle of the stupidity, slavery, barbarism, and extravagance of mankind; and the friend of humanity can find unmixed pleasure only in tasting the sweet delights of hope for the future.

Such are the subjects that ought to enter into a historical sketch of the progress of the human mind. In presenting it, we shall endeavor above all to exhibit the influence of this progress on the opinions and the welfare of the great mass of the people, in the different nations, at the different stages of their political existence. We shall endeavor to exhibit the truths they have learned, the errors from which they have been freed, the habits of virtue they have contracted, and the developments in their capacities that have established a more fortunate relation between their wants and these capacities; and, then by way of contrast, the prejudices that have enslaved them, the political or religious superstitions with which they have been infected, the vices with which they have been corrupted by ignorance or tyranny, and the misery to which they have been subjected either by force or by their own degradation.

Up till now, the history of politics, like that of philosophy or of science, has been the history of only a few individuals: that which really constitutes the human race, the vast mass of families living for the most part on the fruits of their labor, has been forgotten, and even of those who follow public professions, and work not for themselves but for society, who are engaged in teaching, ruling, protecting, or healing others, it is only the leaders who have held the eye of the historian.

In writing the history of individuals, it is enough to collect facts; but the history of a group of men must be supported by observations; and to select these observations and to fasten upon their essential features enlightenment is necessary, and, to use them to good effect, philosophy in the same measure.

Moreover, these observations relate to quite ordinary matters, which lie open to every eye, and which anyone who so desires can find out about by himself. Consequently almost all the observations that have been collected have been made by travellers or foreigners; for facts that are regarded as common-place in their own country, become for them objects of curiosity. But unfortunately travellers are nearly always inaccurate observers; they observe things too hastily, through the prejudices of their own country or of that in which they are travelling; they discuss them with those into whose company chance has thrown them, and what they are told is nearly always dictated by self-interest, by the spirit of party, by patriotic pride, or merely by the mood of the moment.

Thus it is not only to the servility of historians, as has been said with justice about the official historians of monarchs, that we must attribute the scarcity of records that would allow us to follow this, the most important chapter in the history of man.

These records we can supplement, but only imperfectly, by a study of legal systems, of the practical principles of politics and public economy, and of religion and superstition in general. For there can be such a vast discrepancy between the law in writing and the law applied, between the principles of rulers and their practice as modified by the will of their subjects, between a social institution in the minds of those who conceive it and the same institution when its provisions are realized in practice, between the religion of books and the religion of the people, between the apparently universal acceptance of a superstition and the support which it can in fact command, that the actual effects may bear no relation whatever to their apparent and generally accepted causes as studied by the historian.

It is this most obscure and neglected chapter of the history of the human race, for which we can gather so little material from records, that must occupy the foreground of our picture; and whether we are concerned with a discovery, an important theory, a new legal system, or a political revolution, we shall endeavor to determine its consequences for the majority in each society. For it is there that one finds the true subject matter of philosophy, for all intermediate consequences may be ignored except insofar as they eventually influence the greater mass of the human race.

It is only when we come to this final link in the chain that our contemplation of historical events and the reflections that occur to us are of true utility. Only then can we appreciate men's true claims to fame, and can take real pleasure in the progress of their reason; only then can we truly judge the perfection of the human race.

The idea that everything must be considered in relation to this single point of reference is dictated both by justice and by reason. Nevertheless one might be tempted to regard it as fantastic. But one would be wrong. To show this is so, we have only to cite two striking examples.

The man who tills our soil owes his enjoyment of the commonest goods, which plentifully supply his needs, to the long-continued labors of industry assisted by science: and his enjoyment of these goods can be traced even further back, to the victory of Salamis, but for which the shadows of Oriental despotism threatened to engulf the earth. Similarly, the mariner who is preserved from shipwreck by precise observations of longitude, owes his life to a theory which can be traced back, through a chain of truths, to discoveries made in the school of Plato, and thereafter buried for twenty centuries in total disuse.

THE TENTH STAGE: THE FUTURE PROGRESS
OF THE HUMAN MIND

If man can, with almost complete assurance, predict phenomena when he knows their laws, and if, even when he does not, he can still, with great expectation of success, forecast the future on the basis of his experience of the past, why, then, should it be regarded as a fantastic undertaking to sketch, with some pretense to truth, the future destiny of man on the basis of his history? The sole foundation for belief in the natural sciences is this idea, that the general laws directing the phenomena of the universe, known or unknown, are necessary and constant. Why should this principle be any less true for the development of the intellectual and moral faculties of man than for the other operations of nature? Since beliefs founded on past experience of like conditions provide the only rule of conduct for the wisest of men, why should the philosopher be forbidden to base his conjectures on these same foundations, so long as he does not attribute to them a certainty superior to that warranted by the number, the constancy, and the accuracy of his observations?

Our hopes for the future condition of the human race can be subsumed under three important heads: the abolition of inequality between nations, the progress of equality within each nation, and the true perfection of mankind. Will all nations one day attain that state of civilization which the most enlightened, the freest, and the least burdened by prejudices, such as the French and the Anglo-Americans, have attained already? Will the vast gulf that separates these peoples from the slavery of nations under the rule of monarchs, from the barbarism of African tribes, from the ignorance of savages, little by little disappear?

Is there on the face of the earth a nation whose inhabitants have been debarred by nature herself from the enjoyment of freedom and the exercise of reason?

Are those differences which have hitherto been seen in every civilized country in respect of the enlightenment, the resources, and the wealth enjoyed by the different classes into which it is divided, is that inequality between men which was aggravated or perhaps produced by the earliest progress of society, are these part of civilization itself, or are they due to the present imperfections of the social art? Will they necessarily decrease and ultimately make way for a real equality, the final end of the social art, in which even the effects of the natural differences between men will be mitigated and the only kind of inequality to persist will be that which is in the interests of all and which favors the progress of civilization, of education, and of industry, without entailing either poverty, humiliation, or dependence? In other words, will men approach a condition in which everyone will have the knowledge necessary to conduct himself in the ordinary affairs of life, according to the light of his own reason, to preserve his mind free from prejudice, to understand his rights and to exercise them in accordance with his conscience and his creed; in which everyone will become able, through the development of his faculties, to find the means of providing for his needs; and in which at last misery and folly will be the exception, and no longer the habitual lot of a section of society?

Is the human race to better itself, either by discoveries in the sciences and the arts, and so in the means to individual welfare and general prosperity; or by progress in the principles of conduct or practical morality; or by a true perfection of the intellectual, moral, or physical faculties of man, an improvement which may result from a perfection either of the instruments used to heighten the intensity of these faculties and to direct their use or of the natural constitution of man?

In answering these three questions we shall find in the experience of the past, in the observation of the progress that the sciences and civilization have already made, in the analysis of the progress of the human mind and of the development of its faculties, the strongest reasons for believing that nature has set no limit to the realization of our hopes.

If we glance at the state of the world today we see first of all that in Europe the principles of the French constitution are already those of all enlightened men. We see them too widely propagated, too seriously professed, for priests and despots to prevent their gradual penetration even into the hovels of their slaves; there they will soon awaken in these slaves the remnants of their common sense and inspire them with that smoldering indignation which not even constant humiliation and fear can smother in the soul of the oppressed.

As we move from nation to nation, we can see in each what special obstacles impede this revolution and what attitudes of mind favor it. We can distinguish the nations where we may expect it to be introduced gently by the perhaps belated wisdom of their governments, and those nations where its violence intensified by their resistance must involve all alike in a swift and terrible convulsion.

Can we doubt that either common sense or the senseless discords of European nations will add to the effects of the slow but inexorable progress of their colonies, and will soon bring about the independence of the New World? And then will not the European population in these colonies, spreading rapidly over that enormous land, either civilize or peacefully remove the savage nations who still inhabit vast tracts of its land?

Survey the history of our settlements and commercial undertakings in Africa or in Asia, and you will see how our trade monopolies, our treachery, our murderous contempt for men of another color or creed, the insolence of our usurpations, the intrigues or the exaggerated proselytic zeal of our priests, have destroyed the respect and good-will that the superiority of our knowledge and the benefits of our commerce at first won for us in the eyes of the inhabitants. But doubtless the moment approaches when, no longer presenting ourselves as always either tyrants or corrupters, we shall become for them the beneficent instruments of their freedom.

The sugar industry, establishing itself throughout the immense continent of Africa, will destroy the shameful exploitation which has corrupted and depopulated that continent for the last two centuries.

Already in Great Britain, friends of humanity have set us an example; and if the Machiavellian government of that country has been restrained by public opinion from offering any opposition, what may we not expect of this same spirit, once the reform of a servile and venal constitution has led to a government worthy of a humane and generous nation? Will not France hasten to imitate such undertakings dictated by philanthropy and the true self-interest of Europe alike? Trading stations have been set up in the French islands, in Guiana, and in some English possessions, and soon we shall see the downfall of the monopoly that the Dutch have sustained with so much treachery, persecution, and crime. The nations of Europe will finally learn that monopolistic companies are nothing more than a tax imposed upon them in order to provide their governments with a new instrument of tyranny.

So the peoples of Europe, confining themselves to free trade, understanding their own rights too well to show contempt for those of other peoples, will respect this independence, which until now they have so insolently violated. Their settlements, no longer filled with government hirelings hastening, under the cloak of place or privilege, to amass treasure by brigandry and deceit, so as to be able to return to Europe and purchase titles and honor, will now be peopled with men of industrious habit, seeking in these propitious climates the wealth that eluded them at home. The love of freedom will retain them there, ambition will no longer recall them, and what have been no better than the counting-houses of brigands will become colonies of citizens propagating throughout Africa and Asia the principles and the practice of liberty, knowledge, and reason that they have brought from Europe. We shall see the monks who brought only shameful superstition to these peoples and aroused their antagonism by the threat of yet another tyranny, replaced by men occupied in propagating among them the truths that will promote their happiness and in teaching them about their interests and their rights. Zeal for the truth is also one of the passions, and it will turn its efforts to distant lands, once there are no longer at home any crass prejudices to combat, any shameful errors to dissipate.

These vast lands are inhabited partly by large tribes who need only assistance from us to become civilized, who wait only to find brothers among the European nations to become their friends and pupils; partly by races oppressed by sacred despots or dull-witted conquerors, and who for so many centuries have cried out to be liberated; partly by tribes living in a condition of almost total savagery in a climate whose harshness repels the sweet blessings of civilization and deters those who would teach them its benefits; and finally, by conquering hordes who know no other law but force, no other profession but piracy. The progress of these two last classes of people will be slower and stormier; and perhaps it will even be that, reduced in number as they are driven back by civilized nations, they will finally disappear imperceptibly before them or merge into them.

We shall point out how these events will be the inevitable result not merely of the progress of Europe but also of the freedom that the French

and the North American Republics can, and in their own real interest
should, grant to the trade of Africa and Asia; and how they must of
necessity be born either of a new-found wisdom on the part of the
European nations, or of their obstinate attachment to mercantilist
prejudices.

We shall show that there is only one event, a new invasion of Asia by
the Tartars, that could prevent this revolution, and that this event is now
impossible. Meanwhile everything forecasts the imminent decadence of
the great religions of the East, which in most countries have been made
over to the people, and, not uncontaminated by the corruption of their
ministers, are in some already regarded by the ruling classes as mere
political inventions; in consequence of which they are now powerless to
retain human reason in hopeless bondage, in eternal infancy.

The progress of these peoples is likely to be more rapid and certain
than our own because they can receive from us everything that we have
had to find out for ourselves, and in order to understand those simple
truths and infallible methods which we have acquired only after long
error, all that they need to do is to follow the expositions and proofs that
appear in our speeches and writings. If the progress of the Greeks was
lost to later nations, this was because of the absence of any form of
communication between the different peoples, and for this we must
blame the tyrannical domination of the Romans. But when mutual needs
have brought all men together, and the great powers have established
equality between societies as well as between individuals and have raised
respect for the independence of weak states and sympathy for ignorance
and misery to the rank of political principles, when maxims that favor
action and energy have ousted those which would compress the
province of human faculties, will it then be possible to fear that there are
still places in the world inaccessible to enlightenment, or that despotism
in its pride can raise barriers against truth that are insurmountable for
long?

The time will therefore come when the sun will shine only on free
men who know no other master but their reason; when tyrants and
slaves, priests and their stupid or hypocritical instruments will exist only
in works of history and on the stage; and when we shall think of them
only to pity their victims and their dupes; to maintain ourselves in a state
of vigilance by thinking on their excesses; and to learn how to recognize

and so to destroy, by force of reason, the first seeds of tyranny and superstition, should they ever dare to reappear among us.

In looking at the history of societies we shall have had occasion to observe that there is often a great difference between the rights that the law allows its citizens and the rights that they actually enjoy, and, again, between the equality established by political codes and that which in fact exists among individuals: and we shall have noticed that these differences were one of the principal causes of the destruction of freedom in the ancient republics, of the storms that troubled them, and of the weakness that delivered them over to foreign tyrants.

These differences have three main causes: inequality in wealth; inequality in status between the man whose means of subsistence are hereditary and the man whose means are dependent on the length of his life, or, rather, on that part of his life in which he is capable of work; and, finally, inequality in education.

We therefore need to show that these three sorts of real inequality must constantly diminish without however disappearing altogether: for they are the result of natural and necessary causes which it would be foolish and dangerous to wish to eradicate; and one could not even attempt to bring about the entire disappearance of their effects without introducing even more fecund sources of inequality, without striking more direct and more fatal blows at the rights of man.

It is easy to prove that wealth has a natural tendency to equality, and that any excessive disproportion could not exist or at least would rapidly disappear if civil laws did not provide artificial ways of perpetuating and uniting fortunes; if free trade and industry were allowed to remove the advantages that accrued wealth derives from any restrictive law or fiscal privilege; if taxes on covenants, the restrictions placed on their free employment, their subjection to tiresome formalities, and the uncertainty and inevitable expense involved in implementing them did not hamper the activity of the poor man and swallow up his meager capital; if the administration of the country did not afford some men ways of making their fortune that were closed to other citizens; if prejudice and avarice, so common in old age, did not preside over the making of marriages; and if, in a society enjoying simpler manners and more sensible institutions, wealth ceased to be a means of satisfying vanity and ambition, and if the equally misguided notions of austerity, which condemn spending money in the cultivation of the more delicate pleasures, no longer insisted on the hoarding of all one's earnings.

Let us turn to the enlightened nations of Europe, and observe the size of their present populations in relation to the size of their territories. Let us consider, in agriculture and industry the proportion that holds between labor and the means of subsistence, and we shall see that it would be impossible for those means to be kept at their present level and consequently for the population to be kept at its present size if a great number of individuals were not almost entirely dependent for the maintenance of themselves and their family either on their own labor or on the interest from capital invested so as to make their labor more productive. Now both these sources of income depend on the life and even on the health of the head of the family. They provide what is rather like a life annuity, save that it is more dependent on chance; and in consequence there is a very real difference between people living like this and those whose resources are not at all subject to the same risks, who live either on revenue from land, or on the interest on capital which is almost independent of their own labor.

Here then is a necessary cause of inequality, of dependence, and even of misery, which ceaselessly threatens the most numerous and most active class in our society.

We shall point out how it can be in great part eradicated by guaranteeing people in old age a means of livelihood produced partly by their own savings and partly by the savings of others who make the same outlay, but who die before they need to reap the reward; or, again, on the same principle of compensation, by securing for widows and orphans an income which is the same and costs the same for those families which suffer an early loss and for those which suffer it later; or again by providing all children with the capital necessary for the full use of their labor, available at the age when they start work and found a family, a capital which increases at the expense of those whom premature death prevents from reaching this age. It is to the application of the calculus to the probabilities of life and the investment of money that we owe the idea of these methods which have already been successful, although they have not been applied in a sufficiently comprehensive and exhaustive fashion to render them really useful, not merely to a few individuals, but to society as a whole, by making it possible to prevent those periodic disasters which strike at so many families and which are such a recurrent source of misery and suffering.

We shall point out that schemes of this nature, which can be organized in the name of the social authority and become one of its greatest benefits, can also be the work of private associations, which will be formed without any real risk, once the principles for the proper working of these schemes have been widely diffused and the mistakes which have been the undoing of a large number of these associations no longer hold terrors for us.

[We shall reveal other methods of ensuring this equality, either by seeing that credit is no longer the exclusive privilege of great wealth, but that it has another and no less sound foundation; or by making industrial progress and commercial activity more independent of the existence of the great capitalists. And once again, it is to the application of the calculus that we shall be indebted for such methods.]

The degree of equality in education that we can reasonably hope to attain, but that should be adequate, is that which excludes all dependence, either forced or voluntary. We shall show how this condition can be easily attained in the present state of human knowledge even by those who can study only for a small number of years in childhood, and then during the rest of their life in their few hours of leisure. We shall prove that, by a suitable choice of syllabus and of methods of education, we can teach the citizen everything that he needs to know in order to be able to manage his household, administer his affairs, and employ his labor and his faculties in freedom; to know his rights and to be able to exercise them; to be acquainted with his duties and fulfill them satisfactorily; to judge his own and other men's actions according to his own lights and to be a stranger to none of the high and delicate feelings which honor human nature; not to be in a state of blind dependence upon those to whom he must entrust his affairs or the exercise of his rights; to be in a proper condition to choose and supervise them; to be no longer the dupe of those popular errors which torment man with superstitious fears and chimerical hopes; to defend himself against prejudice by the strength of his reason alone; and, finally, to escape the deceits of charlatans who would lay snares for his fortune, his health, his freedom of thought, and his conscience under the pretext of granting him health, wealth, and salvation.

From such time onwards the inhabitants of a single country will no longer be distinguished by their use of a crude or refined language; they will be able to govern themselves according to their own knowledge; they will no longer be limited to a mechanical knowledge of the procedures of the arts or of professional routine; they will no longer depend for every trivial piece of business, every insignificant matter of instruction on clever men who rule over them in virtue of their necessary superiority; and so they will attain a real equality, since differences in enlightenment or talent can no longer raise a barrier between men who understand each other's feelings, ideas, and language, some of whom may wish to be taught by others but, to do so, will have no need to be controlled by them, or who may wish to confide the care of government to the ablest of their number but will not be compelled to yield them absolute power in a spirit of blind confidence.

This kind of supervision has advantages even for those who do not exercise it, since it is employed for them and not against them. Natural differences of ability between men whose understanding has not been cultivated give rise, even in savage tribes, to charlatans and dupes, to clever men and men readily deceived. These same differences are truly universal, but now they are differences only between men of learning and upright men who know the value of learning without being dazzled by it; or between talent or genius and the common sense which can appreciate and benefit from them; so that even if these natural differences were greater, and more extensive than they are, they would be only the more influential in improving the relations between men and promoting what is advantageous for their independence and happiness.

These various causes of equality do not act in isolation; they unite, combine, and support each other and so their cumulative effects are stronger, surer, and more constant. With greater equality of education there will be greater equality in industry and so in wealth; equality in wealth necessarily leads to equality in education: and equality between the nations and equality within a single nation are mutually dependent.

So we might say that a well-directed system of education rectifies natural inequality in ability instead of strengthening it, just as good laws remedy natural inequality in the means of subsistence, and just as in societies where laws have brought about this same equality, liberty, though subject to a regular constitution, will be more widespread, more complete than in the total independence of savage life. Then the social art will have fulfilled its aim, that of assuring and extending to all men enjoyment of the common rights to which they are called by nature.

The real advantages that should result from this progress, of which we can entertain a hope that is almost a certainty, can have no other term than that of the absolute perfection of the human race; since, as the various kinds of equality come to work in its favor by producing ampler sources of supply, more extensive education, more complete liberty, so equality will be more real and will embrace everything which is really of importance for the happiness of human beings.

It is therefore only by examining the progress and the laws of this perfection that we shall be able to understand the extent or the limits of our hopes.

No one has ever believed that the mind can gain knowledge of all the facts of nature or attain the ultimate means of precision in the measurement or in the analysis of the facts of nature, the relations between objects, and all the possible combinations of ideas. Even the relations between magnitudes, the mere notion of quantity or extension, taken in its fullest comprehension, gives rise to a system so vast that it will never be mastered by the human mind in its entirety, that there will always be a part of it, always indeed the larger part of it that will remain forever unknown. People have believed that man can never know more than a part of the objects that the nature of his intelligence allows him to understand, and that he must in the end arrive at a point where the number and complexity of the objects that he already knows have absorbed all his strength so that any further progress must be completely impossible.

But since, as the number of known facts increases, the human mind learns how to classify them and to subsume them under more general facts, and, at the same time, the instruments and methods employed in their observation and their exact measurement acquire a new precision; since, as more relations between various objects become known, man is able to reduce them to more general relations, to express them more simply, and to present them in such a way that it is possible to grasp a greater number of them with the same degree of intellectual ability and the same amount of application; since, as the mind learns to understand more complicated combinations of ideas, simpler formulae soon reduce their complexity; so truths that were discovered only by great effort, that could at first only be understood by men capable of profound thought, are soon developed and proved by methods that are not beyond the reach of common intelligence. If the methods which have led to these new combinations of ideas are ever exhausted, if their application to hitherto unsolved questions should demand exertions greater than either the time or the capacity of the learned would permit, some method of a greater generality or simplicity will be found so that genius can continue undisturbed on its path. The strength and the limits of man's intelligence may remain unaltered; and yet the instruments that he uses will increase and improve, the language that fixes and determines his ideas will acquire greater breadth and precision and, unlike mechanics where an increase of force means a decrease of speed, the methods that lead genius to the discovery of truth increase at once the force and the speed of its operations.

Therefore, since these developments are themselves the necessary consequences of progress in detailed knowledge, and since the need for new methods in fact only arises in circumstances that give rise to new methods, it is evident that, within the body of the sciences of observation, calculation, and experiment, the actual number of truths may always increase, and that every part of this body may develop, and yet man's faculties be of the same strength, activity, and extent.

If we apply these general reflections to the various sciences, we can find in each of them examples of progressive improvement that will remove any doubts about what we may expect for the future. We shall point out in particular the progress that is both likely and imminent in those sciences which prejudice regards as all but exhausted. We shall give examples of the manner and extent of the precision and unity which could accrue to the whole system of human knowledge as the result of a more general and philosophical application of the sciences of calculation to the various branches of knowledge. We shall show how favorable to our hopes would be a more universal system of education by giving a greater number of people the elementary knowledge which could awaken their interest in a particular branch of study, and by providing conditions favorable to their progress in it; and how these hopes would be further raised, if more men possessed the means to devote themselves to these studies, for at present even in the most enlightened countries scarcely one in fifty of the people who have natural talents, receives the necessary education to develop them; and how, if this were done there would be a proportionate increase in the number of men destined by their discoveries to extend the boundaries of science.

We shall show how this equality in education and the equality which will come about between the different nations would accelerate the advance of these sciences whose progress depends on repeated observations over a large area; what benefits would thereby accrue to mineralogy, botany, zoology, and meteorology; and what a vast disproportion holds in all these sciences between the poverty of existing methods which have nevertheless led to useful and important new truths, and the wealth of those methods which man would then be able to employ.

We shall show how even the sciences in which discovery is the fruit of solitary meditation would benefit from being studied by a greater number of people, in the matter of these improvements in detail which do not demand the intellectual energy of an inventor but suggest themselves to mere reflection.

If we turn now to the arts, whose theory depends on these same sciences, we shall find that their progress, depending as it does on that of theory, can have no other limits; that the procedures of the different arts can be perfected and simplified in the same way as the methods of the sciences; new instruments, machines, and looms can add to man's strength and can improve at once the quality and the accuracy of his productions, and can diminish the time and labor that has to be expended on them. The obstacles still in the way of this progress will disappear, accidents will be foreseen and prevented, the insanitary conditions that are due either to the work itself or to the climate will be eliminated.

A very small amount of ground will be able to produce a great quantity of supplies of greater utility or higher quality; more goods will be obtained for a smaller outlay; the manufacture of articles will be achieved with less wastage in raw materials and will make better use of them. Every type of soil will produce those things which satisfy the greatest number of needs; of several alternative ways of satisfying needs of the same order, that will be chosen which satisfies the greatest number of people and which requires least labor and least expenditure. So, without the need for sacrifice, methods of preservation and economy in expenditure will improve in the wake of progress in the arts of producing and preparing supplies and making articles from them.

So not only will the same amount of ground support more people, but everyone will have less work to do, will produce more and satisfy his wants more fully.

With all this progress in industry and welfare which establishes a happier proportion between men's talents and their needs, each successive generation will have larger possessions, either as a result of this progress or through the preservation of the products of industry; and so, as a consequence of the physical constitution of the human race, the number of people will increase. Might there not then come a moment when these necessary laws begin to work in a contrary direction; when, the number of people in the world finally exceeding the means of subsistence, there will in consequence ensue a continual diminution of happiness and population, a true retrogression, or at best an oscillation between good and bad? In societies that have reached this stage will not this oscillation be a perennial source of more or less periodic disaster? Will it not show that a point has been attained beyond which all further improvement is impossible, that the perfectibility of the human race has after long years arrived at a term beyond which it may never go?

There is doubtless no one who does not think that such a time is still very far from us; but will it ever arrive? It is impossible to pronounce about the likelihood of an event that will occur only when the human species will have necessarily acquired a degree of knowledge of which we can have no inkling. And who would take it upon himself to predict the condition to which the art of converting the elements to the use of man may in time be brought?

But even if we agree that the limit will one day arrive, nothing follows from it that is in the least alarming as far as either the happiness of the human race or its indefinite perfectibility is concerned; if we consider that, before all this comes to pass, the progress of reason will have kept pace with that of the sciences, and that the absurd prejudices of superstition will have ceased to corrupt and degrade the moral code by its harsh doctrines instead of purifying and elevating it, we can assume that by then men will know that, if they have a duty toward those who are not yet born, that duty is not to give them existence but to give them happiness; their aim should be to promote the general welfare of the human race or of the society in which they live or of the family to which they belong, rather than foolishly to encumber the world with useless and wretched beings. It is, then, possible that there should be a limit to the amount of food that can be produced, and, consequently, to the size of the population of the world, without this involving that untimely destruction of some of those creatures who have been given life, which is so contrary to nature and to social prosperity.

Since the discovery, or rather the exact analysis, of the first principles of metaphysics, morals, and politics is still recent and was preceded by the knowledge of a large number of detailed truths, the false notion that they have thereby attained their destination, has gained ready acceptance; men imagine that, because there are no more crude errors to refute, no more fundamental truths to establish, nothing remains to be done.

But it is easy to see how imperfect is the present analysis of man's moral and intellectual faculties; how much further the knowledge of his duties which presumes a knowledge of the influence of his actions upon the welfare of his fellow men and upon the society to which he belongs, can still be increased through a more profound, more accurate, more considered observation of that influence; how many questions have to be solved, how many social relations to be examined, before we can have precise knowledge of the individual rights of man and the rights that the state confers upon each in regard to all. Have we yet ascertained at all accurately the limits of the rights that exist between different societies in times of war, or that are enjoyed by society over its members in times of trouble and schism, or that belong to individuals, or spontaneous associations at the moment of their original, free formation or of their necessary disintegration?

If we pass on to the theory which ought to direct the application of particular principles and serve as the foundation for the social art, do we not see the necessity of acquiring a precision that these elementary truths cannot possess so long as they are absolutely general? Have we yet reached the point when we can reckon as the only foundation of law either justice or a proved and acknowledged utility instead of the vague, uncertain, arbitrary views of alleged political expediency? Are we yet in possession of any precise rules for selecting out of the almost infinite variety of possible systems in which the general principles of equality and natural rights are respected, those which will best secure the preservation of these rights, which will afford the freest scope for their exercise and their enjoyment, and which will moreover insure the leisure and welfare of individuals and the strength, prosperity, and peace of nations?

The application of the calculus of combinations and probabilities to these sciences promises even greater improvement, since it is the only way of achieving results of an almost mathematical exactitude and of assessing the degree of their probability or likelihood. Sometimes, it is true, the evidence upon which these results are based may lead us, without any calculation, at the first glance, to some general truth and teach us whether the effect produced by such-and-such a cause was or was not favorable, but if this evidence cannot be weighed and measured, and if these effects cannot be subjected to precise measurement, then we cannot know exactly how much good or evil they contain; or, again, if the good and evil nearly balance each other, if the difference between them is slight, we cannot pronounce with any certainty to which side the balance really inclines. Without the application of the calculus it would be almost impossible to choose with any certainty between two combinations that have the same purpose and between which there is no apparent difference in merit. Without the calculus these sciences would always remain crude and limited for want of instruments delicate enough to catch the fleeting truth, of machines precise enough to plumb the depths where so much that is of value to science lies hidden.

However, such an application, notwithstanding the happy efforts of certain geometers, is still in its earliest stages: and it will be left to the generations to come to use this source of knowledge which is as inexhaustible as the calculus itself, or as the number of combinations, relations, and facts that may be included in its sphere of operation.

There is another kind of progress within these sciences that is no less important; and that is the perfection of scientific language which is at present so vague and obscure. This improvement could be responsible for making the sciences genuinely popular, even in their first rudiments.

Genius can triumph over the inexactitude of language as over other obstacles and can recognize the truth through the strange mask that hides or disguises it. But how can someone with only a limited amount of leisure to devote to his education master and retain even the simplest truths if they are distorted by an imprecise language? The fewer the ideas that he is able to acquire and combine, the more necessary is it that they should be precise and exact. He has no fund of knowledge stored up in his mind which he can draw upon to protect himself from error, and his understanding, not being strengthened and refined by long practice, cannot catch such feeble rays of light as manage to penetrate the obscurities, the ambiguities of an imperfect and perverted language.

Until men progress in the practice as well as in the science of morality, it will be impossible for them to attain any insight into either the nature and development of the moral sentiments, the principles of morality, the natural motives that prompt their actions, or their own true interests either as individuals or as members of society. Is not a mistaken sense of interest the most common cause of actions contrary to the general welfare? Is not the violence of our passions often the result either of habits that we have adopted through miscalculation, or of our ignorance how to restrain them, tame them, deflect them, rule them?

Is not the habit of reflection upon conduct, of listening to the deliverances of reason and conscience upon it, of exercising those gentle feelings which identify our happiness with that of others, the necessary consequence of a well-planned study of morality and of a greater equality in the conditions of the social pact? Will not the free man's sense of his own dignity and a system of education built upon a deeper knowledge of our moral constitution, render common to almost every man those principles of strict and unsullied justice, those habits of an active and enlightened benevolence, of a fine and generous sensibility which nature has implanted in the hearts of all and whose flowering waits only upon the favorable influences of enlightenment and freedom? Just as the mathematical and physical sciences tend to improve the arts that we use to satisfy our simplest needs, is it not also part of the necessary order of nature that the moral and political sciences should exercise a similar influence upon the motives that direct our feelings and our actions?

What are we to expect from the perfection of laws and public institutions, consequent upon the progress of those sciences, but the reconciliation, the identification of the interests of each with the interests of all? Has the social art any other aim save that of destroying their apparent opposition? Will not a country's constitution and laws accord best with the rights of reason and nature when the path of virtue is no longer arduous and when the temptations that lead men from it are few and feeble?

Is there any vicious habit, any practice contrary to good faith, any crime, whose origin and first cause cannot be traced back to the legislation, the institutions, the prejudices of the country wherein this habit, this practice, this crime can be observed? In short will not the general welfare that results from the progress of the useful arts once they are grounded on solid theory, or from the progress of legislation once it is rooted in the truths of political science, incline mankind to humanity, benevolence, and justice? In other words, do not all these observations which I propose to develop further in my book, show that the moral goodness of man, the necessary consequence of his constitution, is capable of indefinite perfection like all his other faculties, and that nature has linked together in an unbreakable chain truth, happiness, and virtue?

Among the causes of the progress of the human mind that are of the utmost importance to the general happiness, we must number the complete annihilation of the prejudices that have brought about an inequality of rights between the sexes, an inequality fatal even to the party in whose favor it works. It is vain for us to look for a justification of this principle in any differences of physical organization, intellect, or moral sensibility between men and women. This inequality has its origin solely in an abuse of strength, and all the later sophistical attempts that have been made to excuse it are vain.

We shall show how the abolition of customs authorized, laws dictated by this prejudice, would add to the happiness of family life, would encourage the practice of the domestic virtues on which all other virtues are based, how it would favor the progress of education, and how, above all, it would bring about its wider diffusion; for not only would education be extended to women as well as to men, but it can only really be taken proper advantage of when it has the support and encouragement of the mothers of the family. Would not this belated tribute to equity and good sense put an end to a principle only too fecund of injustice, cruelty, and crime, by removing the dangerous conflict between the strongest and most irrepressible of all natural inclinations and man's duty or the interests of society? Would it not produce what has until now been no more than a dream, national manners of a mildness and purity, formed not by proud asceticism, not by hypocrisy, not by the fear of shame or religious terrors but by freely contracted habits that are inspired by nature and acknowledged by reason?

Once people are enlightened they will know that they have the right to dispose of their own life and wealth as they choose; they will gradually learn to regard war as the most dreadful of scourges, the most terrible of crimes. The first wars to disappear will be those into which usurpers have forced their subjects in defense of their pretended hereditary rights.

Nations will learn that they cannot conquer other nations without losing their own liberty; that permanent confederations are their only means of preserving their independence; and that they should seek not power but security. Gradually mercantile prejudices will fade away: and a false sense of commercial interest will lose the fearful power it once had of drenching the earth in blood and of ruining nations under pretext of enriching them. When at last the nations come to agree on the principles of politics and morality, when in their own better interests they invite foreigners to share equally in all the benefits men enjoy either through the bounty of nature or by their own industry, then all the causes that produce and perpetuate national animosities and poison national relations will disappear one by one; and nothing will remain to encourage or even to arouse the fury of war.

Organizations more intelligently conceived than those projects of eternal peace which have filled the leisure and consoled the hearts of certain philosophers, will hasten the progress of the brotherhood of nations, and wars between countries will rank with assassinations as freakish atrocities, humiliating and vile in the eyes of nature and staining with indelible opprobrium the country or the age whose annals record them.

When we spoke of the fine arts in Greece, Italy, and France, we observed that it was necessary to distinguish in artistic productions between what belonged properly to the progress of the art itself and what was due only to the talent of the individual artist. We shall here indicate what progress may still be expected in the arts as a result of the progress in philosophy and the sciences, of the increasing number of observations made about the aim, effects, and methods of the arts, of the destruction of those prejudices which have formerly narrowed their sphere and even now hold them within the shackles of authority, shackles that science and philosophy have broken. We shall ask, whether, as some have thought, these means are exhausted, and the arts condemned to an eternal, monotonous imitation of their first models since the most sublime and moving beauty has already been apprehended, the happiest subjects treated, the simplest and most arresting ideas used, the most marked or most generous characters delineated, the liveliest intrinsic passions and their truest or most natural manifestations, the most striking truths and the most brilliant images already exploited.

We shall see that this opinion is a mere prejudice, born of the habit, which is prevalent among artists and men of letters, of judging men, instead of enjoying their works. If the more reflective pleasure of comparing the products of different ages and countries and admiring the success and energy of the efforts of genius will probably be lost, the pleasure to be derived from the actual contemplation of works of art as such will be just as vivid as ever, even though the author may no longer deserve the same credit for having achieved such perfection. As works of art genuinely worthy of preservation increase in number, and become more perfect, each successive generation will devote its attention and admiration to those which really deserve preference, and the rest will unobtrusively fall into oblivion; the pleasure to be derived from the simpler, more striking, more accessible aspects of beauty will exist no less for posterity although they will be found only in the latest works.

The progress of the sciences ensures the progress of the art of education which in turn advances that of the sciences. This reciprocal influence, whose activity is ceaselessly renewed, deserves to be seen as one of the most powerful and active causes working for the perfection of mankind. At the present time a young man on leaving school may know more of the principles of mathematics than Newton ever learned in years of study or discovered by dint of genius, and he may use the calculus with a facility then unknown. The same observation, with certain reservations, applies to all the sciences. As each advances, the methods of expressing a large number of proofs in a more economical fashion and so of making their comprehension an easier matter, advance with it. So, in spite of the progress of science, not only do men of the same ability find themselves at the same age on a level with the existing state of science, but with every generation, that which can be acquired in a certain time with a certain degree of intelligence and a certain amount of concentration will be permanently on the increase, and, as the elementary part of each science to which all men may attain grows and grows, it will more and more include all the knowledge necessary for each man to know for the conduct of the ordinary events of his life, and will support him in the free and independent exercise of his reason.

In the political sciences there are some truths that, with free people (that is to say, with certain generations in all countries) can be of use only if they are widely known and acknowledged. So the influence of these sciences upon the freedom and prosperity of nations must in some degree be measured by the number of truths that, as a result of elementary instruction, are common knowledge; the swelling progress of elementary instruction, connected with the necessary progress of these sciences promises us an improvement in the destiny of the human race, which may be regarded as indefinite, since it can have no other limits than that of this same progress.

We have still to consider two other general methods which will influence both the perfection of education and that of the sciences. One is the more extensive and less imperfect use of what we might call technical methods; the other is the setting up of a universal language.

I mean by technical methods the art of arranging a large number of subjects in a system so that we may straightway grasp their relations, quickly perceive their combinations, and readily form new combinations out of them.[2]

We shall develop the principles and examine the utility of this art, which is still in its infancy, and which, as it improves, will enable us, within the compass of a small chart, to set out what could possibly not be expressed so well in a whole book, or, what is still more valuable, to present isolated facts in such a way as to allow us to deduce their general consequences. We shall see how by means of a small number of these charts, whose use can easily be learned, men who have not been sufficiently educated to be able to absorb details useful to them in ordinary life, may now be able to master them when the need arises; and how these methods may likewise be of benefit to elementary education itself in all these branches where it is concerned either with a regular system of truths or with a series of observations and facts.

A universal language is that which expresses by signs either real objects themselves, or well-defined collections composed of simple and general ideas, which are found to be the same or may arise in a similar form in the minds of all men, or the general relations holding between these ideas, the operations of the human mind, or the operations peculiar to the individual sciences, or the procedures of the arts. So people who become acquainted with these signs, the ways to combine them and the rules for forming them will understand what is written in this language and will be able to read it as easily as their own language.[3]

It is obvious that this language might be used to set out the theory of a science or the rules of an art, to describe a new observation or experiment, the invention of a procedure, the discovery of a truth or a method; and that, as in algebra, when one has to make use of a new sign, those already known provide the means of explaining its import.

Such a language has not the disadvantages of a scientific idiom different from the vernacular. We have already observed that the use of such an idiom would necessarily divide society into two unequal classes, the one composed of men who, understanding this language, would possess the key to all the sciences, the other of men who, unable to acquire it, would therefore find themselves almost completely unable to acquire enlightenment. In contrast to this, a universal language would be learned, like that of algebra, along with the science itself; the sign would be learned at the same time as the object, idea, or operation that it designates. He who, having mastered the elements of a science, would like to know more of it, would find in books not only truths he could understand by means of the signs whose import he has learned, but also the explanation of such further signs as he needs in order to go on to other truths.

We shall show that the formation of such a language, if confined to the expression of those simple, precise propositions which form the system of a science or the practice of an art, is no chimerical scheme; that even at the present time it could be readily introduced to deal with a large number of objects; and that, indeed, the chief obstacle that would prevent its extension to others would be the humiliation of having to admit how very few precise ideas and accurate, unambiguous notions we actually possess.

We shall show that this language, ever improving and broadening its scope all the while, would be the means of giving to every subject embraced by the human intelligence, a precision and a rigor that would make knowledge of the truth easy and error almost impossible. Then the progress of every science would be as sure as that of mathematics, and the propositions that compose it would acquire a geometrical certainty, as far, that is, as is possible granted the nature of its aim and method.

All the causes that contribute to the perfection of the human race, all the means that ensure it must by their very nature exercise a perpetual influence and always increase their sphere of action. The proofs of this we have given and in the great work they will derive additional force from elaboration. We may conclude then that the perfectibility of man is indefinite. Meanwhile we have considered him as possessing the natural faculties and organization that he has at present. How much greater would be the certainty, how much vaster the scheme of our hopes if we could believe that these natural faculties themselves and this organization could also be improved? This is the last question that remains for us to ask ourselves.

Organic perfectibility or deterioration among the various strains in the vegetable and animal kingdom can be regarded as one of the general laws of nature. This law also applies to the human race. No one can doubt that, as preventive medicine improves and food and housing become healthier, as a way of life is established that develops our physical powers by exercise without ruining them by excess, as the two most virulent causes of deterioration, misery and excessive wealth, are eliminated, the average length of human life will be increased and a better health and a stronger physical constitution will be ensured. The improvement of medical practice, which will become more efficacious with the progress of reason and of the social order, will mean the end of infectious and hereditary diseases and illnesses brought on by climate, food, or working conditions. It is reasonable to hope that all other diseases may likewise disappear as their distant causes are discovered. Would it be absurd then to suppose that this perfection of the human species might be capable of indefinite progress; that the day will come when death will be due only to extraordinary accidents or to the decay of the vital forces, and that ultimately the average span between birth and decay will have no assignable value? Certainly man will not become immortal, but will not the interval between the first breath that he draws and the time when in the natural course of events, without disease or accident, he expires, increase indefinitely? Since we are now speaking of a progress that can be represented with some accuracy in figures or on a graph, we shall take this opportunity of explaining the two meanings that can be attached to the word *indefinite*.

In truth, this average span of life which we suppose will increase indefinitely as time passes, may grow in conformity either with a law such that it continually approaches a limitless length but without ever reaching it, or with a law such that through the centuries it reaches a length greater than any determinate quantity that we may assign to it as its limit. In the latter case such an increase is truly indefinite in the strictest sense of the word, since there is no term on this side of which it must of necessity stop. In the former case it is equally indefinite in relation to us, if we cannot fix the limit it always approaches without ever reaching, and particularly if, knowing only that it will never stop, we are ignorant in which of the two senses the term "indefinite" can be applied to it. Such is the present condition of our knowledge as far as the perfectibility of the human race is concerned; such is the sense in which we may call it indefinite.

So, in the example under consideration, we are bound to believe that the average length of human life will forever increase unless this is prevented by physical revolutions; we do not know what the limit is which it can never exceed. We cannot tell even whether the general laws of nature have determined such a limit or not.

But are not our physical faculties and the strength, dexterity, and acuteness of our senses, to be numbered among the qualities whose perfection in the individual may be transmitted? Observation of the various breeds of domestic animals inclines us to believe that they are, and we can confirm this by direct observation of the human race.

Finally may we not extend such hopes to the intellectual and moral faculties? May not our parents, who transmit to us the benefits or disadvantages of their constitution, and from whom we receive our shape and features, as well as our tendencies to certain physical affections, hand on to us also that part of the physical organization which determines the intellect, the power of the brain, the ardor of the soul or the moral sensibility? Is it not probable that education, in perfecting these qualities, will at the same time influence, modify, and perfect the organization itself? Analogy, investigation of the human faculties, and the study of certain facts, all seem to give substance to such conjectures which would further push back the boundaries of our hopes.

These are the questions with which we shall conclude this final stage. How consoling for the philosopher who laments the errors, the crimes, the injustices which still pollute the earth and of which he is often the victim is this view of the human race, emancipated from its shackles, released from the empire of fate and from that of the enemies of its progress, advancing with a firm and sure step along the path of truth, virtue, and happiness! It is the contemplation of this prospect that rewards him for all his efforts to assist the progress of reason and the defense of liberty. He dares to regard these strivings as part of the eternal chain of human destiny; and in this persuasion he is filled with the true delight of virtue and the pleasure of having done some lasting good which fate can never destroy by a sinister stroke of revenge, by calling back the reign of slavery and prejudice. Such contemplation is for him an asylum, in which the memory of his persecutors cannot pursue him; there he lives in thought with man restored to his natural rights and dignity, forgets man tormented and corrupted by greed, fear, or envy; there he lives with his peers in an Elysium created by reason and graced by the purest pleasures known to the love of mankind.

NOTES TO ''SKETCH FOR A HISTORICAL PICTURE OF THE PROGRESS OF THE HUMAN MIND''

1. The reference is to Renaissance Italy, whose achievements in science and philosophy Condorcet compares with the tyranny and superstition of the Reformation and Counter-Reformation.
2. In a draft chapter developing his ideas on this subject, Condorcet proposed a decimal system of classification similar to that which we know as the Dewey decimal system. Such a system, he argued, would make it possible to store information accurately,

retrieve it easily, and organize it to test hypotheses from any point of view. It would also have the advantage that much of this work could eventually be done mechanically. See K. M. Baker, "An Unpublished Essay of Condorcet on Technical Methods of Classification," *Annals of Science* 18(1962): 99–123.

3. Again, Condorcet drafted (but never finished) a chapter developing his ideas for a universal symbolic language of the sciences. See G.-G. Granger, "Langue universelle et formalisation des sciences: un fragment inédit de Condorcet," *Revue d'histoire des sciences* 7(1954): 197–219.

Fragment on the New Atlantis, or Combined Efforts of the Human Species for the Advancement of Science (1793)

From his earliest years as secretary of the Academy of Sciences, Condorcet had been advocating the reorganization of scientific activity in France. When he came to write the *Historical Picture of the Progress of the Human Mind*, he devoted a chapter of that unfinished work to his vision of an association of scientists (first in France and then, perhaps, beyond) to fulfill the Baconian dream of a collective assault upon nature in the service of human progress. Condorcet spent much time in the *Fragment on the New Atlantis* emphasizing that the association must be free and independent of government activity, while organized in such a way that scientific truth alone would be served. The following selection from that essay represents his last statement on the relationship of science and society in the new social order. The *Fragment on the New Atlantis* was first published in 1804.

Bacon conceived the idea of a society of men devoted solely to the search for truth. His plan embraced all the parts of human knowledge. He envisaged a host of observers ceaselessly traversing the globe to gain knowledge of the animals that inhabit it, the vegetables it nourishes, the substances spread over its surface and those that it contains deep within. These observers would study the external form and the organization of these phenomena. They would seek to identify the vestiges and the proofs of the ancient upheavals of the earth, to seize the traces of those peaceful revolutions insensibly brought about by the slow hand of time. Other observers, settled in the various regions, would follow with a daily precision the phenomena of the sky and those of the terrestrial atmosphere. Vast edifices would be consecrated to experiments which, forcing nature to reveal what the course of her ordinary operations would hide from our sight, would wrest from her the secret of her laws. These investigations would not be limited to efforts successful in a few hours or a few months. One would know how to employ a weapon so powerful that nature had seemed to reserve it to herself: the weapon of time. Results to be realized only by distant generations would be silently prepared; the object of study would embrace everything that must enlighten man, and everything that can preserve him and serve him. All the apparatus, all the instruments, all the machines by which we have been able to add to our senses or to our industry, to increase our powers or multiply our means of observing, knowing, or producing, would come together for the instruction of the philosopher as for that of the artisan. Love of truth would unite in this society men whom the sacrifice of the common passions had rendered worthy of it. And the enlightened nations, knowing all that such a society could do for the happiness of the human species, would lavish upon genius the means of deploying its activity and its forces.

Such is the plan that a creative mind dared to conceive in a century still covered with the darkness of a superstitious ignorance. For a long time it seemed to be merely a philosophical dream. Today the rapid progress of society and enlightenment gives hope of seeing it realized by future generations, and perhaps undertaken by ourselves.

Bacon wrote at a time when events had not yet determined whether the inevitable fall to which kings had been condemned by reason would be the peaceful work of enlightenment or the rapid effect of the indignation of peoples freed from deception. It was then still possible to think that chance would perhaps one day inspire a monarch with a passion for science to the same degree that his fellow monarchs had so often carried the furor of the hunt or the passion for building. This monarch would have chosen among those great enterprises whose very extent seemed to obliterate even the idea of attempting them, among those problems that isolated genius could not conquer even with the help of time, the ones that most appealed to his fancy or flattered his pride. One would have seen the execution of those vast undertakings which demand the conjunction of the obscure and arduous efforts of a great number of men directed toward a single goal. One would have seen the execution of those researches demanding that nature be interrogated at the same time and by the same method in all climates, under all aspects, at all heights. Here, to arrive at the knowledge of some truths, one would have equalled the efforts and suffering to which men have been inspired by the love of gold; there, instruments so costly in their construction that they are beyond the means of an individual fortune would have wrested from the sky some of its secrets. There is no science which, at certain periods, and for some of its parts, cannot be halted for the lack of these extraordinary resources. There is no science in which a systematic investigation does not reveal problems which await and demand them.

But had this hope been accomplished, one would still have obtained only a part of what one can hope for from the common association of enlightened men in favor of scientific progress.

There are obstacles which can only be conquered by time; there are investigations the success of which nothing can accelerate, requiring a long-sustained determination directed toward a consistent goal as well as vast means and the combined efforts of a great number of scientists. The personal fantasy of a monarch would have thrown light only at random and on a few isolated areas. But that constancy, that coherence of views embracing a long sequence of generations and extending to the entire system of the sciences, is beyond the power of kings to promise. It can only be expected from a people whose laws have been dictated and institutions contrived by a strong and pure reason.

However, let us not hope for this even yet from the public power. In feeble or harsh souls, and in narrow or empty heads, the spirit of equality often degenerates into base envy. Hypocritical ambition hates a rival still dangerous, fears a penetrating and severe judge, in even the most modest talent. The more those who govern remain at the general level of the citizens, the more their authority is transitory, partial, and limited, and the more the personal superiority conferred by genius and enlightenment offends their pride. Even when they do not prefer the charlatanry which flatters and rants to the merit which keeps its place and knows how to put others in theirs, what force can confine within the same route that mass of influential men made up of ceaselessly changing elements; what force can imprint upon them a constant will; what force can ensure that the opinions and the confidence regarding a plan of scientific research will be perpetuated despite their rapid succession?

In matters of legislation these men are restrained by the necessity to respect the rights of man, by the fear of fatiguing the citizens by too rapid changes, and by the check of public opinion, which becomes formidable to them as a result of the ease of instructing the peoples in the harmful consequences and the dangers of a bad law. But when it comes to the institutions of public instruction, and the incentives that it would be their duty to provide to those who cultivate the sciences, they can have only a single guide: the opinion of men enlightened on these questions, which are necessarily foreign to the greatest number. Now it is necessary to be endowed with a superior reason, and to have acquired much knowledge oneself, to be able to listen to this opinion or to be able simply to understand it well.

Assuming a good method of election among a people instructed in all that it is possible to teach the generality of citizens, one can hope that the choice will generally fall upon men possessing, in the affairs entrusted to their care, that common capacity sufficient to prevent them from rejecting through pride that which is good, and adopting that which is bad, in the general judgment of men to whom the public voice grants a superiority of enlightenment.

But the capacity to decide on the means of arriving at new truths can never have the people as judge and should not even be the grounds for their choice of representatives. An enormous distance will always separate the man who wishes only to acquire knowledge useful to himself and necessary for the functions with which he might be charged, and the man for whom the search for truth is the goal, the occupation of his entire life. There will always be an enormous difference between the man of sound mind capable of receiving a limited instruction, and the man who joins the force and the activity of genius to the knowledge and the means of enlightenment conferred by the passion for study and the ability to learn.

Thus all these hopes of one day seeing human efforts combine to penetrate what nature has persisted in hiding from us, to attain what she seems to have placed beyond our feeble powers, will remain relegated to the class of fantasies, if there does not form among men who are raised above the common level by their enlightenment, by their genius, by the force of their reason, a voluntary association of views and of principles. This association must be such that the same plans followed with a long constancy can be perfected, corrected, and expanded, without being either abandoned through frivolity or disgust, or changed through vanity or the spirit of system. If this association is possible, all the difficulties disappear, and success even becomes independent of the public power.

Let us then examine this possibility in first considering a single great nation, whether it find itself united (like France) in a single people, or divided (like Germany or English America) into several states interrelated by a more or less intimate federation; or whether these states (like those of Italy) have no other links than proximity, use of the same language, and the easy and multifarious communications which result from it. I will then speak of the general association of the scientists of the world in a universal republic of sciences, the only such republic the project and utility of which would not be a puerile illusion.

I find myself in a truly free country, where real equality reigns, where the simplicity of laws and administration makes it unnecessary to multiply the number of public officials and entrust them with functions that can excite greed and flatter ambition. Here public positions conferred for a very short time and distributed in such a way that each of them can be fulfilled by an individual of ordinary capacity, can become neither the object nor the exclusive occupation of a class of men who prepare for them by studies foreign to the rest of the citizens. Here, finally, there no longer exist those institutions, those laws, uniquely contrived to offer the means of acquiring opulence and great wealth. Now in such a country, the glory of the talents must soon become preeminent; and study must become the almost general occupation of men who have conceptual ability, an active temperament, and a measure of leisure time.

I find myself in a country where general enlightenment and knowledge of the rights of man make it impossible to fear that one should ever wish to found public happiness on the equality of ignorance and stupidity. Here no one could ascribe the narrow limits of his own intelligence to human reason itself, or have his own prejudices taught as the only truths worth knowing.

I can demand these conditions, because it is a question here of the progress of the human species freed at last from its grossest errors.

As soon as the true methods of studying the sciences and of making progress in them are known, there cannot fail to exist, among all those who cultivate them with some success, a common opinion and avowed principles from which they cannot diverge without betraying their interior sentiment, without giving themselves over to a reputation for ignorance or bad faith.

These men are certainly not exempt from the pettiness of egotism, nor are they strangers to jealousy; but they will not sacrifice to the impulses of these miserable passions the very object which excites them. Since they enjoy different levels of talent and reputation, it follows that a man of genius who finds himself in the first rank has as his defender against those who follow him most closely the more numerous class which comes behind these latter. Sufficiently instructed to pronounce between those more renowned, without being able to pretend to rival them, this class is more disposed to recognize their superiority than to combat it. It is very rare that young men, if they have a true talent, are hurt at not sharing equally in the advantages they are permitted to regard as the prize of experience. They are rarely jealous of a reputation enhanced by time, or of a status which they hope one day to attain for themselves. In the sciences, the generation which is beginning its work—starting from the point at which the preceding generation is stopping, to follow a certain route in its footsteps—has no need to disparage that generation in order to establish itself. No matter how far the preceding generation has advanced the limits of science, the succeeding can aspire with justice, and with assurance of success, to advance them even further. Finally, the scientists of each country have as their judges the scientists of all the enlightened nations. It is the common judgment of the latter, which can be neither escaped nor challenged, that dispenses glory and enduring fame; impartial, like posterity, it is no less infallible.

Now we only have need here of an approximate justice.

Whether jealousy distinguishes badly the relative merits of men of genius is of little importance. It is enough that it does not accord the honors to mediocrity or charlatanism.

Inconstancy or error will be no more of a threat than the passions. A plan of researches formed by enlightened men and necessarily in conformity with the common opinion of the class of scientists which it interests, will not be so bad that the following generation is forced to abandon it or unable to correct it. Nor will it be so good that the progress of knowledge will not make these corrections necessary. There will always be glory for those who follow the plan while reforming and perfecting it; and there will always be charges of presumption or charlatanism to fear, if one wishes to attempt a useless reorganization simply to win fame. Moreover, one can count enough on that policy which leads skillful men to husband the work of their predecessors, to be sure that what they prepare will be respected by their successors. The partisan spirit sometimes replaces this policy with the passion to destroy everything; but the spirit of sect (or of school, which represents it in the sciences and produces the same effects) no longer exists since true methods have been discovered and recognized in all branches of the system of the sciences.

Will the men who cultivate the sciences desire to create such a plan and have the means of executing it? Without any doubt. In the state of society which we have supposed, their number is too great for each one of them to think of making study a means of obtaining more than mere esteem. For the majority, curiosity will be the primary motivation of their researches, and the pleasure of knowing new truths by forming common undertakings cannot be foreign to them. Can one imagine that they would not wait impatiently for the moment of each year in which were announced the results of the observations, experiments, investigations, and calculations undertaken and directed according to their views? Can one believe that they would not experience a lively and pure enjoyment in seeing that one of their conjectures had been verified, that one of their doubts had been resolved, that a truth long pursued in vain had been unable to escape their constant and zealous investigation? Where is there even now a scientist, an enlightened scientific amateur, who can learn without transports of joy that far from him an important experiment has been carried out, that certain means have been utilized to enlighten obscure questions, that great researches or extensive voyages have been undertaken? Now all that does not yet exist, in what I have supposed, can only be realized by rendering this sentiment (which already exists) more general and more active, by separating interest, ambition, and personality from the passion for the sciences, by rendering the usurpation of fame more difficult, by putting the intellectual pleasures within the grasp even of common souls.

One could still fear the kind of rivalry which reigns between the sciences. It is in the interests of truth that they all combine, because there is not one among them which is not related to all the other parts of the scientific system by a more or less immediate dependence. There is not one of them that provides a point at which one can break the chain without harming the two portions thereby separated. Thus, for example, the metaphysical sciences are related to the mathematical sciences both by their theory (whether it be the theory of combinations or of probabilities) and by the indispensability of the study of these same sciences for just, extensive, profound ideas concerning quantity and mass, movement and its general and necessary laws, in short concerning the nature of the mechanical and physical laws of the universe. How useful still to the metaphysical sciences is not observation of the habits of animals, of their intelligence, of their industry, and of their passions?

Are the social sciences not related to the mathematical and physical sciences? Is there one of the latter which does not offer truths applicable to the needs of men and to the well-being of societies? Would it not be impossible, without their help, either to resolve completely a great portion of the questions that the social sciences present, or to obtain the data necessary for their solution? Are not those who cultivate a science avid to multiply its applications, to exercise their genius on matters which excite a more general interest by their novelty or importance? Will they not therefore search to relate the science they cultivate to those which may need to borrow its principles or its methods, to employ its procedures or its theories?

If it became a question of bringing scientists together, either to confer in common deliberations or to execute common researches, it would doubtless be necessary to divide them into several classes. Otherwise, since each matter would interest only a fraction of the men forming this too-extensive gathering, one would lose for the sciences all the time they were obliged to devote reciprocally to matters too indifferent or too foreign to them. In condemning them to this periodic idleness, to this boredom that they would suffer and inflict in their turn, one would create among the sciences a kind of rivalry, and among those who cultivate them a kind of thoughtless disdain absolutely contrary to the purpose of their gathering.

But it is a question here of uniting only the determination and the means of these men for the progress of the sciences in general. And, from this point of view, none of the sciences is irrelevant to him who cultivates another.

It is not demanded of each scientist that he follow the investigations, that he crawl through the petty details, of a science which is foreign to him. It is simply demanded that he contemplate attentively the important results and useful applications.

Certainly all rivalry between men cultivating the sciences will not be destroyed. Nor must we hope, or even desire, that the more active zeal motivating each scientist toward the object of his studies can be counterbalanced to the point of a complete equilibrium. Is not the motivation inspiring his preference the same attraction that animates his efforts and sustains his work? But one can preserve minds from an overexaggerated, too-exclusive preference. The idea of extending the domain of all the sciences at one and the same time is so grand and so elevated, its goal so useful, that it will be enough to excite in truly philosophical minds an enthusiasm capable of balancing personal inclinations and interests. These interests and inclinations, divided among different objects, are not the same in different individuals. This enthusiasm, on the contrary, directs them all toward the same point: even if it is more feeble in each individual, it will exercise over the whole body a single force superior to these divided forces. That general philosophy which embraces in its views, goals, and achievements the principles, effects, and totality of human knowledge—that general philosophy which is only reason expanded and fortified by study—will necessarily become the common attribute of enlightened men in all countries where human intelligence has reconquered its rights and its liberty.

Moreover, if one examines the causes of the rivalry which seems to exist among the various sciences, one will see that it is due much less than one thinks to the rigorous necessity of preferring the object to which one has consecrated one's life, of wishing to place the glory to which one aspires in the first rank. The true causes of this rivalry are to be found in that vicious order which makes the cultivation of the sciences not an individual occupation but an estate from which one can hope to derive other advantages than the celebrity due to talent and the pure pleasure attached to intellectual activity. They are to be found also in a social system contrived for vanity, a milieu in which it was not at all astonishing that men had come to attach a sense of pride not only to the progress or the discoveries they made, but to their very choice of occupations. They are to be found, finally, in the vices of the common instruction, which, by leaving almost all men in a profound ignorance of the sciences to which they have not been powerfully attracted, made it almost a necessity for them to concentrate all their activity and all their ideas on a single science. Thus this spirit of rivalry revealed itself above all in those who, far from having penetrated to the frontiers of the science they cultivated, needed to find consolation for their inferiority in the preeminence of the kind of occupation in which they engaged. It was also more common among those whose mind is completely circumscribed by a single science. In almost all cases, it was the consequence of that extreme disproportion between pretensions and talent which is the work not of nature but of bad institutions.

After having disposed of the obstacles that the will and the passions can oppose to the establishment of a perpetual society for the advancement of the sciences, it remains to be seen whether, in such an association, the means of action would match the extent of the plan to be embraced. These means can be divided into three categories: those which must ensure the quality of the plan and the choice of men capable of executing its various parts; those necessary to triumph over external obstacles; those, finally, of acquiring funds sufficient for the expenses necessary to the success of so vast a plan. But in order to evaluate the adequacy of the means that such an association can employ, it is first of all necessary to determine more precisely the plan whose possibility I am examining. It would be enough to know the object of this plan to see also that it could only be fulfilled by the free and spontaneous will of those who cultivate the sciences; and that the honor of having contributed to such an undertaking, the pleasure of seeing its success realized, that of abandoning oneself to more extensive hopes, would be motives powerful enough to inspire the will, to give it all the force, all the activity, and all the constancy necessary for success.

This plan must embrace the parts of the diverse sciences. Otherwise the discovery of truth would remain dependent upon chance. And the happy effects of the sciences would become probable only after a long succession of centuries, if they relied for their progress only on the successive or simultaneous researches of isolated men linked only by fleeting communications.

One must count among the objects of research all those investigations, both daily and perpetual, which it is necessary to follow with a constant precision without ever stopping or interrupting them. Such are astronomical observations, meteorological investigations, observations of the natural history of man, and observations of the rural economy. . . .

[At this point in the essay, Condorcet begins a discussion, here omitted, of some of the investigations to be undertaken by the new scientific organization. It is indicative of his interests that the greater part of this discussion is devoted to research into what Condorcet calls "the natural history of man." With appropriate methods of investigation, observers in all regions would examine the effects of climate and environment on the physical constitution and socioeconomic organization of mankind. Detailed tables of mortality and medical statistics would be compiled, together with data on economic and social life. The physiological and psychological factors in the development of the moral and intellectual faculties would be investigated, the factors leading to the degeneration of the human organism discovered. Such investigations would enable scientists to answer fundamental questions concerning the limits of the human lifespan, the nature of the differences between the sexes, and the extent of man's capacity for moral, intellectual, and social progress.]

Finally, we lack a general table of known truths, from which could be discovered at a glance the current state of each science, the stage at which it has come to a halt, the discoveries that are most necessary to its progress, and those it can hope for most quickly. Such a table would allow one to distinguish proven and recognized truths; truths which are almost as certain but, because they are still surrounded by some obscurity, appear so only to impartial and penetrating eyes; those whose indirect or contested proofs still permit a reasonable doubt; and those, finally, that imposing probabilities, attestations of great weight, or the common opinion have consecrated as true, but which must nevertheless be left in the category of mere conjectures until time and new researches assign them a definitive place, either in the system of the sciences or among that mass of errors which have momentarily usurped the name of truths.

This table, while it should only contain the simple exposition of truths, would indicate where one could find their details, their developments, their discussion, and their proofs. It could be formed, even for a single science, only by a number of men who between them had profoundly cultivated all its branches. It would demand, at least in respect of several sciences, knowledge extensive enough that no object could escape it. At the same time, it would require a philosophy sure enough not to confuse truths with opinions; to distinguish, in any fact, that which is properly the fact itself from that which is really only a conjectural explanation; to separate, in any proposition, the true meaning which results from proofs, and that presented by the hypothetical language employed by scientists.

But it is useless to multiply these examples. I have said enough to show both the extent and the importance of the plan that a numerous society would have to form for the progress of the sciences. I can now proceed to examine whether that society would be able to work out the particulars and the overall organization of this plan, to direct its execution with success, to persist in it constantly, to provide for the expenses involved, and to triumph over the alien obstacles that it might encounter. And I can do so knowing that I have said enough that no one can accuse me of having understated the difficulties by restricting this plan within too narrow limits.

It is necessary here not to lose sight of the hypothesis that I first established, that of a great nation truly free. By that I not only mean a nation in which the entire mass of the people has retained the sovereignty and the citizens exercise their political rights in all their extent. I also mean one in which the entire system of the laws respects the natural rights of the individual, who can be forbidden nothing that does not violate the particular right of another individual; in which a right that is common to all, since it belongs to each individual as member of the society, cannot be violated in respect of a single individual without being violated in respect of all, and therefore appears to be a right of society itself. The closer a people approaches this point, the fewer the obstacles to the realization of the plan that I am here considering.

It is first of all necessary that one or several men together propose to form the association, and propose it under provisional conditions. These conditions would be simple. They would consist in this alone, that all those who would like to cooperate in the project sign their name and consent to elect, according to the procedures indicated to them, a small number of scientists charged to draw up the very plan of the association.

This election, like all those to be carried out by the totality of the members, must be organized in a way that does not require that they meet in the same place, or even as separate groups in separate places. It is necessary in general to avoid any numerous assembly: this is the only way of obtaining a true equality, of avoiding the influence of intrigue, charlatanry, and verbiage; of preserving for the simple truth all its empire, of being guided by reason and not by the passions.

Two letters and two responses would be sufficient for each election.

Once the project of association was formed, it would be made public. Since those who had agreed to choose the drafters of the plan would retain the freedom not to enter into the association or to form another one, it would be useless to submit the project to their approval after it had been drawn up. Since in this matter the will of the majority cannot impose itself as a law upon the minority; since other individuals can arbitrarily join one or another society, it is evident that such a procedure would be absolutely pointless. It says nothing more, and it even says something less, than the simple resolution to contribute to the execution of the plan or to refuse to do so.

Is it not permissible to suppose that this project of association would be drawn up in such a way as to inspire men truly zealous for the advancement of enlightenment with the desire of becoming useful members; that it would provide effective means of choosing both the men who would be charged with the responsibility of drawing up a general system of observations to be followed, or of experiments to be undertaken, and those to whom these observations and experiments would be entrusted?

Would it be difficult to find a method of election that would give to all of the individuals in this association an influence sufficient to sustain their interest, while nevertheless taking necessary precautions to ensure that these choices would fall only on men capable of the work with which they would be charged, possessed of the vigor required by it, and the leisure and the will to devote themselves to it constantly?

As for the means of providing for the necessary expenses, one would first institute a general subscription among all the associates, a modest subscription in return for which they would receive monthly, and annually, a collection of observations and memoirs that a committee of the association would be charged to publish. If the subscribers were very numerous, these volumes would be almost the equivalent of their expenses. Furthermore, they would give subscribers the advantage of seeing their own researches published in a work necessarily widely circulated.

Once the general scientific table had been formed, one would publish every tenth year a table of the truths with which the sciences had been enriched. One would be careful to insert here only discoveries already some years old. An annual publication would demand that the philosophical spirit of the editors, their impartiality, and the control of scientists over the impulses of their own egotism, had attained a level still too far from us.

To the product of the subscriptions, one would join the voluntary offerings of members of the association. These would be received either to support the general object of the association, or one or another of its particular divisions. In this latter case, two conditions would be imposed. The first would be that a tenth of the contribution (for example) would always be regarded as destined to fulfill the general aims of the association. This would ensure that its utility could be extended to the entire system of human knowledge, and that the dominant spirit at each period, by favoring some parts more than others, would condemn none to absolute abandonment.

The other condition must be that these particular applications will be defined by general divisions determined by the association, which must not expose itself to the temptation of submitting them to the views and ideas of an individual. Ten or twelve divisions would be enough to satisfy the tastes of men combining real enlightenment with a true zeal for the advancement of the sciences.

The plan of research necessarily contains two kinds of investigation which it would be difficult to sustain on the basis of the uncertain and changing support of subscriptions. One of these is comprised of researches which become useless unless they are perpetual or continued for a very long time; the other is comprised of those investigations which require a very considerable initial investment. But one can correct the inequality or the inadequacy of these resources by establishing two reserve funds drawn from the annual income, the one intended for the initial expenses required to undertake a new investigation, the other devoted to forming a fixed revenue. This precaution supposes laws relating to mortgages as wise as those which existed, twenty-two centuries ago, in the republic of Athens; but it is not too much to demand of the state of civilization to which I suppose the human species has attained.

Thus parts of the social system that appear to be most distant join together at some points. Thus in order for reason to exercise its empire entirely over a single part, it is necessary for it to have extended its rule over all the parts. It is equally impossible for good or evil to be isolated in society, just as in an organized body there is no local ill which does not affect the whole organism, and the good only exists by half if it does not embrace the whole.

The government could contribute to these expenses. But it is necessary for the association to feel, in all its dignity, the independence belonging to the individual in a free people; for it to refuse benefactions, or for such benefactions to be subject to common rules. It would be too dangerous to allow any authority to introduce itself into an empire where truth must hold undivided sway; to allow external views, even when they are useful, to trouble the pure worship a free will had devoted to it.

Certainly one could expect and desire that the public power would provide facilities for correspondence, the means of executing long voyages, the use of sites (some of which can be strictly necessary), or the mediation of its external or internal agents (interventions indispensable for certain researches, such as those concerned with the formation of general tables of mortality). Without doubt all these would establish relations between the public power and a free association, the goal and recompense of which would establish relations between the public power and a free association, the goal and recompense of which would be the advancement of the sciences and the general utility. But if those entrusted with that power are not enlightened enough to recognize that they must not direct these researches but second them, that they must not command discoveries but profit from them, they will be much more incapable still of combining support with just, extensive, and profound views. In such a case, it is permissible to doubt whether their influence would not be more harmful than their support useful.

It is for the association alone to judge, in an independent manner, what it believes should be undertaken to accelerate the progress of the sciences. It is for the public power to judge, with the same independence, what among the association's projects seems to merit its cooperation or its munificence. Let us not despair of a time when this division could be effected by reason alone, without the hand of pride weighing too heavily on either side of the balance.

One can ask at this stage what will assure the constancy and the perfection of the general plan, and what will assure the same constancy in its execution? These means will be found in the regulations of the association, and it will be enough to introduce into them the practice of requiring decisions by a greater or lesser majority. The nature of the questions to be examined requires that deliberations always be carried out among a very small number of men. It is impossible not to suppose that these men, necessarily chosen from among the number of scientists known throughout a great territory, even if they have only that feeble portion of natural wisdom necessary to make progress in one or another branch of the system of the sciences, will be in a position to understand and to follow forms of decision-making contrived with some care. Thus one will be able to graduate the majorities required according to the nature of the questions. It will also be necessary for each committee of the association, taken as a whole, to be able to embrace the entire extent of human knowledge, or at least not to overlook any important branch. It will be necessary to assign a certain number of members to each of the great divisions of the sciences; and then their votes can be given a greater influence in any deliberation relative to this branch, though without ever allowing it to be really exclusive.

Thus, for example, if it were a question of eliminating a certain phenomenon from a plan of observations, of having no further regard for a particular circumstance, one could only carry out this suppression by a great majority. On the contrary, the most feeble majority would have to be enough to demand greater extent and detail in the observations.

In the first case, the scientists to whose researches this suppression is most relevant should have a greater influence; but they should have a lesser influence on the establishment of an addition that they must naturally desire; and they would have an equal influence if they voted to reject this addition.

The principles according to which these forms must be regulated are not the same as those which must direct analogous institutions in political societies. The goal of the association is not the same: that of a society is the maintenance of the equal rights of each of the members in their greatest extent; that of a scientific association is the advancement of the sciences. In the one, the forms must be within the grasp of the least enlightened individuals; in the other, one must suppose only men accustomed to following a chain of reasoning and to organizing ideas. In the one, a false decision can violate the most important rights of the electorate or of the minority; in the other, it can violate no right, since each individual has entered the association voluntarily for a determinate length of time, since he knows in advance the conditions and laws of the association. In the one, an equal influence is a right for each individual in every decision; in the other, inequality can be in conformity with reason, and it is in conformity with justice, especially when it is reciprocal.

An annual renewal of a third [of each committee] would assure consistency of views while preventing the danger of personal opinions or sectarian prejudices.

The same advantages in the execution will be assured by putting obstacles in the way of changing observers that would prevent caprice or personal passions from multiplying changes without motive, but would nevertheless not prevent them when they became necessary to remedy bad choices.

Since every year all members of the association would be informed of the results of the researches undertaken, and since it is impossible that the great majority would have any other interest than that of the success of these researches, it would be difficult for its influence on the choices not to correct very quickly the abuses which time always brings in its train. Finally, since intrigue, charlatanism, and overexaggerated pretensions always find shame and ridicule even in a temporary success, one would soon find them disgusted at attempts that too constantly have such an effect.

This association of all those in a single nation who take care to cultivate their reason, to enhance their enlightenment, their occupation, or their pleasure, can be extended to all the enlightened nations. In each, a national association would carry out its investigations in an independent manner. But the comparison of these same investigations among diverse nations; their combination to form a common result; the undertaking of some vaster enterprises such as the establishment of a universal language, the construction of a monument that would shelter the sciences even from a general cataclysm of the globe: all these objects would be reserved to a more general association. The establishment of such an association, embracing all the peoples who have attained more or less the same degree of enlightenment and liberty, would meet no obstacles; and it would assure among all the sciences and all the arts directed by their principles, as among all nations, an equilibrium of knowledge, industry, and reason necessary for the progress and the happiness of the human species.

Index

Academy of Sciences (Paris), viii, ix, xiii, xxxix, 31 (n. 2)

Alembert, Jean le Rond d', viii, ix, x, xxxix, 3, 31 (n. 1), 32 (n. 7), 240

America, xviii, xxxix, 9–10, 32 (n. 5), 71, 76–82, 102, 146, 234–235, 236, 237

Ancients, 35, 122, 123, 125, 240, 253

Arnauld, Antoine, 93, 96 (n. 2)

Bacon, Sir Francis, 19, 283, 284

Balance of powers, xxxii, xxxiii, 35, 80, 32 (n. 4), 86–87, 155, 162, 178, 237

Bastille, fall of, xxiv, xl

Bernoulli, Jakob, xv, xxxvii (n. 10), 69 (n. 3)

Brienne, Etienne-Charles de Loménie de, archbishop of Toulouse, xl, 84

Brissotins, xxx, xxxiii, xl

Calonne, xxiv

Cartesianism, xvii, 237–238, 239, 242

Colbert, Jean-Baptiste, 28

Commerce, theory of, 200–201

Condorcet, Sophie de Grouchy, marquise de, xxv, xxxix

301